A Year in the
Life and Death
of the
Melbourne Rebels

Geoff Parkes

BookReality

Helping Writers Become Independent Authors

About the Book

Iain Payten, Sydney Morning Herald

From hope to heartbreak in a matter of months, Geoff Parkes captures the tumultuous final season of the Melbourne Rebels with brilliant, fly-on-the-wall insight. Already one of the leading analysts of rugby's precarious state in Australia, Parkes documents the journey of a club in its final - and most successful - campaign with a perfect blend of the macro and micro; the political and the personal. Through the coaching personalities, to Rebels fringe players never in the limelight and even the stories of unsung staff members, Parkes provides a timely reminder that even at the professional level, at the heart of all rugby clubs are good people, passion for the game and a love for their shared community.

Harry Jones, 8/9 Combo Rugby Podcast

Rugby writer Geoff Parkes has written a book about a club which finds its most vivid life in the year of its demise. The Melbourne Rebels of 2024 fought inevitability, history, futility, and for a place in sporting history within Australia. In so doing, Parkes has delved deeply into the fibre of the people — the folklore — of a club: the way an embattled community led, fed, judged, and found purpose. We learn in vibrant and yet studied prose how a rugby club condemned, rose to the occasion. How every part of the enterprise functions within the whole. Parkes has contributed an invaluable and perhaps cautionary tale to add to the canon of sports-writing, Unerring and unsparing, yet always with a loving and respectful eye for the game.

Ubuntu

An ancient African word meaning 'humanity to others'

It is often described as reminding us that:
'I am what I am because of who we all are'

Melbourne Rebels Staff and Players 2024

This list includes staff and players present for all or part of the 2024 season, in a full-time, part-time or contracted capacity. In addition, recognition is due the numerous, unnamed volunteers who contributed to the season.

Staff

Baden Stephenson, CEO

Nick Stiles, general manager of rugby
Kevin Foote, head coach
Tim Sampson, assistant coach
Geoff Parling, assistant coach
Brad Harris, assistant coach
Rob Taylor, specialist coach
John Batina, head analyst
Jarrod Rutley, analyst
Will Nicholson, team manager
Denver Murnane, rugby operations manager

Luke Vella, head of strength and conditioning
Luke Trewhella, S & C coach
Jared Hoare, S & C coach
Emma Hall, S & C intern
Leslie Payne, S & C intern
Alexandra Parr, nutritionist

Katherine Rottier, head of medical
Kristian Waller, physiotherapist
Simon Lumb, physiotherapist
Andrew Waterson, psychologist

Bryn Savill, club doctor
Tracy Peters, club doctor

Moana Leilua, player development manager

Jason Rogers, Super W coach

Rachel Mitrione, GM consumer and marketing
Hayley O'Callaghan, GM people and culture
Emily Riseley, commercial manager
Cameron McFarlane, head of commercial
Jimmy Christo, commercial consultant
Alex Pozzobon, partnerships executive
Jarrod Overend, partnerships executive
Ben Trupiano, memberships operations manager
Jordan Horvat, member services officer
Mitchell Cawsey, consumer and memberships co-ordinator
Sam Richards, media and content manager
Neilson Campbell, marketing and brand manager
Shamila Maralande, brand manager and creative lead
Cameron Carr, graphics designer
Afa Polo, videographer
Ebony McQuinn, match day coordinator
Kate O'Sullivan, office and events manager
Annika Jamieson, marketing contractor
Jerrhyd Hipolito, finance consultant

Men's team

Alex Mafi

Jordan Uelese

Ethan Dobbins

Ottavio Tuipulotu

Sam Talakai

Matt Gibbon

Pone Fa'amausili

Taniela Tupou

Isaac Aedo Kailea

Cabous Eloff

Timma Fainga'anuku

Kohan Herbert

Josh Canham

Lukhan Salakaia-Loto

Angelo Smith

Luke Callan

Tuaina Taii Tualima

Stuart Tualima

Rob Leota, (captain)

Brad Wilkin

Josh Kemeny

Daniel Maiava

Maciu Nabolokasi

Vaiolini Ekuasi

Zac Hough

Wyatt Ballenger

Judah Saumaisue

Leafi Talataina

Ryan Louwrens

Jack Maunder

James Tuttle

Carter Gordon

Mason Gordon

Jake Strachan

Joey Fowler

David Feliuai

Nick Jooste

Divad Palu

David Vaihu

Lebron Naea

Matt Proctor

Lukas Ripley

Filipo Daugunu

Darby Lancaster

Glen Vaihu

Lachie Anderson

Andrew Kellaway

Joe Pincus

Women's team

Laiema Bosenavulagi

Ana Mamea

Hayley Glass

Jiowana Sauto

Paula Ioane

Jayme Nuku

Mary Tuaana

Easter Savelio

Tiarah Minns

Laetitia Bobo

Fapiola Uoifaleahi

Mel Kawa

Sui Pauaraisa

Hollie Twidale

Sydney Niupulusu

Grace Hamilton

Lucy Brown

Sarah Hogan

Millicent Scutt

Cassie Siataga

Grace Freeman

Ashley Marsters, (captain)

Georgia Fowler

Crystal Mayes

Harmony Vatau

Tamsin Barber

Halley Derera

Tyra Boysen-Auimatagi

Mia-Rae Clifford

Chanelle Kohika-Skipper

Tuelia Pritchard

Samantha Treherne

Chapter One

6th November, 2023

In a rugby career which included captaining South Africa in sevens, Melbourne Rebels head coach, Kevin Foote once played flanker in the South African domestic competition, for the Natal Wildebeest. With a blue male typically weighing in at 250kgs and capable of running at speeds up to 80 km/hr, the Wildebeest is an animal that commands respect, even if it lacks the allure of some of Africa's big-ticket attractions. Among their characteristics, Wildebeest are known for 'swarm intelligence', whereby the animals systematically explore, collaborate and overcome obstacles, such as river crossings, as one. They also engage in the defensive tactic of 'herding', where the young are shielded by the older, larger animals, whenever they run as a group.

On a sunny November morning, the Melbourne Rebels players, staff and board members have retired to a theatrette in the depths of Melbourne's AAMI Park, to watch and listen to Foote launch the 2024 pre-season, espousing some of these themes, and others also distinctly African in origin.

Margins in professional rugby are fine. There are few, if any, secrets and with no real edges to be found these days in conditioning, nutrition and skills development, intangibles like the development of team culture and identity have grown in importance. When the Wallabies jetted off to France for the 2023 World Cup dressed in Akubras and RM Williams, that was an attempt to define, for the team and its supporters, their Australian-ness. Who they were and what they stood for. The team's spectacular failure - becoming the first Wallabies side in ten World Cups not to qualify from pool play - was not the result of No. 8 Rob Valetini looking ridiculous trying to settle an Akubra on top of his vast mop of hair, although it did speak to how an effective team culture is not something that can be manufactured on a whim. Organisational culture needs time to seed and develop and, most of all, it must be authentic. Players, staff, everyone in the organisation, cannot be cajoled into embracing it. They must inherently understand it, align with its values, recognise their place in it, and be self-driven to contribute to its maintenance.

The packed room bristles with anticipation and excitement as Foote calmly commands the floor. Working from side to side, speaking softly but firmly, Foote oozes authenticity. It is clear that his core theme, '*Ubuntu*', whatever its African-ness, is one hundred percent authentic for the Rebels organisation.

"Do whatever you can for the people around you," he urges. "Every single day, show your character. Build trust through your character, competence, connection and love; for each other and for the club."

Everywhere there are nodding heads. These are strong messages, well received. Importantly, they are already familiar, not lifted from an MBA slide deck. Foote has been defining standards and laying down culture markers since he took on the head coach role, in 2021.

"What drives me is the selfless service of love," Foote explains later. "Not romantic love, but doing good for others. I was never a scholar, but rugby has done so much for me, it's opened up a lifetime of opportunity. I love the game and I love what it does to change people's lives. I love the humility of rugby, the passion it generates, and the traditions."

In terms of how Foote integrates those values into his coaching, he sees it as a natural, easy extension.

"I'm a coach who enjoys empathising with players and support staff, and I get excited when I see other people's passion for the game shine through. My role is to provide an environment where people can freely express those emotions and values."

Not for a minute is Foote downplaying the technical and tactical aspects of coaching. He simply believes that for players and coaches to perform at their optimum level, individually and collectively, he needs to ensure that they feel what he feels.

As the presentation continues, what emerges is Foote's gratitude - personal and on behalf of his team - for the role others in the club play. He thanks the board members; for their belief, not just in him, but also for fighting to keep the Rebels entity alive. In its short history, the club has been to the precipice twice already; in 2017, when the Western Force were ultimately cast from Super Rugby, and in 2020, when COVID delivered almost insurmountable logistical and financial challenges. While the club has never adopted a siege mentality or contrived underdog persona, everyone present is acutely aware that if the Rebels, demonstrably unsuccessful on the field so far and considered by many in other states to be a financial millstone, did happen to be cast adrift, those people would consider Australian rugby to be in a better place.

Whatever happens in the coming season, there will be no excuses. Because that's not in Foote's nature nor his vocabulary, and because the people who back the club have refused him nothing in the way of resources. He highlights the quality of his support staff, including brand new arrivals: assistant coaches, Brad Harris and Rob Taylor, psychologist Andrew Waterson, even singling out Ju-Jitsu coach Ivan Voronoff for mention. The appreciation is genuine. The attention to detail highly impressive.

Focus switches to the playing group. "Everyone at the club can draw self-belief in the strength of the roster," he says.

The club has seven current Wallabies, more than at any time in its history. Another five players represented Australia with distinction in the Under 20 World Cup earlier in the year. Australian's sevens star Darby Lancaster is a new signing. New halfback Jack Maunder is an English Premiership winner. To illustrate the point even further, Foote identifies two local club players, parked sheepishly in the front row, Maciu Nabolakasi and Folau Finau. Without formal contracts, they have been invited to continue training with the squad for a period of time; something that may or not pay off for either party in the future. But right now, contract or not, the looming return of the Wallabies players or not, in this moment, these young men are Rebels. On the recently completed short tour of Japan, Nabolakasi was called into action early in the match against Kintetsu Liners. Foote's eyes light up as he tells the assembly about his contribution. In other years, Nabolakasi would simply have been a non-contracted player helping out in a pre-season match. Here today, Nabolakasi is celebrated as if he had just made the play that won the Rebels the Super Rugby final. That's Ubuntu.

Then, a reality check.

"There's no hiding from the fact," Foote tells the club. "We are 11th."

Where to set the goal from there? It would be easy for Foote to try to convince everyone they are going to win the competition, and to have the players parrot this. But it simply wouldn't be authentic. Teams that finish 11th in a 12-team competition, that have never made a bona-fide finals series in their 13-year existence, don't suddenly start winning Super Rugby just because they want to. Instead, Foote settles on "the greatest Rebels team ever."

It's a clever delineation; enough to cover finals qualification and to leave the door open for further progress into the top reaches of the ladder. Nobody ever climbed Everest by sprinting from the bottom to the top. They establish themselves at camps, each one higher than the last. The goal is not enough for Foote to hang himself or the team by, nor for players to pay lip service to, as something unrealistic or unattainable.

There's more. This goal turns out to be just one of what Foote calls the "four big rocks."

- the greatest Rebels team ever
- ingrain winning behaviours
- leaders set the culture
- the most physical, fearless, resolute and connected team in the competition

Foote is clearly wary of dumping too much detail, but he sprinkles a few hundreds and thousands on top:

- clarity in the game model
- every day, every person brings a positive attitude and passion
- mental strength (last season the Rebels lost six matches where they were leading into the final quarter)
- love: for the game, for the club, for each other

There are no other speeches. No over-egging. Nobody adding their piece where it doesn't need to be added. No dilution of the message.

Outside, on Gosch's Paddock, with Punt Road's every-day, endless caterpillar crawl of vehicles on the near horizon, there are cones already in position. It's barely 9am, but the temperature is beginning to rise and the players know they are about to be physically flogged. Those final quarter fade outs of last season weren't all mental.

Filing out, there is an overwhelming sense that if it wasn't training aids but the Crusaders waiting out on the field, the Rebels players would be primed and ready to deal to them. It will be a challenge keeping a lid on things until February.

For everyone else present, some in suits and in heels, some who have never played the game, others whose playing days are decades behind them, the feeling is the same. The buzz is palpable. Without exception, everyone is ready to jump through walls. To do whatever it takes to make this the greatest Rebels team ever. *Ubuntu.*

'Wicked Game' that stops everyone in their tracks.

Clarke's modus operandi is laid bare. His passion is to build things and to help build things. Things that connect people emotionally. At their stage of development, the Rebels are a perfect fit.

The gathering is an eclectic mix of Rebels staff, players, sponsors, and financial, industry and political backers. Liberal state MP David Hodgett is a long-term supporter of the club. State Labor MP Belinda Wilson's constituency is Narre Warren North, a developing rugby heartland. Melbourne Football Club's (AFL) longest serving captain, 306-game legend David Neitz, is co-founder of Brewmanity, the Rebels' beer sponsor. Sandith Samarasinghe, Consul General for Sri Lanka, is an avowed rugby fan, excited at the potential for the Rebels to forge closer ties to the burgeoning Sri Lankan community in Melbourne's south-east.

Long-term sponsor Ralph D'Silva, is another Sri Lankan connection. For the 2024 season, both the men's and women's teams will sport the Ralph D'Silva Motors logo on the left chest of their jerseys.

Men's main jersey sponsor, one-stop finance house Ebury, are represented by Managing Director Rick Roach, who has flown in from Sydney. Front of jersey sponsor for the women's 2024 season is innovative cyber security company, CyberCX: Kevin O'Sullivan and members of his team are among those acknowledged by Stephenson.

Dotted amongst the gathered sponsors are a sprinkling of players. Rebels' Director of Rugby, Nick Stiles, introduces all of them by name - well, almost all, omitting James 'Bobby' Tuttle from his list. Tuttle shakes off the snub as just another case of a sad ex-front-rower committing halfback abuse.

Promising Rebels Super W lock Tiarah Minns, who missed all of the 2023 season with a lower-leg injury, stands tall above most of the crowd. She is fit and itching to return to action.

Winger Lachie Anderson proves a popular target, having recently returned from an eight-week northern hemisphere trip that saw him play for Australia A against Portugal, then join the Barbarians. Anderson's story is a prime example of how player progression should work; coming to the Rebels from sevens rugby, initially struggling to get recognition and game time, getting a starting opportunity in 2023 and making the most of it, scoring six tries and becoming one of the Rebels most consistent performers throughout the season. Newly engaged, Anderson is proud and grateful for how Australia A selection is reward for his efforts, but acknowledges how the onus is on him to take another step forward in the coming year.

The roll call of partners continues. Latrobe University will host the state rugby centre of excellence, and has just extended their partnership for a further five years. Brokerage firm, Shaw and Partners, is the principal partner for the Rebels' elite pathways program. BRC Capital, headed by Docherty, is a familiar, long-term supporter.

Victorian Responsible Gambling Foundation, infrastructure labour hire business Rail Co, kit supplier Dynasty Sport, Bells Hotel, Taylors Wines, We Are Mobilise, Asta Solutions, Dulux... all are acknowledged, all of them valued supporters of rugby in Melbourne.

One guest however, stands out from the rest. With McLennan now gone, and new Rugby Australia chairman Daniel Herbert making it clear that he intends to adopt a more traditional non-executive chairman role and leave operations and front-facing communication to the CEO, all of a sudden Phil Waugh has clear air and an opportunity to stamp his vision for the game. He takes the microphone and talks about his determination to better connect the professional and amateur game, scoring extra points for recognising how Victoria and Melbourne are leading the way in that regard.

His catchphrase resounds: "One team from club to country".

Waugh also explains how he has a special connection to the Rebels, having played in their first ever match, in 2011, at AAMI Stadium. Kindly, he neglects to mention the score-line, 43-0 in favour of his Waratahs, although raises a laugh when he tells of celebrating out on the town afterwards with colourful Rebels import, English fly-half Danny Cipriani.

Emphasising his optimism for Australian rugby, Waugh also says he will embrace relationships with other codes, including putting an end to the overt, unseemly conflict with rugby league that marked McLennan's tenure. That too hits the mark with the local audience. Little do they know it will take less than a fortnight for that goodwill to begin to be eroded.

More than any of Australia's rugby franchises, the Rebels are acutely aware of the need to find a niche in Melbourne's impossibly crowded sports market; there being more than 20 professional teams across a number of sports, all competing for airtime and sponsorship and broadcast dollars. Even the Rebels' home base, AAMI Park, is shared with the Melbourne Victory (Soccer), Melbourne Storm (Rugby League) and the Melbourne Football Club (AFL), with training times on Gosch's Paddock needing to be constantly negotiated with the Storm. As always, the AFL's shadow looms large: the Collingwood Magpies having subsumed what was Olympic Park next door, for their training complex and, just across the railway line, Punt Road Oval, the home of the Richmond Tigers, like Collingwood, a club with a 100,000-strong membership base. Alongside sits the grandaddy of them all, the Melbourne Cricket Ground; host to a Bledisloe Cup match in July and the Boxing Day cricket Test, but effectively a giant shrine to the AFL.

Everywhere there are reminders of rugby's low standing in Melbourne's sporting eco-system. The notion that the Rebels can or should compete head on with local entities with profoundly more tradition, history, members and money, is ridiculous. The real competition lies within rugby itself. There's a sense that if the Rebels can turn their Super Rugby fortunes around, there's a latent supporter base - some old, some new - waiting to attach itself to a successful rugby franchise. Nobody knows exactly how many people this is. But everyone present knows it is time to find out.

A late arrival catches the eye. Cadbury Mondelez is Rugby Australia's main sponsor, replacing Qantas, who flew the coop in 2021. While the size of the Cadbury deal has never been disclosed, it is known Qantas were paying $5m a year for similar jersey naming rights for both the Wallabies and Wallaroos. With so much negative energy surrounding McLennan's forced departure, there are media reports that Cadbury will use the current turmoil as an opportunity to make its own exit.

Cadbury Mondelez' Australian President is Darren O'Brien, rugby tragic and a local referee, still active in Melbourne's whistleblower ranks. O'Brien is amongst friends, and he joins Waugh and others in amiable discussion. When it is his turn to speak, in the context of what has played out this week, O'Brien's body language and words are reassuring and important. The current sponsorship agreement is in place until 2026 and he gives every indication that it will run its course.

As vital as that financial arrangement is for Australian rugby, it is neither O'Brien or Waugh who is the most important person in the room tonight. New Rebels lock forward, Lukhan Salakaia-Loto, 30-times capped for the Wallabies, quietly announces his departure. He is en route to Tullamarine Airport to collect another new Rebels' signing, star Wallabies prop, Taniela Tupou. Advice flies freely about precious cargo and taking care to bypass KFC (another Rebels sponsor, locked in until 2025) on the journey home.

But there is also a serious undertone. Since joining the club and returning from a rocky pre-season tour to Japan, Salakaia-Loto has impressed everyone with his transition to senior club man, his appetite for hard work, and calm, understated leadership skills. At 27, now having played 51 Tests, Tupou is no 'wet behind the ears' greenhorn. His experience will be valuable too, but there are variables around his personality. At times extroverted, the team joker; at other times, prone to what he himself terms as "having a sook".

Other than the challenge of keeping a 140kg beast with the biggest calves in world rugby humming along physically, the Rebels aren't anticipating any problems managing Tupou and drawing him into the club culture. But they also can't be 100% certain what they will be getting. If Tupou's signing was a masterstroke on the part of Stiles, the signing of Salakaia-Loto, not just a high-quality, mature, experienced lock forward, but a friend, mentor and confidante for Tupou, might prove to be the best move of all.

Chapter Three

5th December, 2023

An early-morning human horseshoe forms inside the Rebels' gymnasium. A warm, modern facility, the walls adorned with motivational messages and oversized colour prints of the city and players in action, it wasn't always this way - just two years ago weights sessions were conducted out of an airless shipping container located in the car park outside. The playing group sits obediently, the staff standing, forming an outer ring behind them. It's officially the first day back at training for the seven Wallabies players, following a designated break after the completion of the World Cup, and their arrival isn't being allowed to pass unnoticed.

In truth, most have been in and around the club for a few days - some easing their way back into individually tailored conditioning programs, others, like hulking prop Pone 'Bones' Fa'aumasili, subjecting himself the day before to a 'Yo-yo' fitness test. An aerobic endurance fitness test, a near-relative of the ubiquitous 'Bronco', Fa'amausili ruefully rates it as "one of the hardest things I've ever done." Nevertheless, he sports a broad smile, happy to be back today for more.

Wallaby flanker, and Rebels captain-elect, Rob Leota, is not so sprightly, sporting a calf niggle which is expected to keep him from full training until after Xmas. And winger Andrew Kellaway has been busy for other reasons, he and his partner having just celebrated the birth of their first child.

With the club conscious of the negative publicity and sentiment surrounding the Wallabies' World Cup campaign, everyone is keen to make a point of celebrating all seven players upon their official return. One by one, the players are called up to receive a personalised gift; Jordan Uelese, Fa'amausili, Taniela Tupou, Leota, Josh Kemeny, Carter Gordon, and Kellaway. Their appreciation, and the recognition from their teammates, is heartfelt.

From there, the day's program clicks into action. Players and staff work to a schedule that is mapped out on a shared app called Kairos. Everyone knows well in advance what they will be doing, where and when.

The 'why' becomes apparent as the forwards split off into the changing room. There might be eleven and a half weeks remaining until their round one kick-off against the Brumbies, but there is barely a minute to waste.

Forwards coach Geoff Parling takes charge, asking the players to form groups of four, to identify and report back on what they want their forward pack to be recognised for. It is barely a minute before answers are fired back, and consensus achieved;

> 'Fearless' - to have the confidence to kick to the corner to attacking line outs, and to back themselves to execute
> 'Goal-line defence' - to develop confidence and trust in each other in stressful defensive situations, to be able to hold out for repeated phases
> 'Switched on' - to start games fast and to stay fast
> 'Scrum pressure' - hardly a surprise with the resources they have at their disposal, but to be feared by opposition scrums

Defence coach Brad Harris swings straight into a technical session on line out maul defence. The system is simple and repeatable, and works similarly whether the opposition throws to the front, middle or back. This is no talk-fest: players act out their roles on the centre of the floor, and are chosen at random to explain, not just what the patterns are, but why they are employed.

Then comes the kicker - Harris emphasising that the changing room is where the learning is done. "There will be no 'walk throughs' out on the field; that is where we execute, and we do it at speed."

The message is strong and clear: "From today, we lift our on-field training standards to above game standard," he urges.

Harris shifts to 'pick and go' defence, utilising clips taken from the World Cup. He highlights the visual clues from the ball carrier which signal to defenders when to apply a double tackle - to put dual shoulders into the runner to halt his progress. Unsurprisingly, there is a focus on body height, and the execution of what Harris calls a 'crack tackle'; drop the knee, lead with the arms, shoulder under the ball. Springbok RG Snyman is singled out in a perfect example, snuffing out an Irish raid.

"If someone as tall as Snyman can do it, anyone can," implores Harris.

The backs meeting, in an adjacent room, is just as detailed. Attack coach Tim Sampson lays out some basic principles to begin with, around trust (don't repeat mistakes), respect (no short cuts), understanding (each other as people and as players), and enjoyment (walking in the building in the morning with a smile and walking out at night with the same smile).

If anything, Sampson is slightly less prescriptive than Parling and Harris next door, saying, "I will provide the tone and form the basic principles, but you boys have licence to set the agenda and make decisions during a match, 80/20."

To illustrate, he rolls a clip from last season's match against the Blues. During play, Reece Hodge has noticed the Blues' open side flanker slow to react off the side of the scrum, and with the Rebels feeding a defensive 5m scrum, he is standing at second receiver on the goal-line instead of his standard position in the in-goal pocket, ready for a clearing kick. Hodge has a quick word to Carter Gordon and Ryan Louwrens inside him, calling for a pass direct to him from the scrum. The scrum is solid, Louwrens feeds cleanly, Hodge runs straight at his man and pops a soft ball on the inside to Gordon, who is running at full pace. As Hodge predicted, the covering defender is a fraction too slow off the scrum and Gordon easily busts the one-arm tackle attempt. Play sweeps upfield, well into the Blues' half and, multiple phases later, Andrew Kellaway plunges over the try-line for a wonderful team try. It's a clear example of what happens when a player, given licence, uses his initiative on the field - not to take an unnecessary risk from his own goal-line, but to recognise an opportunity, and to take responsibility to act upon it.

This hits another of Sampson and Foote's principles: to be 'fearless'.

As Sampson explains to the players: "We play to score, not to set up."

He repeats it, slowly, for effect: *"We play to score, not to set up."*

Again, there are examples from the 2023 season, the side scoring tries from first phase ball, striking off moves that have been pre-planned, or called on the field in response to how the defence is set up against them.

Then, another non-negotiable: "We compete to win," stresses Sampson. "Every single battle."

To hammer it home, Sampson quickly sets up a team game on a table, inside backs versus outside backs, flipping plastic cups in a relay. It's fun, good humoured and loud, and highly competitive. Which is exactly the point

- whatever the situation, this Rebels side fights to win. It is the inside backs who celebrate, scoring bragging rights for the day.

The topic shifts to extra effort and outside backs 'swinging' in attack. It's another World Cup winner who is highlighted on video: Willie le Roux, in one passage from fullback against Argentina, swinging hard as the play shifts from side to side, right to left, left to right, right to left, passing, cleaning out, regaining his feet quickly, until he is in position to make the final, scoring pass to his winger on the left touchline. It's brilliant play. World class. Without le Roux's effort and multiple involvements, the try doesn't get scored.

Sampson also uses home grown examples - good and bad - and his main point hits home. The player working hard to swing around behind the receiver, even if he doesn't take the pass, creates a blur in the minds of the defenders; enough to affect their decision making, to entice them onto the wrong man or, at worst, create enough hesitation for a half-gap to open up. Sampson eyes each of the outside backs. Be that man.

With the forwards done, Harris has switched rooms. His message for the day is around communication from the backfield, and to illustrate how, if this drops off at any point, it feeds into slow reactions and passivity at the gain line. The modern rugby pitch is no place for quiet, reserved types, or wingers and fullbacks who prefer to mind their own business in the backfield. On the ball or off the ball, their ability to read the play and communicate with the front line is crucially important.

It's Tuesday morning but it feels like match day. There are three hours remaining before the team hits the training track. That time will be spent doing light gym work, refuelling, preparation and strapping, before another 10-15 minute team talk to ramp up the intensity and re-assert the objectives for the main session.

By the time the first whistle blows outside, every player will know exactly what their role is for the session and the performance expected of them.

Chapter Four

12th December, 2023

In the 28 years of Super Rugby, Australian teams have won just four titles: the Brumbies in 2001 and 2004, the Reds in 2011 and the Waratahs in 2014. In matches against New Zealand sides, the disparity is pronounced: zero Australian wins in 2017, two wins in 2021, and by 2023, the tally 'improving' to six wins. No Australian franchise has ever won a play-off final in New Zealand.

One constant throughout the period has been the claim that New Zealand sides have been much fitter than their Australian counterparts. In part, this is an understandable but misplaced attribution which discounts the cohesion factor derived from New Zealand professionals playing more rugby and more rugby *together* in their NPC, and the emphasis New Zealand rugby placed in the professional era on developing skilful, mobile, ball-playing forwards, quick transition into counterattack, and emphasising try scoring over defence. When players are faced with wave after wave of fast, incisive attack it's easy to appear lead-footed. And yes, unfit.

There are also many people closely involved with the game on both sides of the Tasman, who attest to the fitness disparity being real. Australian players, perhaps satisfied with having made a professional squad, perhaps not under the same pressure to maintain their place because of shallow player depth, perhaps still basking in the afterglow of a comfortable, private school upbringing, perhaps under coaches yet to fully grasp how high the fitness bar had been raised… some or all of those things… weren't as conditioned for Super Rugby as they should have been.

All of which makes Luke Vella, Head of Athletic Performance, one of the most important people in the Rebels' organisation. In December, two months out from round one, possibly *the* most important.

Of short build but with a firm, commanding presence, Vella's career progression, and the timing of his promotion into the top job, suggests he is well placed to deliver a squad that will lack nothing in comparison to any other team in the competition. Having obtained a PHD in Exercise and Nutritional Science, completed part-time while working for the Collingwood AFL club, Vella followed those five years with two at another AFL club, St Kilda, before relocating to the UK to support his wife Laura, a sports psychologist.

"That led to me picking up a job as Strength and Conditioning coach at the University of Bath, working across a range of sports," he explains. "But my really big break came when I was lucky enough to get a position at Edinburgh under Richard Cockerill, a dual English Premiership winning coach with Leicester, and someone I rate very highly."

Always intending to return home to Victoria, Vella maintained contact with the Rebels, before being appointed to assist then S & C head, Will Markwick, who departed at the end of the 2023 season to take on a position at the Western Stormers, in Cape Town.

"Will was in this role for six years: an absolute professional who leaves a strong imprint and legacy, and who is a huge personal influence. For the two years I assisted him we were strongly aligned, and now that I have the head role I don't see any need to make paradigm shifts. My job is to build on that where it's appropriate to do so, and to guide the organisation and the players through what is more like a natural evolution. As much as anything, it's my having a different voice that enables the club to steer its way through change."

Like most things in elite level sport, these are subtle, precise measures. Not change for change's sake. Not wholesale, 'burn it down and start again', change - but adjustments at the margins. Enough to meet the needs of the professional game as it evolves, and to appropriately recognise where things can be improved upon.

"There's two things we know about the new law variations that were introduced into Super Rugby last year," Vella explains, by way of example. "The ball is out of play for eight minutes less, and the ball is in play for two minutes more. That's eight minutes less time for the players to do more work. That explains why we saw, across the competition, much higher incidences of muscle cramping. Which makes it incumbent on me to ensure players are conditioned optimally to meet that changed demand on them."

There's more. "Something we've spoken about a lot here, is around the realisation that getting the players to the start line isn't enough. The players must be much fitter, more than we've ever had them in the past. Ready, at their top, right from round one."

If that sounds simple and obvious and prompts the question, 'why wasn't this done before?' Vella outlines the mindset. "The compulsion, the natural instinct, is always to err on the side of looking after the players. Of course we push them hard, but nobody wants to risk breaking a player - causing an injury that will have them out of the game. Nobody wins when that happens."

It's akin to how a professional road cyclist uses data to manage their output during a stage race. Every rider is acutely aware of their limit, and when their onboard data tells them they are in the red zone, they have little choice but to take their foot off the throttle. Even if they feel like they'd be able to maintain high watts and stay at the front of the race for longer, they would inevitably 'blow up' - what in marathon running is known as 'hitting the wall' - and they would not only lose by a greater distance, but impinge on their ability to back up again the next day.

"So we know what we don't want to happen, but we're certainly looking hard at how we can adjust that balance between risk and outcome. To take advantage of the better player depth we have. To tilt things slightly more in favour of getting a player fitter, whilst understanding the calculated risk associated with that," Vella says.

As it happens, the Wallabies program has experienced a higher than normal incidence of serious soft tissue injuries over the last few seasons. Commonly thought to be an S & C issue, it's more likely to be a result of a communication breakdown between S & C, Medical and coaching staff, all pursuing slightly different objectives.

"That alignment imperative is something we take very seriously," says Vella. "We run regular 'push and protect' meetings, where it is the job of myself and Kat (Katherine Rottier, head physiotherapist) and her support staff to be completely candid with each other around where players are at, before informing the coaching staff of our recommendations. Kat is very experienced and level-headed, and we both understand that it's our job to serve the head coach. We do that by making 100% professional and medically based decisions, telling the coach what he needs to know, not what he wants to know."

Given the regularity with which players swing in and out from their franchise programs into the Wallabies program, there is another layer of complexity added. More opinions, more voices.

Vella again; "It's fair to say that things aren't quite at the level of detail as they were under Dean Benton, when he was involved with the Wallabies, but current S & C head Nigel Astley-Jones is very supportive. And Rugby Australia sent down John Clarke and Kieran Cleary to hand over the seven Wallabies when they resumed training with us, so there's a lot of effort going in from both sides to make sure that the players feel well looked after, whichever program they're in, and that the messaging and the management of the individual player programs is consistent."

An obvious individual test for Vella is how he handles Taniela Tupou, given his importance to the Wallabies, and his newness to the Rebels. "It's an enormous challenge and responsibility," he says. "The key is to manage the relationship first. Build trust and mutual respect, learn from and about each other, and the physical follows from that."

It's sound thinking, but there's more. "It was apparent with the Wallabies this year how much of a positive influence Will Skelton had on players like Taniela. Will's experience, his personal growth from his success with Saracens and La Rochelle, how he commands respect, his level of professionalism… smart trainers and coaches leverage off those players, using them to reinforce the right messages to the rest of the group. We have a couple of those guys in our group, Sam (Talakai) and Khan (Lukhan Salakaia-Loto) with the same kind of seniority and respect, who already have strong relationships with Taniela, so without me shifting any responsibility, they potentially have a role to play in helping me get the most out of him. Taniela's a great guy, and so far, so good."

That plays nicely into the emphasis Vella is placing on the players who form the tight five. "It's no secret that we have a huge amount of talent and depth in the core group, this season. But with that comes expectation. That other sides will target us, looking to nullify our strength, and from our side, knowing that we have to perform up to those high expectations. So again, if we're talking about building fitness and resilience, it applies even more to the tight five. That's where we can really get things humming."

For now, nearing the end of the current training block, a week out from the players being sent home for a short break over Xmas and New Year, Vella is cautiously optimistic. A number of players are ahead of where they were expected to be, and the list of injured players limited to restricted training programs is mercifully small. But all of that only serves to make Vella more anxious. How much harder can he push? When the holiday arrives and the players get to relax over Xmas lunch with their families and reconnect with friends, it isn't difficult to imagine Vella poring over copious sets of data, looking for any opportunity he can find to wind things up another notch. Whatever happens in 2024, if the Rebels endure another losing season, it won't be because they're not fit enough.

With a club open day scheduled for Saturday, the coaching team meets to discuss what they want to achieve from the day, and how this may impact upon the rest of this week's activities. Nick Stiles provides the outline; there will be an emphasis on combining the men's, women's and academy teams, but with so many players on the pitch at any one time, and a high degree of unfamiliarity among them, expectations of gaining something tangible from the session is compromised. There is unanimous desire within the group to try to meet multiple objectives. To deliver value to the other teams via their direct exposure to the leading men's players and coaches, but also, to schedule in a men's unit component which will extract some value from the day.

Once that is agreed upon, the group adopts a backfilling process. Kevin Foote maintains a grid - essentially a juiced-up daily planner - pre-populated, designed to ensure that all of the skills, strength and conditioning, tactical, teamwork and administration needs are not only methodically ticked off, but blend harmoniously. The objectives and detail for Thursday's session are quickly agreed on. Rob Taylor's kicking program will take precedence - exits from defensive 5m scrums and line outs, all the way down to 35m. Left side and right side. Who is kicking, from where, to where. Attacking kicks. Kick chase formations. Everything done with a purpose. Detail piled upon detail.

There's something else. Foote throws in an observation from yesterday's session: a disconnect in breakdown defence between back row forwards Josh Kemeny and Vaiolini Ekuasi. It's nothing to dwell on, just something to be attended to, and he puts it back onto Geoff Parling and Brad Harris to clarify and fix before the next session.

Using the planning grid as the primary reference point, it is easy to identify, at a glance, anything that has been missed. Any unit forgone on Saturday or today must be accommodated elsewhere. If not, the team risks arriving at round one underdone. Unsurprisingly, Vella's is a dominant voice at the table. He reminds the group that, if time is an issue, he is flexible in allowing conditioning objectives to be met via blending in skills and set-piece components, so that nothing gets left behind. Regardless, everyone understands how, at this stage of the season, data is driving the process. Open day or not, there must be no compromise when it comes to hitting the right conditioning loads.

Chapter Five

13th December, 2023

Like Flinders Street station on a busy weekday morning, the Rebels' gym is buzzing with activity. It feels chaotic but in a controlled way. Staff and players criss-cross between four workstations set up for the day's media activities. They've been set an ambitious mission - to tick off all of the video content required internal and external media, in one hit. Ripples of laughter intersect as players in various parts of the room take turns to pre-record individual messages - mostly, but not all scripted - to fans, local clubs and for the various social media channels.

The messages are cleverly designed so that they cover the whole season. All video content captured will be archived and pulled out for use when required, the obvious benefit being that one arduous day now - long before the season hots up - is far more preferable than going back to players to record grabs each week during the season proper. It's a charade, but one the players are well on top of.

Flanker Josh Kemeny projects an outward confidence that comes with first-time Wallaby selection in 2023, and a trip to the World Cup. More exposure to media duties breeds familiarity in front of the camera, but there is also a noticeable shift in assuredness that comes with him validating himself as a rugby player. With only brief minutes in his two Tests under Eddie Jones and no guarantee that he will be picked up by the new Wallabies coach, Kemeny knows he is far from having 'made it'. Nevertheless, he has established an important foothold. Being one of seven current Wallabies in the club, he commands a higher credibility and level of respect than he did previously, which feeds into the way he confidently handles himself when the 'record' button lights up.

"Hi, Josh Kemeny here… we're looking forward to a big match this weekend against the Waratahs… it's great to know we've got your support, all the players really appreciate it."

Like clockwork, teammates fall in behind.

"Hi, I'm Carter Gordon, thanks for being on board with the Rebels… wishing you all a great Easter."

Some players lap up the opportunity to perform; class clowns Rob Leota and Jordie Uelese are prominent, while others, like emerging lock forward Josh Canham, give the impression they'd rather be at the dentist undergoing root canal treatment. The biggest group however, are the players who claim to dislike it, but who secretly don't mind.

As utility back Nick Jooste explains: "even though some of us might not naturally blend with the camera or like speaking about ourselves publicly, it kind of reinforces our privileged position as professional rugby players. It reminds us that even though there are some things that take us out of our comfort zone, we're still doing something that we love, that we know other people would love to be able to do."

Players not yet in front of the camera are busy elsewhere. The physio room comes off the gym at one end, where three massage tables are set up, side-by-side. Each table is occupied by a mass of player muscle and strategically placed white towels. Willing hands work methodically to soothe aching tissue.

Also, directly off the gym is a team meeting room, today fitted out with portable clothes racks, the kind normally associated with behind the scenes activity at a fashion show. Only there is no catwalk and no fashion editors looking to tap into the next big trend; just players being fitted up for the suits they will wear to selected events and on match nights. It's a rugby truism that those players not in the match day 23 offer a higher grade of support to their teammates when they are dressed in their number ones.

Elsewhere, CEO Stephenson has given up his office for mouthguard fitting. In contrast to the frivolity at the other stations, this is serious business, all franchises having agreed to participate in the trial of new technology to assist with concussion diagnosis. A result of a Euro 2million investment on the part of World Rugby, in conjunction with technology partner Prevent Biometrics, the new smart mouthguard will send information in real time to the independent match day doctor, to indicate where a player has experienced a high acceleration event that has not been picked up by an observing doctor, team medic or broadcast cameras. It's an important enhancement to the existing HIA process, to ensure that all at-risk players, not some, are removed from the field for precautionary assessment.

The Rebels are no different to any other franchise when it comes to head injury: fully cognisant of the seriousness of the issue but not exactly sure where everything is heading. The mouthguard trial is seen by those in rugby as a step forward, but is viewed with scepticism by some prominent advocates in the sports concussion space as being imprecise, and validating an already flawed HIA process. Above all, the Rebels are committed to the protection of their players, happy and eager to comply with whatever measures are asked of them. Not only mouthguards but restrictions around maximum contact times at training, and adhering to the yellow and red card sanctions that come with the constant tinkering around high contact laws. Defence coach Harris is at the forefront: it is one thing to build a tight defensive system and ensure that there is sting in the tackling, but as the All Blacks learned the hard way at the World Cup, there is a premium placed on keeping all 15 players on the field.

"Yes mate," says Harris, in his trademark, laconic way. "It's my job to instil discipline and accuracy. It's a combination of technique and mindset. I'm really proud of how we've achieved that with the Fijian sides I've been involved with. Big, powerful lads with a reputation for heavy hitting. I think we've showed how it's possible to harness that, through developing trusting relationships with them so that we get more consistent outcomes, and keep guys on the field, without taking away the big hits that all the fans love and expect."

Players too, are philosophical and supportive of the new mouthguard initiative. Waiting his turn, halfback James "Bobby" Tuttle, an Australia A representative, outlines how, earlier in his career, he played through head knocks that he now knows would necessitate an assessment and, potentially, time out of the game. "It's the classic situation," he explains. "I've seen it with many other guys too. When you're younger and establishing yourself, looking to impress, keen to get starts, you never want to show anything that might rule you out of contention. Later in my career, sure, I still want to start, but I think more about what comes after rugby. And because of that, I make different decisions when it comes to my body and my health."

Overseeing the day's activities is GM, Consumer and Marketing, Rachel Mitrione. Now in her third year with the Rebels, she comes from an AFL background, working in a similar role with Essendon Football club. She loves the environment and is excited at the potential for rugby, and for the

Rebels in Melbourne. But having seen the other side of the fence, hers is a job full of frustration and 'what ifs?'

"We spend hour after hour looking at what we can do to entice more people into taking up memberships. Some of the ticketing packages we introduced last year (bundled deals for the matches against New Zealand teams, special pricing for Pacific Island family groups) are innovative and we think offer terrific value. Perhaps the club hasn't always done things as well as it could have, and COVID was a terrible inhibitor for us, but in the last few years we've really made an effort to connect better to Melbourne's rugby community. But I really think it's not so much an issue with the Rebels, but a code issue. If we go back to the 2003 World Cup, the sport hasn't really invested in promoting the game of rugby. We don't seem to know how to create heroes. That's the main difference compared to AFL. There, the players are the attraction. At open training sessions we'd get hundreds of parents and kids along, all wanting to touch their favourite player or get a selfie with them. In rugby, even the kids that play, they don't know the names of the players, who the stars of the game are. Because it's nobody's job to make that happen. And there's no budget for it."

But what about sending the players out more into schools and clubs, to talk to youngsters and conduct clinics? Shouldn't the players be doing more to drive interest on the ground? "In a perfect world, yes," says Mitrione. "And some players are better at it than others, and enjoy it more than others. But what a lot of people don't understand, is that it's a challenge around their CBA (collective bargaining agreement). There are restrictions as to what players can do, and for anything above and beyond that, it triggers additional payments that we, and I'm sure most of the clubs, can't afford."

Once again, the comparison with AFL is stark. "They have what is called an additional services agreement (ASA) where 10 players from each club are paid extra for marketing activities," Mitrione explains. "But of course, they have the money to be able to do this."

Since the birth of the Rebels in 2011, many international stars of the game have visited Melbourne to play in Super Rugby. From New Zealand, South Africa, Argentina, Japan, Fiji, Samoa and Tonga. Names roll off the tongue like a smooth Bordeaux red; Carter, Read, Savea, Barrett, Smith, Matfield, Etzebeth, Marx, de Klerk, Matera, Sanchez, Leitch, and many others. It seems faintly ridiculous to expect the Rebels, with their minuscule promotions budget, to be responsible for promoting the global stars of the game. This should be a given - something that the competition itself provides. But, time after time, world-class players slip in and out of AAMI Park, seen only by the hardcore fans, because nobody outside of the rusted-on base understands what Super Rugby is, and where these players fit in the bigger scheme of things.

Even the Bledisloe Cup match in July was another missed opportunity. Stretching across both sides of Melbourne's Tullamarine Freeway, the main route to and from the airport, were two massive billboards, advertising the upcoming match at the MCG. It contained oversized images of two players, one from each side: Michael Hooper for the Wallabies, and Folau Fakatava for the All Blacks. But Hooper was no longer in the Wallabies squad and with the ascension of the Hurricane's Cam Roigard, Fakatava had slipped to New Zealand's 4th ranked halfback, with zero prospect of getting anywhere near the MCG. So much for enticing potential fans along to see the current stars of the game. Anyone can make an honest mistake or be cruelled by a sudden change in circumstances. But it's odds-on that nobody in Rugby Australia nor the marketing company they contracted the job to, either knows or understands how and why this was yet another missed opportunity to promote rugby in a meaningful and effective way.

Nevertheless, Mitrione and her small team soldier on. They also know that the club can help itself by delivering on-field success. "Our research and feedback show that fans were happy with how our side played last year," she says. "That's obviously key, that people feel entertained and proud about the way the team conducts itself, and the style of play. But yes, we know that to build on that, we need to get more wins."

Social media is an important fan connector and, by comparison to the other Australian franchises, the Rebels produce content more often and of better quality, than any of their peers. The data is intriguing, with the number of followers on the different platforms being: Facebook 95,209, Instagram 61,068, Twitter 40,100 and an e-mail database of 18,014.

This year, there is also the addition of a weekly videocast, uploaded onto the club's website. Hosted by Super W captain (and new mum) Mel Kawa, outside back Joe Pincus and hooker Alex Mafi, it's a fun, informative glimpse behind the scenes, with other players taking turns to guest, to share some of their rugby IP and spill their darkest secrets. The finished product is rough and ready - nobody will accuse the club of splurging when it comes to production values - but that's part of its charm. Pincus in particular, takes to the hosting role like a seasoned professional.

Overall, while there are some who follow the club across multiple platforms, the channels listed mostly comprise discrete groups, based around different age and demographics. "Obviously it speaks to the potential that is lurking in the background, and what we can unlock if the side starts winning, and if there can be a wider reconnection of the Australian fanbase with Super Rugby. On the other hand, some AFL and NRL players have multiples more Instagram followers just on their own, so it shows you how far we still have to go," says Mitrione, smiling ruefully.

Saturday's open day comes and goes. Despite plenty of push through the social media channels, spectator numbers are muted, but the event is rated a success by all in the high-performance team, with the objective of mixing the three squads together working a treat. It's hard to quantify just what motivational effect this will have on the careers of the women and junior players, but the number of broad smiles tell their own story.

Outside the ropes, the overall mood is subdued, almost certainly due to a report that surfaced midweek in the Australian Financial Review, claiming that the Rebels are millions of dollars in debt, and raising concerns around the club's viability. Some of the board members named in the article are present, unamused by the tone of the reporting. For CEO Stephenson, acknowledging the substance, it is the twisted context and misrepresentation of facts that grates. As well as coming to terms with where and how the story was sourced. The kind of detailed financial information that is now in the public domain can only have come from one of two places - inside the Rebels' sanctum, or from within Rugby Australia. And Stephenson knows his office well enough to know that it isn't the source.

Chapter Six

19th December, 2023

It's one of the oldest cliches in sport: 'there are just two types of coaches, those who have been sacked and those who are waiting to be sacked'. Setting aside Super W coach Jason Rogers, within the Rebels' ranks there are four men who have held the position of head coach, two of whom left the job the hard way; Nick Stiles, sacked by the Queensland Reds at the end of the 2017 season, and Tim Sampson, sent packing by the Western Force at the end of the 2022 season. Brad Harris enjoyed success as head coach in the NRC, with the Canberra Vikings (runners-up in 2015) and the Fijian Drua (winners in 2018) and is yet to join the ranks of the sacked; something he jokingly puts down to nimbleness, moving to new assignments before anyone gets the chance to swing the axe. The fourth is Kevin Foote, head coach in the NRC with the Perth Spirit in 2017, now entering his third season in the hot seat with the Rebels. (His coaching history also includes teaching Matt Damon how to play rugby for his role as Francois Pienaar in the 2009 film *Invictus*). Although a realist, Foote has no intention of joining that club any time soon.

"I know there's a fascination in the media around sacking coaches, but to be frank, it's the furthest thing from my mind," he affirms. "I'm fully focused on my work, to ensure that myself and the other coaches deliver the best possible outcome for the club. And I'm confident that we're building something special here, and that the work that everyone is putting in will translate into results."

Australian rugby has long harboured an obsession with head coaches. It lauds the successful (Alan Jones, 1984 grand slam tour; Bob Dwyer, 1991 World Cup, Rod McQueen, 1999 World Cup) and hounds out the 'failures', sometimes for emotional or parochial reasons rather than rational. The last Australian coach to win Super Rugby was Michael Cheika, in 2014, with the Waratahs. Subsequently elevated to Wallabies head coach, his team made the World Cup final the next year, losing to a New Zealand side ranked by many observers as their best ever. But by the end of the next World Cup cycle, Cheika was seen as divisive, too hard to manage, too quick apportion blame to match officials. And somewhere along the way, his side had lost connection to an identifiable, discernible style of play.

No Australian coach however, has generated attention and news headlines like Eddie Jones. Parachuted into a second term in the Wallabies role by Hamish McLennan, at the expense of the widely respected Dave Rennie, Jones worked tirelessly after his appointment, to restore Australian rugby's public profile. But within a few short months, his trademark cheeky grin, snappy one-liners and Australia's supposed 'soft' World Cup draw were exposed as a gossamer-thin veil that failed to mask a number of terminal deficiencies. In hindsight, the army of fans seduced by the possibility of a miracle, saw the truth. In the time available - nine months from appointment to the World Cup - Jones was never going to be able to identify the players and coaches he wanted, install a game plan and identity, and turn his Wallabies into a cohesive and credible unit, capable of beating the best rugby nations in the world - most of whom were working within a carefully planned four-year cycle. Among the bevy of coaches approached by Jones for assistant roles, some were genuinely unavailable while others had been warned off by people who had themselves been burned by Jones in previous jobs. By the end of the World Cup, the Wallabies' 2023 record - just two wins against Georgia and Portugal, to set against seven losses - seemed neither here nor there. Jones the man, Jones the story, transcended all of that. History will focus on Jones' deceit and his repeated denials that he was talking to Japan about walking out on the Wallabies for the Japan head coach role - right up until the time he was being introduced to the press pack in Tokyo. But while all of that unedifying circus, and the tone of the media reporting accompanying it, reinforces the notion that the biggest person in any rugby system is the head coach, that's not an accurate portrayal of how things work in practice. Winning and losing head coaches make headlines - for obvious reasons. But what is lost in all of the building up and tearing down is a true sense of how a rugby organisation operates, and the myriad factors that influence whether a franchise is successful of not.

For Foote and the Rebels, the story being less about him, and more about the whole club, is both accurate and healthy. Blessed with an engaging personality, Foote is a willing front-face and is as driven as the next coach, but not to the extent where everything needs to be about him. He has a job description, and it's important to him that it is well defined, with no ambiguity around what he sees as its three main components:

- to provide leadership and define the culture
- to influence and support the assistant coaches
- to provide clarity about how we want to play

Those three components intersect when it comes to Foote delegating 'gatekeeper' responsibility for his three game-style pillars:

- FAST, Geoff Parling, forwards coach
- FEARLESS, Tim Sampson, attack coach
- RESOLUTE, Brad Davis, defence coach

Foote is prescriptive in articulating how he wants these delivered. Ball speed from the forward breakdown unit (FAST); team rules around offloading, intent and execution (FEARLESS); unbending work ethic (RESOLUTE).

It is 'Fearless' that is the hardest to define; the one containing the greyest area. Says Foote, "It can be difficult to show players, 'what does fearless look like?' It's not the same as reckless, but it's also not about players stopping to think about what is a calculated risk. Take the contrast between two players in the back three this (2023) season, Monty Ioane (since transferred to Lyon in the French Top 14), and Andrew Kellaway. Kells values fundamentals and sound decision making. He can always be trusted to make good decisions and execute well, in defence and attack. With Monty, you didn't always know what he was giving you. High work rate, a willingness to make things happen, an ability to create something out of nothing; yes. But winning outcomes? Not every time. In a perfect world, you would blend those two guys."

Foote is philosophical about the things that change when you become head coach. "Take club coaching. You do everything: all the technical coaching, the organisation, the emotional support... everything. It's exhausting, but it's all down to you and it can be exhilarating when you enjoy success. From there, the great thing about assistant coaching in a professional franchise is that this is where you really get to help make players better - working with them on their skills development, establishing trust and the close personal bonds necessary to help them develop emotionally and as a rugby player. The big difference when you become head coach is that you don't get as much time with players individually. Your door is always open, you're still a big influence, obviously, but on a different level. Not with every player, not every day."

Instead, Foote's is a bigger picture, overarching role, managing the whole program, always with his grid as a reference point. The head coach also carries primary selection responsibility. The Rebels' coaching group may be furiously democratic and collaborative, but there are occasions, when it comes to final selection, where Foote is required to make a call, in the process reminding everyone who is in charge.

"I don't waste the opportunity either, if it comes off, to subtly remind everyone," he grins. "Take David Feliuai, who came straight to us from playing in Romania. Not everyone understood what we were getting, but I could see what he had. In his character and his physical attributes. And he's been huge for us."

Foote's biggest role by far is the work he puts into and with his coaches; sounding them out and being a sounding board, constantly checking in, individually and collectively, sharing every scrap of information, aligning and re-aligning, making sure nothing is missed or left to assumption, asking and answering questions, always trusting, always challenging each other. 'What is it that we can be doing better?' is a recurring question. As important as the playing list is, Foote leaves no doubt as to how highly he views the importance of the coaching team. It is their cumulative expertise and the level of respect and trust afforded each other in their communication, that is integral to the success of the side.

It's a busy morning, with the schedule front-loaded to allow the players to be on their way by lunchtime, into their Xmas break. The players are stripped and on the field by 7.45am, already split into two teams, warming up separately, as they would for a real game. It's as close to a match simulation as is possible to replicate for this time of year; two 15-minute halves: opposed but not full contact, with the line outs and mauls fully live, overseen by local referee, Oli Kellett on the whistle. Not only does Kellett provide an air of authenticity and helps cement in a higher level of intensity, his presence also enables the coaches to concentrate fully on observing the players' skill execution and combinations. It's dynamic, with the emphasis very much on keeping things moving and playing at tempo.

At the end of it, Foote is delighted. There are no injuries, the players have never been as fit at this time of year, and some of the younger brigade - he singles out forwards Tavi Tuipulotu and Wyatt Ballenger - are making exceptional progress.

The players showered and fed, all that is left to do is to gather for one more team meeting, but not before Geoff Parling steps in to fulfil his other important role, on top of his forward coaching responsibilities. Looming large as club rubbish monitor, players are reminded by Parling, in plain language, to ensure that food scraps, paper plates and utensils end up in the correct bin. "Some of these boys can be a bit lazy," Parling grumbles under his breath, like a grizzled, worn parent.

The meeting is a final opportunity for Foote to send the squad away with the right message foremost in their minds. But first, the floor is handed to Luke Vella, to outline his do's and don'ts for the Xmas period, and to acknowledge some of the physical achievements in the pre-season blocks to date. An award for the biggest strength gain goes to fly-half Jake Strachan, while the fastest player is no surprise - seven's recruit Darby Lancaster, at 9.98 metres/sec edging Lachie Anderson. Stuart Tualima, younger brother of utility forward Tuaina, is honoured for the biggest Bronco improvement, while the player who has completed the most sessions unmodified is Bobby Tuttle. Over the course of this training block, Tuttle has logged an impressive 14 kilometres more in distance than any other player. With competition red hot for a starting place at halfback this season, he is doing everything he can to put himself into the frame.

Also singled out is Lukhan Salakaia-Loto. Second placed in a number of categories, his numbers speak to how much he has taken to the Rebels' environment since his arrival in Melbourne; 4kgs heavier with a 21mm reduction in skin fold; a 19 second reduction in his Bronco time; and an impressive 20kg improvement to his max squat lift. Everyone knows it counts for nothing until it is transferred into performance on the field, but Vella's acknowledgement clearly goes down well with Salakaia-Loto and the rest of the playing group.

It's a nice segue into Foote's final act. He asks for contributions from the floor, for players to single out a teammate, to provide examples of where that player exhibits character, competence, connection and trust. There is no shortage of takers. The full group, including Wallabies and new signings, has only been together for a fortnight, but they have come together quickly, on-field and off.

As the last of the players file out, some to tackle their Xmas shopping, some on their way to the airport, more stories about the club are breaking, this time in the News Ltd and Nine media. There are no new revelations, but with the initial story in the Australian Financial Review largely hidden from wider view, and the Eddie Jones story in Japan finally running out of legs, the two big media players have turned their attention to the domestic scene, and the sniff of blood in Port Philip Bay. A kind reading paints the Rebels' financial situation as 'parlous'. Another interpretation might be 'untenable'.

The dichotomy between the success of morning session, the team meeting and the mood of the playing and coaching group, and the press headlines couldn't be starker. It is impossible to observe the former and believe the latter.

Thrust into the middle of a firestorm, Chairman Docherty and CEO Stephenson face a huge test of their resolve and competencies. With Rugby Australia vowing not to restore the annual grant made to franchises to pre-COVID levels, not only do they have to cauterise what now appears to be a gaping financial wound, they have to maintain the confidence of the staff and players, sponsors and fans.

Media who normally wouldn't touch rugby with a 40-foot barge pole buzz their phones, seeking comment. Even if certain reporters aren't genuinely interested in rugby or the health of the sport in Melbourne, they must still be respectfully attended to.

The next morning, it feels bizarre to hear references to the Rebels on Melbourne breakfast radio news - something that simply never happens. If only the old adage 'any publicity is good publicity' was actually true.

Stephenson draws breath, insistent that much of what has been reported is overblown and misconstrued. "We are in the process of finalising an arrangement with the ATO, we have an extremely competent and supportive board, and we are managing our situation," he insists.

Despite media-driven speculation, he insists the Rebels aren't about to fold or, as some reports speculate, be sent up the Hume Highway into a forced merger with the Brumbies. But any thoughts of a quiet, relaxing Xmas with family have been swept by the wayside.

Chapter Seven

22nd December, 2023

"Our intent is to have five Super Rugby teams and a presence in our biggest markets, and Melbourne is clearly one of the biggest markets."

Out and about on ABC breakfast television, it is Rugby Australia CEO Phil Waugh's careful use of the word "intent" that hits Rebels fans in the solar plexus. As ever, the instability in Australian rugby is laid bare, and Waugh's qualification makes it evident that for as long as there is a chopping block, the Rebels will remain squarely on it.

There are no new revelations added to the story that came to light last week, but for anguished chairman Paul Docherty, this is a hardening of the battle-lines. "Myself and my board, we've given years of volunteer service and loads of cash, to grow and support the game… we're in the process of working with Rugby Australia to show how we and the Victorian government help get rugby out of its mess, and… we get leaked on to the newspapers? Including disclosure of private information that has nothing to do with rugby? How does that help change the game for the good? They withdraw funding after it is committed, then tell us, 'just do your best'. And if you don't succeed, we will kill you. What does that say about what Rugby Australia thinks of its member states and the game's stakeholders and fans?"

Waugh heads straight to a press conference, to confirm the appointment of Peter Horne as Rugby Australia's new director of high performance and, to follow later in 2024, the return from Ireland of successful performance consultant David Nucifora, in an advisory role. It's a rare good news story for Australian rugby, but in typical fashion, it doesn't take long for questioning to stray into familiar, combative territory: Eddie Jones, and Australia's capacity to support five Super Rugby teams.

Waugh tiptoes deftly, attempting to justify the failure of his organisation to restore funding to the franchises that was cut as a COVID austerity measure. With annual grants at $5.5m pre-COVID, cut to $3.8m for the third year running, and restoration off the table for 2024 as well, that's a

$6.8m revenue hole that all franchises are faced with - highly problematic given the $5m annual salary cap they are operating under.

"It's not just the absence of the money," explains Stephenson, "but that we were given assurances it would be reinstated. That's the basis for our cashflow management, and to have the rug pulled from under us in that way clearly causes problems for us with respect to our creditors."

If Waugh is sympathetic, he isn't letting on. With only a modest TV deal in place, an anticipated private equity injection failing to materialise and costs rising, including the need to fund an expanding women's program, Waugh is merely cutting his cloth to suit. As far as Rugby Australia is concerned, funding to the franchises isn't being restored because the money isn't there to do it. Waugh is prosecuting the argument in public merely to signify how serious he is about it.

In principle, the same situation applies to all five franchises. But after being cut adrift by Rugby Australia in 2017, the Western Force have re-emerged stronger, due to the financial backing of two of Australia's wealthiest people, Andrew ('Twiggy') and Nicola Forrest. Benefitting from the awarding of hosting rights for the 2032 Olympic Games, the Queensland Reds have worked closely with a Queensland state government eager to build sporting infrastructure and underpin their future success. Also with strong private backing, and with their Ballymore home converted into a 'state of the art' centre of rugby excellence, with government funding attached, they too are less reliant on Rugby Australia.

The remaining franchises, the Waratahs, Brumbies and Rebels, albeit with differing pressure points, are similarly impecunious. Already, the Waratahs have waved their problems away, handing themselves over, lock, stock and barrel to Rugby Australia, under the guise of a 'centralisation' strategy advocated by the parent body, designed to deliver efficiencies and shared purpose throughout the high-performance layers. Tellingly, there is no public transparency around the numbers involved. But because of their similar natures and structures, the franchises know each other's businesses, one Rebels director noting: "It's in the millions, and there'll be another $4 million or so shortfall this year, that Rugby Australia will pick up on their behalf."

It's one thing for a Sydney franchise to hand over the keys to its henhouse to the Moore Park foxes. Representing Australia's biggest rugby market, no matter how broke, the Waratahs aren't going anywhere. Everyone knows that rugby in Sydney is never going to be cast adrift. Financially, the Waratahs may have had little option other than to acquiesce but - importantly - for them, there is no risk. The Rebels and the Brumbies have no such luxury or guarantee. They have concerns around expertise and Rugby Australia's capacity to manage their businesses. They also know that reversion to four or even three professional franchises is a real possibility. An issue of finances has also become an issue of trust and survival.

"We were actually very open to an aligned or centralised model for the commercial operations - because this is all about the game as a whole, and if people could do it more efficiently, better, cheaper, we're all for it - but those conversations have all stopped in their tracks," Stephenson tells reporters.

It is as if, suddenly, the Rebels are a fifteen-year-old teenager, ostensibly under the control of their parents, reliant on them for food, shelter and support, being told if you want new clothes, or to play school sport, to go and find a job and earn the money to pay for it yourself. And if you don't like it, tough. Further, because it is not just the Rebels, but the Brumbies who are also fragile, it is potentially like two siblings being set against each other by their parents. (By July, with the Rebels safely terminated, unable to find new revenue sources, the Brumbies too agree to hand over their commercial operations to Rugby Australia).

Nowhere is there evidence offered as to how a reduction to four franchises will provide better outcomes for Australian rugby. Potentially, any saving in annual grant money withheld would be more than offset by a reduction in broadcast rights revenue, commensurate with a reduction in content and loss of subscriptions due to the lack of presence in a major market. And nowhere is it explained how the reduction in contracted Super Rugby players from just over 200 nationwide, to around 160, shrinking the pool of elite players and coaches by 20%, is going to improve Australia's on-field performances.

One doesn't need to look far for precedent - the summary dismissal of the Force in 2017. While the Rebels were the beneficiary of a number of players and coaches (including Foote) relocating east, there was no noticeable improvement to the performance of the four remaining franchises. Many of the players cut free simply took up contracts overseas. And, as successful franchises like the Crusaders, Chiefs, and even the Brumbies - Australia's most consistently competitive side - have shown, it is not the random or indiscriminate casting of players here and there that makes a difference. Rather it is stability and cohesion across the whole organisation, the development over time of an unimpeachable culture, and a shared commitment and understanding of what it means to be part of that franchise and to enact the behaviours and actions befitting. How can this even begin to happen if the long-term security of the franchise isn't assured?

Instead, the franchises are effectively being told: 'if you want to play, find the money yourselves. From government, from sponsors, from benefactors. To cover the debt and to cover forward shortfalls. And if you don't find it, your place in Super Rugby won't be guaranteed beyond 2025'.

Waugh's other challenge is that with no competition and broadcast deal in place for 2026 and beyond, a new Super Rugby commission only just coming to fruition (and no inkling as to how it will be resourced), Rugby Australia doesn't have the luxury of allowing things to play out over time. How can it finalise an optimal broadcast deal without offering the bidding companies certainty around the content being offered? Is it Super Rugby Pacific, with 12 competing teams? Or with 10 or 11 teams? Or is it something else altogether - a domestic competition with 10, 11 or 12 teams, a mix of the Force, Rebels, Brumbies and existing clubs from Sydney and Brisbane, with some kind of crossover play-off system with New Zealand and, potentially, Japan? Given that there is a participation agreement in place up until the end of the 2025 season, which guarantees five Australian teams, then extending to 2030, is this even a conversation that should be happening?

Not for the first time, Rugby Australia is the proverbial deer in the headlights: joined at the hip to New Zealand out of commercial necessity and an understanding that high performance rugby is a global construct, while at the same time, trying to appease and accommodate stakeholders in the game who lost interest in Super Rugby long ago, and who look enviously at the AFL and NRL and pine for a healthy, vibrant domestic competition. All the while, seeing the respective merits and necessities from both sides, realising that it can't shut itself off from the rest of the rugby world, but also understanding the psyche of Australian sports fans and media, and their predilection for domestic competitions that they can easily understand and relate to. And so, in the process, finding itself unwilling or unable to make decisions to take the game forward.

For Stephenson, another thing that grates is the notion pushed by some in the media that the Rebels shouldn't be reliant on a handout from Rugby

Australia. "There's a narrative, completely false and misplaced, that somehow the Rebels are a drain on Australian rugby. The franchises clearly have obligations with regard to obtaining sponsorship and membership, but overwhelmingly, it's the sport itself that generates the bulk of the revenue to underpin the game. It's not a handout, it's a normal distribution of funds generated by the competition to the competing franchises. And for that, we produce players and coaches for Australia's high-performance programs, we provide pathways for talented local juniors to become Wallabies and Wallaroos," he says.

For contrast, consider the Melbourne Storm, their headquarters directly opposite, on the western side of AAMI Stadium. Their annual grant (along with all other 16 NRL clubs) is $17m. Most AFL clubs receive around $11m annually, with equivalent expansion clubs in developing markets, the Gold Coast Suns and Greater Western Sydney, said to receive $25m annually. It's hard to imagine a less even playing field.

Tasked with competing against New Zealand franchises containing many of the best players in the world, the Rebels have already been set an enormous task. Now, with $1.7m per year cut from an already modest distribution, they will have to perform in an environment where any misfortune - a loss, an injury to an important player - will quickly be framed by media as 'another nail in the Rebels coffin'. Hardly a context conducive to building a successful professional rugby franchise.

That's some kind of Christmas cheer for Stephenson and Docherty. Neither is old enough to have been served Christmas pudding with thruppence and sixpence coins hidden inside. But whatever the contemporary equivalent is, they will need to find it. Thruppence and sixpence. Many of them. And fast. There are bills that must be paid, payment plans to be solidified, and negative speculation that needs to be dampened. Failure to do so will render all of the good work across the pre-season, and the anticipation of on-field success in 2024, moot.

Chapter Eight

9th January, 2024

It's 8.00am and Kevin Foote and his small group of coaches are huddled around a table. These daily meetings are ostensibly about confirming details for the day's on-field training but this morning, before they get to that, there is other business to attend to.

"I want to start by addressing the matter from yesterday. Make sure we get the tone of the response right," Foote says, calmly but authoritatively.

Hooker Jordie Uelese is the subject - there are concerns about him not channelling his fight into the right areas. In yesterday's opposed session, Uelese was penalised for a breakdown offence by the acting referee and reacted by denying, complaining and throwing the ball away. It's the second instance in as many training sessions.

"We all know Jordie can be prone to negative body language when things don't go his way," says Foote. "But he's a senior player, a Wallaby. And he was clearly in the wrong, both times. Obvious penalties. He reacts like that in a game and we're down a man trying to defend a 5m line-out. It's a killer."

Foote pauses before he articulates how he'd like the group to respond. "Obviously, we need to demonstrate to the rest of the players how this behaviour is unacceptable. But there's no point in shouting at him. He needs more clarity on when things are good, and when they are bad. And he needs to show us that he understands the differences."

The coaches resolve to involve Rob Leota, captain and a close friend of Uelese. That way, their message will be better reinforced. Forwards coach Geoff Parling takes responsibility for seeing that the issue is promptly knocked on the head.

Eyes then turn to the large screen, where the afternoon's session is mapped out in detail. One by one, all of the modified/restricted players are discussed: Luke Vella explaining what activities are ruled in and out. Key flanker, and last year's captain, Brad Wilkin, has got through his first team sessions well and his load will be increased again today, with a view to having him in full contact by next week. And this afternoon will be Leota's first jumping session.

On the negative side, hulking prop Cabous Eloff reported back from the Xmas break with a calf strain and is being managed outside of the team sessions. With Pone Fa'amausili still working his way back into full contact, and Taniela Tupou off sick for the second day running, they decide to park any meaningful scrum sessions for a couple of days.

"It just goes to show how easily plans get turned on their head," Foote says later. "A couple of niggly calves, a guy gets the flu and suddenly we can't get the scrum work in we'd hoped for. So we have to adapt, come up with something else. But then you worry about having to chase things to catch up what's been missed."

Foote plays a clip from yesterday's training, captured from the drone that is a constant presence at every outdoor session. It's not a player issue he's highlighting but attack coach Tim Sampson, who is seen stepping in to fix a positioning and alignment issue that nobody else spotted, and delivering clear messaging to the players.

"Look at that," says Foote. "That's superb coaching, Sambo. World class."

But before he gets too comfortable, Foote gives Sampson another job. "We've talked about this before, but Pone's handling is a priority work-on. It's not where it needs to be."

Sampson is also the 'selector' for the day, sorting the players into two teams - in some cases trying to maintain combinations that were first tried prior to Xmas, and in others, pitting new combinations together, to see what happens. As always, the emphasis is on training at tempo, and players being given full clarity in their roles.

When the music stops and all the chairs are taken, two of the new players with Emerging and Developing Squad (EDS) contracts are without a position in either of today's two teams. In addition to kicking skills, Rob Taylor's other job is to oversee the emerging players. It's quite a responsibility, being heavily influential in the development of a young professional player, bringing along through a whole season where they are unlikely to receive any game time, but still have an important role to play in training and in support of the playing squad, and to be ready to go next year.

"Got it," says Taylor. "I'll run with them myself, off to the side. I've got plenty for them to do."

Taylor also comes to the fore when the conversation shifts to a try from the weekend's English Premiership, where Exeter halfback Harry Randall had a kick charged down at the base of a ruck, despite his forwards providing a 4-man 'caterpillar'.

"Does this have implications for our set-up?" asks Sampson. "No kick without a block in place?"

"Personally, I don't like using a blocker," says Taylor. "Leave it with me, I'll speak to all three guys and I'm happy to run with whatever the halfbacks want."

The meeting ends with the coaches agreeing on the communication points for the pre-training meeting. This is where, before every single session, detailed objectives are set and, importantly, the tone for the session is set - whether or not the intensity needs to be wound up, or things lightened up a touch.

In light of yesterday's events, Foote wants more clarity and discipline around the breakdown, and he'll be pushing the players hard on it.

"But I have a nice clip from yesterday. Make sure we start with a positive."

From there, Parling, Harris and Sampson head straight into a forwards unit meeting. All players are seated and ready, before the appointed start time.

Parling is an expert at 'war-gaming' different game scenarios - always asking the players to think the solution through for themselves. This morning he poses the question, "what happens when we lose a lock to a yellow card? Three different cases; first one, our exit scrum; second one, attacking line out, our feed; last case, a restart, our receive."

With the players in groups of three, they are given a minute before being asked to respond.

Parling likes what he hears. Everyone present is aware and aligned.

"Good. Anyone not a hundred percent, before we move on?"

Sampson steps up. He runs a clip from yesterday's training, showing two examples, side by side, of the forwards hitting it up off ruck ball. In one, the first receiver is almost 10 metres from the halfback.

"Too wide," he mutters.

In the other, the receiver is positioned closer, around six or seven metres from the halfback.

"Much better," he says. "Less margin for error. In these situations, too much ball-in-air time is an invitation for a defender to fire out of the line. We lose the collision."

On his second day back after the Xmas break, CEO Stephenson is working his way through a series of meetings. His is the ultimate 'jack of all trades' job, overseeing a broad range of functions across financial, commercial, marketing, HR and rugby. Not to mention managing relationships with stakeholders such as sponsors, his board and Rugby Victoria. And yes, Rugby Australia.

The events leading into Xmas haven't been forgotten, but neither is Stephenson allowing himself to be bogged down by the situation.

"It's not the issue it's been painted as in the media," he says. "And our board has been terrific. It's like the bear has been poked. In the long run, don't be surprised if this turns out very differently than what people expect. This isn't about any particular failing of the Rebels, it's about the state of the game."

Stephenson explains how, since the story broke, internally, the club hasn't missed a beat. "We've had one resignation in the admin team, which may or not be related, but on the rugby side, not one person has shown any disquiet or asked me to explain. They trust me, they trust the board, and we're all getting on with business."

Fighting words. Stephenson's demeanour is unmistakably calm and assured. Nothing is flaky or fake, nothing is said that isn't meant.

The next day, at the team meeting prior to stepping out onto Gosch's Paddock for training, an additional, unscheduled speaker steps up. Jordie Uelese addresses the group, not at the request of any of the coaches, but because he has had time to figure out when and how to repay the debt he owes his teammates. His message is simple and on point: an apology and humble acknowledgement of how his on-field behaviour fell short of what everyone in the group has committed to, and a vow to do better next time.

Foote is quietly delighted. A firm believer in the equation $E + R = O$ (Event plus Reaction equals Outcome), Uelese has changed what was an untidy, unsatisfactory outcome, into a positive one. He will, of course, need to back up his words with actions. But for now, it's another little mini-crisis ticked off, on the way to the February 23rd start-line.

Chapter Nine

17th January, 2024

One of the key ingredients to the success of any sporting organisation is to make certain the environment is made fun and interesting. A rugby season is not only hard on players' bodies, it challenges their minds. An avalanche of on-field skills and team sessions, weights sessions and team meetings soon blur, and the repetition can become a chore if the program is not kept fresh and the players' minds and bodies not kept sharp and stimulated.

Today, the afternoon is set aside for completion of the season's media tasks: this time all of the individual photography for the website and accreditation passes, jersey and ball signings, television and scoreboard profile shots and, to finish the day, along with the women's team and staff, the official team photographs.

A continued pain point for the Rebels is that they don't get enough access to the AAMI Stadium pitch to help them cement in the advantages people normally associated with a home venue.

"It's enormously frustrating," says coach Foote. "In fact, because of competition regulations which provide for visiting teams to have a captain's run on the match-day pitch, it feels sometimes like we end up on there less than our opposition!"

Today however is a little bit different. Not for any training, because with soccer's A-League in full swing, and Melbourne Victory and Melbourne City both using AAMI as their home ground, that's a bridge too far, but because the players will walk out onto the arena for their team photo.

Foote is big on the use of visualisation as a tool for affirmation, and he doesn't waste the opportunity. At the end of the morning session he gathers the players together and asks them to think about what it means to walk onto the AAMI Stadium turf as a Melbourne Rebel.

"Think about it this afternoon when you're dressing up, just like you would before a game," he exhorts. "So that when we go out there as a group, we feel like we own the field."

In the meantime, the players move en masse to an upstairs function room, to begin their rotations. At the long, narrow autograph table, the pace is searing. Initials, not full names, are the order of the day; Tuaina Tai Tualima and Lukhan Salakaia-Loto resorting to longhand would see them still chipping away at midnight. Nearby, Taniela Tupou, in front of a video camera, is given the choice, in one minute, to recite as many KFC menu items or rugby positions as he can. He selects the rugby option and starts off; "Hooker, prop... um, reserve prop," before stumbling into a fit of laughter, wishing he'd taken the easy route and chosen the chicken instead.

The morning run was conducted in steady, at times driving, rain. A blessing according to Tim Sampson, who says: "It went really well. The rain helps sharpen everyone up. Players have to focus more on their basic skill execution."

But the monsoonal weather also comes at a cost. No sooner than Foote has delivered his message and the players are released for a light lunch, word comes through from stadium management that, because of the wet, nobody will be allowed on the playing surface. Murphy's Law has kicked in, with a vengeance. Foote's words have been wasted. The team photos, scheduled for 5.30pm, will need to be moved.

With his own photo and signing session ticked off, Foote takes a moment to reflect on an opportunity he had earlier in the pre-season, to observe up close, the Queensland Ballet.

"What a privilege that was," he enthuses. "They were preparing for 'Mao's Last Dance' so not only was the story inspiring, but so was the process and the people, from the head coaches and development coaches, through to the dancers. What really hit home was their work ethic, and their humility. Even though it's a tiered system, where lead dancers and beginners observe a hierarchy, there's absolutely no entitlement on the part of anyone - just respect and commitment. And as it turns out, their program isn't that much different to ours: skills and technique sessions in the morning, followed by 'match simulation' in the afternoon."

The task for Foote was not only to observe and learn, but to carry the lessons across to his own team.

"I'd like to think I've been able to do that," he says. "Overall, the values are very similar, but the sacrifices made by some of the dancers - in terms of their lifestyle, diet and so on - are profound. I hope I was able to get across to the players that, as hard as we work, there is in fact no upper limit to what they can do, in terms of their individual preparation and commitment to their career as a rugby player."

In typical Melbourne fashion, the afternoon weather undergoes a sudden transformation from biblical deluge to something more usually associated with summer. The grey clouds disperse and, in no time at all, the sun makes its presence felt. So rapid is the transition, by mid-afternoon, Stephenson bounds back into the building, having come direct from the AAMI Park superintendent's office.

"We're back on!" he gushes. "I had to promise that we'll keep to the Astroturf on the edges, but they're happy that it's dry enough now we won't cause any damage."

The mood lifts noticeably, and at 5.30pm everyone in the club makes their way to the eastern race, walks up the twenty-metre rise onto AAMI Stadium and then places themselves at the mercy of the photographer.

The late timing tells its own story about where rugby is placed in the national sporting landscape. It's been a long day for the men's team, and in ideal circumstances they would have been on their way home well before now. But the players who make up the clubs' Super W team aren't remotely close to fully professional, and can't walk out of their jobs for an afternoon photo shoot. The level of excitement amongst the women is palpable; they don't get to play many games and aren't often made to feel the centre of attention. Everything that Foote said to his team about visualisation and positive affirmation is amplified tri-fold for the women.

There isn't a player in both teams who doesn't scuff their feet on the turf - away from the view of the ground superintendent - and imagines being back here in a few short weeks, doing it for real. Early in its history, AAMI Stadium was an embarrassment, every scrum creating a sandpit deep enough to lose small children in. Those days are now a distant memory, the turf as it is presented today, is pristine. World class.

Sampson gazes across the playing field to the main tunnel opposite and sums up what many are thinking. "If we can't play good rugby on this, we may as well give up and go and do something else."

Chapter Ten

23rd January, 2024

Ryan Louwrens. Jack Maunder. James Tuttle.

The Rebels boosting their squad depth means that, in a number of positions, competition for playing spots is fierce - far more so than it has been in the past. One of those hot spots is halfback. Three highly motivated and capable rugby players are all desperately keen to wear the #9 jersey, and all have been tearing it up throughout the preseason.

Having started every match in 2023, Louwrens is the incumbent. Highly respected for his work ethic and, pound for pound, possessor of the biggest biceps in world rugby, he's a popular figure amongst the team, answering to "Hundy".

"That came from my time at the Western Force," he explains. "Alby Mathewson was the 'Hundy', but after he left, the title was vacant and the boys were keen for someone else to take it. Somehow it all came down to a wrestling match between me and Brynard Stander, where it was agreed that the loser would be crowned 'Hundy'. Anyone who knows Stander knows how he's just this immense physical beast, right? And I wrestle him, I lose, so I become the 'Hundy'. Someone who gives everything a go at 100%, but also, isn't 100% right in the head."

When his laughing subsides, Louwrens ponders; "There's a lot worse names around. I'll take that."

South African raised, a product of a strong school system, like so many of his countrymen, Louwrens emigrated to Perth with his family, as a teenager, and eventually, after a brief return to South Africa which culminated in a two-year ban for steroid use, found himself contracted with the Force.

"At that stage I had these ambitions of trying to make the Wallabies, but then events took their course and in 2017, just as I was establishing myself as starting halfback, the Force was cut from Super Rugby. That was a chaotic time, players and coaches dispersing in all directions, and I ended up in

Japan, with the Kintetsu Liners, which was a fairly big deal at the time, because of the restrictions Japan had in place on the number of overseas players."

His connection with coach Dave Wessels saw Louwrens join the Rebels in 2020, on a one-year contract, before he landed in Austin, Texas, playing for the Austin Gilgronis. "I loved it there," he says. "Austin is a great city, not too big, but with lots of great restaurants and so on. And we had a really good team too, sitting at the top of the competition before events took their turn."

Those events were team owner, Australian entrepreneur Adam Gilchrist, and the club, being done for salary cap infractions. Not only were competition points docked, Gilchrist's effective ostracising from the game led to the Gilgronis, and his other team, the Los Angeles Giltinis, folding.

It wasn't hard for Louwrens to decide where to turn to next.

"With a young family, my wife was keen to return to Melbourne, get a bit more settled, and there was an opening there for the 2023 season."

Starting all 14 matches, scoring five tries, Louwrens was a solid contributor in a promising - albeit unsuccessful - season.

With other senior players involved with the Wallabies at the World Cup, or Australia A or the Barbarians, Louwrens took on a leadership role for the Rebels' short tour to Japan, in October.

"It was a real honour to be asked to captain the side. To go to Osaka as a group (to play sister club, Kintetsu Liners), a mixture of established guys, some newer guys at the club, some up and comers… to be asked to lead that team, and to come away with a win, it was a real highlight for me."

Satisfied with how things went in 2023, and still a pace-setter in the gym, Louwrens is clearly in a good place. But he's also experienced and mature enough to know that a month out from the start of the season, with Tuttle and Maunder more than nipping at his heels, what has happened in the past counts for nothing, as far as this season is concerned.

At a rugby club, everyone loves an old head on young shoulders. Someone who brings youthful vitality, but also exudes maturity and calm. Someone who is low maintenance, who the coaches can rely upon to always contribute constructively, and be a good influence on the rest of the team.

Jack Maunder is one of those people. Despite only having been in Melbourne for a short time, the genial Englishman with an already well-developed taste for fine red wine, has made quite an impression, on field and off. Arriving at the Rebels via a connection with forwards coach Geoff Parling - ex-teammates at Exeter - so far, it feels like a marriage made in heaven.

In an era where professional rugby players are often criticised for carrying an overweight sense of entitlement, Maunder is naturally humble and appreciative of how his upbringing laid a path for his rugby career.

"I was very lucky that my dad played rugby, so there was this clear path for me into the game as a junior, and lots of support at home. All my best mates played rugby, and right through Devon there's this terrific pathway, and if you're good enough you can go from there to the southwestern England trials and then to England trials, so I guess I always knew that I wanted to play rugby, and play in my home area with Exeter, and I was lucky there was this great environment to help make that happen."

Like many successful players, there was an element of luck involved.

"I missed most of my first senior season with Exeter because of a skateboard accident, and then at the start of the second year I had a good pre-season match, which coincided with a couple of the other nines getting injured, so it all kind of fell into place after that."

'Falling into place' meant elevation into Eddie Jones' England squad and selection for a tour to Argentina in 2017, where he gained his sole Test cap.

"Obviously everyone in England and Australia has a view on Eddie, but for me, as an 18-19 year-old, I loved playing under him. His style was very much a teacher-pupil relationship, and because I'd just come from school I didn't know any different, so I never had any problem around him talking down to me. But for some of the older guys that had been around the traps for a lot longer, I can see why that wasn't so much fun for them."

In total, Maunder appeared 149 times for Exeter, with one match standing out, the 2019/20 English Premiership final, at Twickenham, where Exeter defeated Wasps 19-13.

"We'd had a massive six weeks, going through the European Championship Cup quarters, semi's and then winning the final against Racing 92. And then we had to lift ourselves up again the next week, for the premiership final. It's incredibly difficult - look at how a side as good as Leinster has struggled to go all the way in dual competitions over the last few years. But somehow we managed to drag ourselves up. Winning that match and sharing it with all those boys was the best feeling ever."

It's that hard-nosed winning experience that Maunder has been charged with bringing to AAMI Stadium.

"This is a pretty young group: really talented but in a few places still inexperienced, so my job is to help add some voice, a little more awareness to the exit kicking game, and help with how the team builds and relieves pressure. The other big thing for me is understanding my role as halfback, which is to link and serve. I want to give Carter as much time as possible, to make things as easy as possible for him. Do all of the shit things that need to be done, not transfer any pressure to my outside. I'll still get my chances to run and do things, but he's the class player and I need to make sure he stays fresh and has the space to dominate."

There's also plenty for Maunder to learn.

"Obviously I have to be totally open to the fast and fearless model, which I'm absolutely loving. But yeah, I can't tell you how different it all is. There's obviously a lot fewer games here too, compared to the European season, so it all feels a lot more like a sprint than a marathon."

The third piece in the Rebels' half-back puzzle is 9th year professional player, James "Bobby" Tuttle. Tuttle's early claim to football fame came as a Queensland under-12 Australian Rules Football representative, marking up against star Melbourne Demon Christian Petracca, in a match against Victoria. It wasn't the 100-point thrashing that pushed Tuttle in a different direction, but him attending the well-regarded rugby nursery of Nudgee College, Brisbane, from where he joined future Rebels' teammates Alex Mafi, Andrew Kellaway, Matt Gibbon and Brad Wilkin on a five-week Australian Schoolboys tour of the UK and Ireland. That led him to the Reds' academy and two years in the Australian Under-20 team, the second as captain, before making his first Super Rugby appearance for the Reds in 2016, in the same debut match as another current teammate, Lukhan Salakaia-Loto.

With the Reds having burned through three head coaches in his first three years, Tuttle notes, with a wry nod to the current financial situation, how he's no stranger to instability. His facility for soaking up and riding adversity would be tested by three major injury events, the first in 2015, when Tuttle was king hit in a match and had his jaw broken in three places, the offender receiving a six-month prison sentence. Then in 2018, Tuttle ruptured his

Achilles tendon, before, in 2019, five months into rehab, suffering a re-rupture.

"Twice in the same place is usually considered to be a career-ending injury, but I never felt like throwing it away," he explains. "After I came out of contract with the Reds, still injured, the Rebels took a punt on me and eventually, after what someone figured out was 846 days in between games, I made my debut for the Rebels in a win against the Brumbies at Leichhardt Oval, during the COVID season when we were based at Terrigal. The thing is, now that I look back at all of that time off, I'm twenty-seven but I actually feel two years younger in rugby years."

Higher recognition has followed, with Tuttle selected for Australia A in 2022 and 2023, as understudy to captain Ryan Lonergan. It's a reflection of what he sees as his core strengths: "For me, it's mostly about communication and organisation. This year, I'm really enjoying working with Brad Harris on developing how I help with the front-line defence."

He sneaks another one in for good measure. "I work pretty hard on my goal-kicking too. That's an important string to have to my bow."

Like Maunder, who has a commercial degree behind him which he anticipates will serve him well in taking over management of the family butchery business, Tuttle finished a commerce degree last year.

"My wife is in dental practice, so who knows where all that will go," he says. "But I'm very grateful to her for enabling me to follow my rugby career and, along with her father, to have such a supportive family environment. The only real downside is the unsolicited rugby advice I get from my father-in-law; he's an ex-Churchie fly-half who reckons he was pretty good back in the day, so he enjoys keeping me in my place!"

For now however, Tuttle is happy to keep working hard, supporting and competing with the other halfbacks.

"Halfbacks and hookers are always competitive positions, because squads will always carry three of each. I mean, you can see it right across the squad, the physical and mental application is higher than it's ever been before. The competition is dialled right up. But in a good way. To be selfless is one of our team pillars, something that we breed right across the group. And halfback is no different."

Selflessness. In an adjacent office, the coaching group is meeting with Paul Roos, ex-AFL Premiership winning coach with the Sydney Swans, now highly regarded as a coaching consultant and mentor. Roos' client list is small and selective, but includes Kevin Foote, who, up until now, has been connecting with Roos via zoom, at his home in Hawaii. With Roos on a flying visit to Melbourne and on a tight schedule, it would be easy for Foote to ring-fence that face-to-face time for himself. Instead, he has chosen selflessly, to give over his mentor to his assistant coaches, because he thinks that will provide better value for the club.

Chapter Eleven

26th January, 2024

Australia Day. Since its high-water mark in 1988, when brilliant weather framed a re-enactment of the first fleet sailing into a Sydney harbour ringed with quintessential bronzed Aussies, tanked to the gills on Tooheys New, belting out Cold Chisel classics, Australia's national day has degenerated into an increasingly messy, potentially unsolvable, muddle.

Thirty-six years on, Australia Day is not so much a clash of culture - the flag-draped, bogan 'old', versus a progressive 'new' demanding more appropriate indigenous recognition - but a magnet for the disaffected and disadvantaged; those who view Australia as anything but the lucky country.

As the morning unfolds, thousands of protesters congregate in front of the steps to state parliament. As if to prove the point about confusion, there are as many Palestinian flags brandished as there are Aboriginal flags. Elsewhere, in the CBD and across suburban offices, there are businesses closed for the day, with employees observing the national holiday. In other workplaces, employers have allowed any staff uncomfortable with observing the 26th January, the option to come in to work and to take another, different day off, in lieu.

The Rebels' playing group is among those who are hard at work, but theirs is not a political or moral stance. They have a date with the Brumbies on February 23rd, and no day, public holiday or otherwise, is getting in the way of their preparation.

Before they strap up and hit the training track, the squad is called to a meeting in the gym. Media reporting around the ongoing viability of the Rebels has intensified. So much so that the night before, a hastily arranged meeting was called by the player's association (RUPA) to address, in private, any concerns the players might have. CEO Stephenson has no choice but to stay on the front foot, to keep everyone informed and aligned as best he can, given that the situation, and the story mushrooming around it, has taken on a life of its own. He stands directly in front of the tightly-formed group, close enough so they can see the truth in his eyes and, unscripted, calmly and authoritatively delivers a twenty-minute summary of events. Nothing is glossed over.

"My commitment to you boys is to be fully transparent. These are obviously difficult days for the club, nobody wants to be going through what we are going through and it's particularly difficult for some of the board members right now. But as tough as the situation is, we believe we have a way through it, the board has been unbelievable in the way they are tackling this, we are continuing to work very closely with Rugby Australia, we have an assurance that nothing will change for this season, and we'll continue to work with RA to determine how things are going to go from next year onwards."

Stephenson goes on to explain the likely process should the club go into voluntary administration. Contrary to media reports, an administrator is yet to be appointed, although Stephenson says that he anticipates this will happen in the next couple of days.

Next, he addresses the media reporting, and the impact that is potentially having on wives, girlfriends and family.

"A lot of the reporting on this is untrue, some of it is grossly misleading, but I understand that, true or not, how this makes people feel uneasy. That's only natural. Not everybody is our friend, and that kind of destructive reporting is something we can't control. All I can do is reiterate to you guys is that we have your backs, your contracts are all safe, and that as soon as possible, we hope we'll be able to get some clarity for you and your families around next year and beyond. One thing that I expect will happen from here is that, as soon as the administrator is appointed, or straight after, we'll be able to get a joint statement out, with Rugby Australia that we hope will be a bit more definitive and hopefully will set people's minds at ease, at least for the short term."

Stephenson calls for questions or concerns from the floor but there are none. For many of the players, mention of administrators, creditors and boards of management flies straight over their heads. Others have already posed questions at last night's meeting with their player's association. A small handful will take Stephenson up on his offer to meet with him privately. The rest simply want to get out on the field and play rugby.

With building blocks already in place for the 2024 season, and the pre-season humming along nicely, it is evident that the risk to the club, and the biggest fear for everyone involved, is that all of the promise, the hard work, and the feeling that the club has finally matured, learned what is required to succeed, and has turned a corner, will all go to waste.

"We're doing everything that's been asked of us," says Nick Stiles. "Everyone in Australia is sick of playing second fiddle to the New Zealand sides, everyone is sick of the Rebels losing, the Wallabies losing, and they don't care about how hard it is to turn that around, they just want us to get on with it and fix it. And that's what this club is in the process of doing. Making the Melbourne Rebels a desired destination, where players want to come and play, to join the best program in Australia, and to have success. And while we haven't achieved that yet, because it takes time to cement that continuity and TWI (team work index) into the club, blind Freddie can see the progress we're making, how our roster is strengthening, how our coaching group is developing, how fit the guys are, and how they're performing out on the track."

Stiles' frustration is evident. More than any individual, it is he who has sold the dream that has seen a raft of players approach the Rebels wanting in; not all of whom have been able to be accommodated.

"Obviously we've got Taniela here now, he'd been hearing lots of positive feedback from other players, and he was very keen to come down. And now here we are, he hasn't even played a game for us yet, and all this blows up and he's already being approached by clubs in the UK with offers to jump ship."

There's more. "We've got a number of contracts out with players for 2025 onwards, important players like Wilkin, Daugunu, the Gordon brothers, a number of others… they all want to stay, they're all basically ready to sign, and now everything has to go on hold, and of course, then we get their agents thinking, 'well hang on, do I need to start having a look around elsewhere?' Vaiolini (Ekuasi) has moved across from Auckland. We're busting our arse trying to get him to stay, he's everything that a Rebel player should be. And he's got family over visiting, checking it all out, and now they're all going 'what the fuck?' That's where all the real damage is being done. What say we manage to get through all of this, but because it takes so long, and player agents and families get spooked, we lose a heap of guys and then we have to start all over again?"

Seeing the prospect of all his work go up in smoke, Stiles becomes emotional, and he steps away to take a moment to compose himself. Media outlets intent on little more than out-trumping each other's headlines about the potential demise of the Rebels, exist in a kind of parallel universe game. They neither know or care that the human cost is real and considerable.

Chapter Twelve

30th January, 2024

It's an occurrence that Baden Stephenson has become all too familiar with - standing in front of a weights rack in the gym, addressing a full staff and player's meeting. Events have moved along since Australia Day, with the anticipated voluntary administration now a reality. Stephenson is tasked with walking a very fine line: maintaining a sense of 'business as usual' around the club, whilst meeting the reality head on that, with the appointment of PwC Australia as administrators, things are in fact, materially different.

Stephenson reinforces the themes from the Australia Day player's meeting. "You have my commitment that we will be completely transparent with you and we'll keep updating everyone as soon as anything happens or changes. You can rely on us to be a source of truth, and in the meantime, we'll all keep working on controlling the things we can control."

He thanks RUPA president Justin Harrison for flying in from Sydney to be in attendance, then introduces the two executives present from PwC Australia, Martin Ford and Aaron Sonnberger.

It's a nervy moment. This is a rugby club, none of the players or staff have experience at this sort of thing. Will the administrators be heartless, intimidating hatchet men, here to get on with carving up what is left of the commercial heart of the club? Or do they understand the human element - the fact that there is a rugby season about to start, and another one next year, that everyone present dearly wants to be a part of?

To Stephenson's relief, Ford's address is conciliatory, human, and reinforces everything he said in his introduction. Whatever hard questions the administrators will have for him personally will be dealt with in time, but for now, it is important that the equilibrium of the club isn't unnecessarily disrupted. They will do their job, but they will do it sensitively.

Representing the board, Director of Finance Owain Stone, takes the floor. Despite his years of business accounting experience, he cuts a nervous figure before clearing his throat: "On behalf of everyone from the board, I just want to reiterate that we have worked incredibly hard and will continue to do whatever we can to see that the future of the club is secure. By reaching the decision we have this morning, to go into voluntary administration, that is without question the most difficult moment of my career. We've taken this path because ultimately, we believe it's in the best long-term interest of the Rebels, and above all else, we want to see a positive outcome for the club."

Stone's voice wavers and his eyes well over before he composes himself. It's a telling moment - on one hand reinforcing the unity and love that exists right throughout the club, from the very top to the bottom, but at the same time, serving as a reminder how, under administration, the club is no longer in control of its own destiny. No matter how cordial and constructive the early engagement with PwC is, financial and strategic decision-making is now out of the board's hands, and in the hands of strangers.

The next morning, most of the office workstations are filled well before 8am. It's business as usual, except that it isn't. Energy levels are lower, the gags are fewer and they don't stick like they normally do. But neither is there any gallows humour. One thing that has marked the whole pre-season is an absence of cynicism. It's just that today, things are merely okay, unlike the last few months, when before this tornado hit, they were *great*.

One shining light in the admin team, a perpetually positive influence on everyone around her, is newly promoted commercial manager, Emily Riseley. A business marketing graduate from a sporting family and a keen Carlton AFL fan, it was always Riseley's ambition to work in a global sport. That saw her land a sponsorship role with the Melbourne Victory, tucked into a similar office on the opposite side of the stadium.

"The biggest difference over there is the culture around the players. Things at the Victory were a bit more formal and there was more separation between players and staff. At the Rebels we share the kitchen and have lunch with the players, so it's quite a different atmosphere."

Being an expert on rugby isn't a pre-requisite for a commercial sponsorship role, nevertheless, Riseley has thrown herself into learning the game.

"It's like, I had to be all-in, right?" she says, enthusiastically. "Last year, when the side had a pre-season trial match in Albury, I got in a car with one of the guys and we drove up there and back in the one day. And right through the match, I'm asking him all sorts of questions about the laws and positions and tactics and so on, and then all the way home (three hour's drive), the same thing, pestering him all the way. I think it's really important that if I'm asking businesses to sponsor the Rebels, and support rugby in Melbourne, I actually know what it is I'm asking them to support."

That commitment, and the personal relationships she has begun to forge might be one of the reasons sponsors have been quick to reaffirm their support for the club, despite the turmoil.

"All of the sponsors got sent the formal statement from Rugby Australia and Baden, and it's my job to fill in any gaps. Obviously, it's a testing time, but the response has been really heart-warming. Nobody is washing their hands of the Rebels. That's because most sponsors are on board because they want to see rugby succeed in Victoria and they want to be part of it."

Others go the extra yard. "Sa1nt offered to come in next week to fit the whole squad out with compression gear, free of charge. It was like, 'anything we can do to help lift the mood, we'll do it'."

Stephenson is acutely aware of how important his demeanour is in setting the tone of the club's reaction. Any dropping of the guard, any defeatist body language on his part, will spread through the organisation in a flash. At the same time, he owes it to everyone not to promise anything he can't deliver. Optimism, yes. False hope, no.

"It's a very fine line," he says, reflecting on the events of yesterday. "I'm calm about how things are because, for one, I've learned that you can only control what you can control. And the other thing is, people are looking to me to provide strong leadership because I've been here before, in 2017 and 2020, when we went through terribly uncertain times. It's never fun, but it's part of what you study for and what you prepare for in your career. Anybody can manage through the easy times. That said, compared to 2017 (when the Rebels narrowly avoided being cut from Super Rugby), and 2020 (when, because of sudden state government lockdowns and travel restrictions the team were given six hours to make a decision, pack and relocate to NSW to avoid being omitted from the competition), this time does feel different."

One of the reasons for that is Stephenson's simmering anger at how things have been allowed to get this point. "We're not at war with Rugby Australia or anyone, but we've consistently been made to feel like we're at fault. The administrators aren't going to find any indiscriminate spending or hidden debt. We run this place lean, we have no choice. If RA says that the game doesn't have the money, then let's all work through that together. If they want to walk away from Super Rugby altogether, then be up front about it. But to leave us hanging in the breeze, like this is all about the Rebels being singled out for not managing their finances properly, then that's just ridiculous. Yet here we are."

Stephenson makes the observation that Phil Waugh hasn't visited Melbourne since the November sponsor evening. He's disappointed. "If this isn't a serious enough matter, if this wasn't worth presenting a front face to players and staff over, then you'd have to wonder what is. After all, it's Rugby Australia who has taken $6.8m out of our revenue. We didn't need it all back, we accept that the situation has changed. But we demonstrated how just $1m would have been enough to cover what we needed, settle the urgent debt, and then work with RA on a handover… all without the need to go into administration."

Stephenson gets to the heart of what is being painted in public: that if all franchises have had their distributions similarly reduced, how is it that it is only the Rebels who are millions of dollars in debt? "Most of that goes back to the deal that was done in 2017 to secure the Rebels' ongoing participation in Super Rugby. Rugby Australia had a financial hole and the Victorian state government stepped up to assist with that. They provided that money, $16.5m, and in return there was an arrangement for Wallabies content in Melbourne and for the ongoing participation of the Rebels in Super Rugby. But - and this is the key point that is missed - the deal was structured so that the Vic government's funding went into RA's coffers. In 2018 and 2019 some of that flowed back to us, but from 2020, nothing came to the Rebels for us to offset against our operational costs. Remember that all the other franchises get a significant annual grant from their governments, $2-$3m in some cases, yet the money that our government puts in, it all goes straight to RA. Throw in the extra expenses we incurred helping keep the game alive during COVID and there's your difference."

"I don't think anyone really understands how impactful COVID was for us," Stephenson continues. "The cost of maintaining a team away from home was massive. No home games for two years obviously hurt gate receipts, memberships and sponsorships. And even in 2022, because of the way COVID was managed in Victoria compared to other states, our first home match was still subject to COVID restrictions, limiting our financial return and our ability to provide value to sponsors."

Stephenson returns to the theme that, by nature of their financial position being leaked to reporters, the Rebels feel they have been unfairly singled out. With their dirty linen aired for all to see, it grates that the Waratahs were dealt with in secret. "All of the franchises have a similar equation. We operate under the same salary cap. It costs roughly $13-$14m per annum to run a franchise, we get the same grant from RA, and we have to make the shortfall up through government grants, memberships, sponsorship and donations. And despite COVID and despite the disparity in how state government assistance is treated, we're clearly not the only ones with a substantial shortfall. But the difference is, other franchises have been allowed to discuss their affairs in private, and come to an arrangement with Rugby Australia in private. We've been transparent about our finances all along, working together with RA. We were totally open to centralisation, doing exactly what they wanted us to do, and talks were well advanced in October - that's all well documented. Yet that wasn't enough for certain people in RA. For whatever reason, they had to let it all go nuclear," he says.

At the same time, Stephenson acknowledges that he and all of the CEO's, have to come to terms with Rugby Australia's insistence that whatever money was available previously, is no longer. "No-one is denying that the funding model for the game is broken," he says. "Least of all, us."

That's the message reinforced by Rugby Australia chairman Daniel Herbert, in an exchange following an article of mine in *The Roar*, that was critical of Rugby Australia's propensity for leaking confidential information. He's unrepentant about the withheld $6.8m and Rugby Australia's refusal to offer any comfort beyond 2024. "Of course we understand how difficult things are down there (Melbourne), and we wish we weren't in this situation," he says. "But that's our reality. There is less money in the game and more demands on the money we do have. Obviously we have to lift our investment in women's rugby too. And until we secure a new broadcast rights deal, we don't know exactly what we'll have to work with moving forward."

It feels like a watershed moment for Australian rugby. For years everyone in the game has talked about how little money the game generates; compared to other rugby nations, compared to rugby league and AFL. But no longer is it the time to talk about it. This is the living embodiment of it.

At the end of a tough day, coach Foote is reflective on where things sit.

"We had a really good session out there this afternoon. I'm so proud of where we've got this team to: from a year ago to now, there's just no comparison. Depth is the key, because we've been able to push the guys harder in their conditioning work. We don't have to tread so carefully and protect individuals because we've got other options who will step up, and then more behind them.

But it's so tough because now we all know that all of this can potentially be ripped away from us, and there's nothing we can do about it."

Chapter Thirteen

3rd February, 2024

It's difficult to imagine a more unassuming location for a professional rugby match than the Harold Caterson Reserve, Keys Road, Moorabbin. Hard core industrial, immediate neighbours include an Amcor packaging materials manufacturing plant, auto parts suppliers and a brothel. First viewing of the Moorabbin Rugby Club must come as a culture shock for some of the Waratahs, as they hop off their bus and take in the spartan surrounds.

"It's not like we've set out to ambush anybody," says Stephenson, a couple of days before. "It's just that it's important we continue to connect with the rugby community, and this is an opportunity to bring the players to a different part of Melbourne. Last time it was Harlequins, this time we're supporting the Rams, and there'll be a big junior clinic on during the afternoon. This is club land, Melbourne style."

The Moorabbin club does themselves proud. What once resembled a turning, day-five Karachi dustbowl is now a first-class playing surface, following a recent re-laying. If you excuse the odd Brisbane Broncos jersey, the junior clinic, teeming with young rugby players, is a resounding success. And with the sun beating down, under the shade of a gazebo at one end of the ground, a makeshift bar is doing brisk trade.

By 4.00pm kick-off time it's a testing 31 degrees - a temperature that won't drop until well after the match ends. Sitting out for a couple more weeks, recovering from a broken jaw, water runner Lachie Anderson will be earning his coin today.

Both teams have named their strongest available sides, albeit the Waratahs have a couple more of their starters, including skipper Jake Gordon, sitting out. Wallaby loose forward Langi Gleeson finds himself on the end of a couple of flashy, improvised passes and dashes 22 metres for the opening try, but that's about as good as it gets for the visitors. The Rebels have a superior kicking game, an efficient set-piece, and by half-time, have edged ahead, 12-5.

It's what transpires in the second half though, that really lifts the spirit of the home supporters. Numerous changes are made to both sides and two things stand out. The Rebels are noticeably fitter and their list runs deeper. Despite the Waratahs playing with a strengthening breeze, the final twenty minutes are played in their defensive half. The Rebels' young, experimental pack delivers in spades: the rest of the squad, huddled together in a dugout, go up as one when a line out maul drive results in a penalty try. On the run of play, the final score, 38-12, flatters the visitors.

Post-game, the field bustles with fans seeking selfies and kids excitedly pushing shirts, posters and rugby balls at the players to be autographed. For a supposedly terminal patient on life support, the Rebels still have a healthy pulse.

The show of solidarity isn't lost on one Rebels board member as he stands in amongst the crowd, soaking in the positive energy. "It didn't have to come to this," he says. "We had an arrangement in place with the ATO. All we needed was Rugby Australia to just be a little more genuine in continuing to work together with us and the ATO, to agree to extend a plan to get us through to the Lions tour. Everything we'd been working with them on over a long period. We weren't asking for much at all - way less than what they're tipping into the Waratahs. But instead of continuing to collaborate they've chosen to be adversarial, and blow it all up. And where are they? They've led the game into crisis, good people who work in the game are hurting, we're getting hammered in the media, and they're nowhere to be seen."

There's no mistaking his steely resolve. "Well, fuck 'em. They're about to find out what we're about. And this is just the start," he says, pointing across to the scoreboard. "Rebels 38, Rugby Australia 12."

For Nick Stiles, it's a satisfying outcome, but, an expected one. "Obviously, you don't exactly know how it's going to go until you get out on the field, but really, this isn't any surprise," he says, without arrogance. "We know we've recruited well, we know we've put in the work, and we know what these players are capable of. This is just an accurate reflection of where we are."

Coach Foote is delighted with the defensive effort. "Brad (Harris) is really making a difference with our 'D'. Just having that clarity across the group, it really helps the guys develop confidence in the system and in each other, and we saw that today."

But the biggest glint in his eye is reserved for his running forwards. "That's something we're putting a lot of work into," he says. "Making sure the ball carrier has running options on both sides. Particularly on the inside, that's the easier ball to get away... safer because of the way they hook their arm towards the runner, not flicking it out the back... but you have to have guys put themselves in that position, to take advantage of it. Those big runs today up the middle from Josh (Canham) and Daniel (Maiava), and to have Robbie (Leota) back, running the ball so strongly... that's a great sign of how hungry and fit we are, and where we want to be as a team."

There's a wee flourish to finish off with. "This is just a trial, they had a long day of travel, and we don't want to get carried away. But I'd say I've gone in too low with the goal. Being the best Rebels team ever isn't enough. It feels like this team is already there. We can be much better than that."

In a period where media coverage has been unrelentingly negative and sensationalist, 'The Age' sports reporter, Roy Ward, can sniff a rugby-led redemption piece. He corners Foote and Moorabbin Rams club president, Arvind David, and the article that goes on line two hours later, and runs in print the following morning, comes as welcome balance.

David sends his message to Rugby Australia about how important rugby is for Melbourne, and how important Melbourne rugby is for Australia. "You're taking away the pinnacle of this sport in this stage, and we just know that for a state that generates elite players that feeds a lot of nations in the World Cup, including Australia, it guarantees you're going to push those players out of the country."

"We're invested in a nation in developing sporting networks that Australia has, so for me, it's an Australian thing. Is Australia going to take rugby seriously but not have a team in the top sporting city in the nation? The growth isn't in the rugby states north of the border. The growth is right here," he says.

For those inside the club, there is one disappointment on the day. With the Rebels going into administration, Paul Docherty has stood down as board chairman. The weekend edition of the 'Australian Financial Review' contains a feature article that is a merciless hatchet job on Docherty, his business interests, and the Rebels. The concluding section illustrates the tone;

"World Rugby boss Alan Gilpin said Melbourne, which had flagged ambitions to host the Rugby World Cup final in 2027, could still do so without a professional team. But the absence of one will no doubt have knock-on effects for the sport in the region.

It's an undesirable outcome for Docherty, whose strong vision for the future of rugby union in Victoria is in tatters. For staff of Docherty's BRC Capital subsidiaries, the demise of the businesses has left most with empty pockets and no jobs. That could end up being the case for the Rebels too.

And when the tide goes out, who is swimming naked? Looks like it was Docherty. Stephenson and Rugby Australia are left holding the towel."

The article ties Docherty's personal and business interests to the Rebels in a way that is speculative and unsupported by facts. After an unflattering photo of Docherty's wife appeared in another newspaper a week beforehand, he fears that there will be photographers sent to the match. Paparazzi stalking him around the Moorabbin pitch like he was the second coming of Christopher Skase would be a disaster for the club. Desperate to attend but adamant he doesn't want to take anything away from the event and the team, he arrives late and, incognito, takes up a position on the far side of the ground, away from most of the crowd. When it is all over, he slips out of the ground quietly, later describing his torn emotions; "Incredibly proud," he says first. Followed by, "heartbroken."

Chapter Fourteen

13th February, 2024

By the measure of recent years it's been a mild, bland summer, weather-wise. Mornington Peninsula businesses, reliant on sun-seeking holidaymakers, would say it's been no summer at all. But today, after a couple of days teasing, Melbourne's weather finally tips over into the type of day everybody dreads. Hot and dry, with a mean wind whipping in from the north.

It's a portent for what is to come. Scared off by the forecast, the Melbourne Storm cancel their morning training session. Immediately, the Rebels claim their slot, so that they can get onto Gosch's Paddock and get all their work done before the worst of it arrives, around lunchtime.

It's taxing and thirst-inducing, but the session is deliberately kept short and sharp. Coach Foote is happy with how the players attack things and maintain their intensity. It's only Tuesday but Foote isn't messing around with selection for Friday's trial match against the Fijian Drua.

"One thing I've decided to do this year is to get the match-day squad named nice and early, at the beginning of the week. No mind games, no messing around. Get our reviews done, make some decisions, and move forward. I think with the squad that we have, it's only fair that the guys have certainty, the coaches have certainty, and everyone gets a full week to prepare properly," he says. "It's something that South Africa has been doing, and it seems to work okay for them," he adds.

He's delighted with his selection - as close to full strength as possible. "Obviously we know there is a risk, playing just a week before opening round. Anyone picks up even a minor knock, or say a concussion, then they'll be out for the Brumbies. But there's much more upside. We've got the guys fit and hungry to play. There's no sense in holding anybody back. We'll be ready to step straight into it against the Brumbies."

As with the Waratahs trial, it's a glance at the second-half 'reserve' team that highlights the work of Nick Stiles in assembling the roster. It's chock-full of proven players, some with Test caps, and youngsters with undoubted promise. Uelese, Talakai, Eloff, Maiava, Ekuasi, Maunder, Tuttle, Jooste, Ripley, Anderson, Gordon (Mason) and more. Everybody wishes it was Friday already.

The players having been given an early mark, office chatter centres around a headline in today's Herald Sun which claims Rebels board members are at risk of losing their houses. Despite the reporter contacting the club for comment and being offered information to balance his story prior to going to print, the emphasis is pure bloodlust. As far as it is true that a director of any company subject to a notice from the ATO and potentially unable to meet its liabilities is at risk, the story carries a kernel of truth. But there is so much more left unsaid. Knowing that there is a lot more still to play out, the directors in the meantime, must suffer the indignity of seeing their names and reputations dragged through the gutter.

That's precisely the reason a detailed board paper, offering a counter to Rugby Australia, found its way into the public domain a couple of days earlier.

"If Rugby Australia believes that we're somehow going to roll over and soak all of this up then they're sadly mistaken," says a board member, his defiance lacking only a swashbuckling cutlass.

With today's newspaper article as a reference point, Stiles shares a gift he received from the estate of his recently deceased grandmother: a mint condition, unopened edition of the Herald Sun newspaper, dated July 7, 2001. The newspaper is blanketed in a full colour, heavy gauge, wrap around, previewing that evening's Test match between the Wallabies and Lions, held at what was then known as Colonial Stadium.

The early years of the millennium were heady ones for Australian rugby. Fresh from winning its second World Cup, about to host its first, possessors of the Bledisloe Cup. Rugby was a sport with enough clout to dominate Melbourne's leading daily newspaper - if only for a day or two - in a way that, twenty-three years later, can only be dreamed of. Despite boasting a large, daily sports section, the Herald Sun has long since cut what was already minuscule coverage of rugby, to nothing. Some of that is down to Australian rugby's slide, and the Rebels themselves: sports media has an appetite for winners. The rest is because the importance of the AFL to the mainstream media channels means both implied and real pressure is applied to push minority sports out of the picture.

The inside of the wrap-around features mini player profiles for the two sides, including one of Stiles himself, which reads: "Great mobility and work rate for a front rower".

The jibes flow thick and fast.

"Mobility? That's code for 'can't scrum'."

"Where did they get that photo from? School?"

"Even twenty years ago, the Herald Sun was full of bullshit."

Rachel Mitrione and marketing contractor Annika Jamieson, do the rounds of the office with a selection of icy poles - handy to help beat the heat. Lemonade is the popular choice. Jamieson announces that tomorrow will be cookie day, her home baking proving a hit with the staff. There is no inkling, no suggestion that she should bake a couple extra, for an unscheduled visitor from Rugby Australia.

By mid-afternoon the wind has gathered strength. Enough to mean that elsewhere across the state, there are large electricity pylons laying on the ground, bent in half like cheap teaspoons in Uri Geller's cutlery drawer, the power supply cut to over half a million households and businesses as a result. It's also eerily dark. A narrow but menacing cloud front delivers pelting rain to pockets of the city in short, violent bursts. Somehow, AAMI Stadium misses most of the rain, but doesn't escape the menace. Dark forces are close at hand.

Stephenson is tetchier than usual, revealing that the 14th of February is the trigger date Rugby Australia has committed funding up to. With consideration of advice from the administrator, Rugby Australia are due to confirm an arrangement for another, interim period. By mid-afternoon, in the midst of the worst of the storm, Stephenson still hasn't heard anything. No news, in this case, can only be bad news.

The office is almost empty by the time Phil Waugh's name lights up on his phone. Rugby Australia will continue to fund the Rebels in 2024. But it will be off a different cost base. Six permanent or permanent part-time positions, plus three contract positions are being made redundant. Instinctively, Stephenson knows what's coming. His name is at the top of that list.

Chapter Fifteen

14th February, 2024

The setting, by now, is all too familiar. Players crowded onto chairs and gym benches in the middle, commercial and high-performance staff circled around the outside. And CEO Baden Stephenson holding court in the centre, ready to deliver the latest update on the Rebels' parlous situation.

Since its establishment in 2022, this gym has been a facility for all in the club to be proud of: not just for its aesthetics and equipment, but because it has become a major part of the club's identity. A warm place, a safe place. Not as high tech as other gyms in the professional rugby world, but from the first day, belonging to the players as they belonged to it.

Today it feels different. Foreign and cold. Stephenson addresses the group in a space that no longer belongs to him or the players or the staff. It belongs to Rugby Australia. In attendance is Rachel Buckling, Head of Human Resources, who has flown down from Sydney to attend the announcement and formally advise Stephenson and the other affected staff members of their termination, effective immediately.

Stephenson confirms what everyone present now already knows. Manfully, he speaks fondly of his time at the club. It is ten years and three days since he arrived at AAMI Stadium. If Buckling happens to be carrying a gold watch to present to Stephenson to mark his anniversary, it remains in her bag.

Those ten years have comprised exactly 150 matches. Kevin Foote takes over and nails the moment.

"This is why we have a love culture at this club," he says, his words overflowing with authority and conviction. "Because our respect for each other, our care for each other, for who we are as people, everything that we go through together, as a team, as a club, carries us through uncertainty, and extends beyond these walls."

Foote presents Stephenson with a special, customised club jersey, to mark his 150 matches. To remind him that, wherever he lands in the future, this will be the place he most belonged.

The players line up and, one by one, hug their CEO goodbye. It's emotional, but above all, it's respectful. A heartfelt thanks to a team-mate gone down.

It is, as Nick Stiles describes, "a gruesome day". Nine good people have lost their jobs; those remaining have been put on notice that they could be terminated in four months, upon completion of Super Rugby. If there is a miracle in the offing, something or someone to carry them into 2025, it feels like they are a universe away. By early afternoon Buckling's work is done and she heads to the airport, and from there, to more familiar surrounds.

And then, there is nothing. The club is now owned and operated by Rugby Australia but, instead of someone senior being stationed at the office to counsel staff and provide a sense of direction, there is only a vacuum.

These are the hardest moments. Some remaining staff immediately switch to guilt mode. Others make the observation that the four months continuation they have been offered will pass very quickly. Nobody believes that Phil Waugh will be walking through the door at the end of those four months to say, 'crisis over, everyone's full contracts are restored'.

For others, confusion quickly turns to anger. With nobody left in charge, with no process to exit or transition the impacted staff, one person turns their rage back at Rugby Australia and begins to delete important files from the system. It will take some days, and a deal of money, for this information to be recovered.

With just ten days before the first home match of the season, realisation hits that some of the people needed to pull all of the detail together, to handle sponsors, membership, logistics and the like, have just been sacked. Nobody is exactly sure what has already started to slip between the cracks.

There is still no facility for members or fans to buy match tickets. For this to happen, there are sign-offs required from Rugby Australia. And now, even if tickets were to go up tomorrow on the Ticketek website, another release of Taylor Swift tickets will render the site un-navigable. Irrational as it may be, some staff claim that there is a conspiracy at work, to hinder fans from buying tickets, then to point to a low crowd number as further justification for shutting down the Rebels.

In a quiet moment, Stiles reflects on what it all means. "Everyone, at every franchise, knows how hard it is to get everything to align. To make a successful team. We have so many good people here, professional people who work for each other. We have a great culture, that's now starting to become organic. A clear game style that everyone inherently understands. It's so rare to get to that point. And we're here. You can see it. Feel it. Smell it. I'm not just talking about this season, but about making a successful organisation across all levels that can and will endure."

His frustration and concern is mostly around 2025 and beyond. "Obviously, I'm concerned for the admin staff, those that have gone and those that don't have a secure future. But as far as the team is concerned, for this season, I think our love and care culture will underpin everything and carry us through any uncertainty. Ask anyone in sport and they'll tell you, the feeling of winning stays with you forever. That's what will bind the group this season, whatever happens off the field."

And for himself and the coaches? After all, they are in the gun too, without a job beyond June. "I think it's different for high performance staff, than it is for ordinary workers," he says. "We operate in an uncertain world. We all hate it, but we understand it, we accept it and we adapt to it."

Stephenson's immediate reflection about the players is less optimistic. "I hope I'm wrong, but today, when I addressed the players, and I saw behind a few eyes, for the first time it all felt a bit vulnerable. They'll come out of the blocks well this season, but I'm worried that the situation and Rugby Australia will suck so much mental and emotional energy out of the tank, there won't be enough there when they need it at the back end."

Foote, as ever, is brave and stoic, but there's no hiding his human side. "We were given assurances that nothing would change for this season. But now, with all these people going, that doesn't feel like 'no change'. I feel so much for them, and for the other coaches. There's families, there's new schools, there's guys and their partners who have turned their lives upside down to come here, because we all want to be part of something special… and now this."

With a young family, he is one of those people. "Of course, it affects me as well. And my wife and my kids. But now, it's more important than ever that I step up as a leader. Me and Stilesy. We're the senior leaders and the role models for the club."

With Rugby Australia now having taken back control of the Rebels' licence, technically, the franchise's senior official is CEO Phil Waugh. Waugh is in Auckland for the day, launching the Super Rugby season along with the captains of each side, including the Rebels' Rob Leota. Asked for comment about the Rebels' situation Waugh calls Leota 'Trevor'. It's a Freudian slip (Waugh used to play against Samoan international Trevor Leota), but the impact immediately reverberates across the Melbourne rugby community. From where fans sit, on such a momentous day for the Rebels and Australian rugby, Waugh has not only delegated the dirty work to a manager, he doesn't even know the name of the Rebels' captain.

The centrepiece of the launch is the release of a short promotional video, designed to pump up interest in Super Rugby Pacific, 2024. Of itself, it's an impressive, inspirational piece of work. In keeping with the pacific theme, prominent players from across the competition are seen to be playing rugby underwater. Cleverly, the video manages to project equal parts calm, grace, and strength. But reporters present are more interested in pinning down Waugh and Super Rugby Commission chairman Kevin Molloy, with questions about the Rebels and the ongoing viability of Super Rugby. Molloy is forced to admit that the tone and substance of discussions about the future of Super Rugby have taken a different turn.

Everyone present knows that is code for 'all bets are off' and 'we know we don't have much time to pull something together for next year'. Unintended metaphor it may be, but telling the story of a competition drowning underwater is surely not what the creators of the video had in mind.

Chapter Sixteen

16th February, 2024

For so early on a Friday evening - a 4.30pm start - a healthy crowd has rolled up to Gosch's Paddock for the Rebels' second trial match, against the Fijian Drua. The early start time proves to be a blessing. Just across the way at the MCG, fresh from celebrating the Kansas City Chief's Super Bowl win, Taylor Swift is opening her Australian tour tonight, in front of almost 90,000 fans. Nearby roads and public transport lines are expected to be chaotic. It's as if rugby fans are the only people in Melbourne not in on the act.

Shortly before kick-off, Baden Stephenson strolls around the car park which separates the Rebels' AAMI Stadium office and the rugby pitch. Suitcase nearby, he isn't staying for the match, instead flying home to the Sunshine Coast for the weekend, and for who knows how long after that. The last few days have been an emotional roller coaster, but he reflects fondly on his ten years and accepts the hugs and well wishes of a smattering of staff - the ones who survived the cut.

"It's time to take a breath. I'm looking forward to a few quiet days at home with the family," he says, relieved to be stepping out of the limelight.

At the same time, it feels like he has unfinished business. "Obviously, it's hard to be confident, but I'm still hopeful for a good outcome for the Rebels, and particularly for all the amazing people involved."

It's almost kick-off time. The players have completed their warm-ups, and are receiving last minute instructions back inside their dressing room. In a few moments they will be back outside, and on the field, ready to play.

Stephenson doesn't wait to watch them take the field. His car has arrived: the airport beckons. His final act as a Rebel is to shake hands with Roma Leota, father of skipper Rob, and show him inside to the men's room.

There's something familiar and comforting about trial matches played outside of large stadiums. The sidelines are roped off, fans stand close to the action, players gently push in between children to make their way onto the pitch. It's classic old school rugby: the only thing missing, a row of utes pulled up to the side of the ground. Among those gathered on the sideline is a man from Hawke's Bay, New Zealand - solid ute country. He is Jimmy Orange, founder of a business called Academy Movement.

A teacher by trade, Orange arrived at Fountain Gate High School in 2010, and over time, realised that there was an opportunity to fix two problems at once: faltering engagement of children from lowly socio-economic groups in their education, and weak participation in rugby, in Melbourne schools.

Earlier in the week, Orange, Stephenson (in one of his last acts as CEO), and Rugby Victoria President Neil Hay, launched a new rugby academy at Lara Secondary College, in Melbourne's west. This was followed by another, a day later, at Mernda Central College, in the north. Since Orange initiated the program in 2015, this now makes eight, the total of public school rugby academies in Melbourne, five of them operating under his Academy Movement banner. Eight public schools with rugby programs, for boys and girls, a meaningful school's competition, and a pathway for the most talented into the Rebels program.

It is clear that the conveyor belt has only just begun: lock Trevor Hosea a notable early recruit, impressive Wallabies Under 20 loose forward Leafi Talataina, among others to more recently graduate into a professional rugby career.

Or not. Should Rugby Australia determine there is no future for the Rebels, repercussions will extend much further than the Super Rugby fixture list. A deeper understanding of how Academy Movement works, sheds light on what is at stake.

"The key to the program is focusing first on academic success. We've seen terrific uptick in student engagement with their schooling, staying on for longer, performing better," says Orange.

"The rugby is an obvious motivator, but it's important that this follows, rather than leads. Not every student is going on to have a professional career, so it's important we don't allow them to tie their whole identity to rugby, and we give them opportunities for academic advancement," he adds.

The model sees Orange work with each school to provide a curriculum. Included is a teacher who is also a qualified rugby coach.

It's equal parts fun and serious business. "This is light years removed from throwing a few cones on the ground, having the kids kick and pass a rugby ball for half an hour, and counting them as 'rugby participants' in an annual report," he says.

As his business matures, Orange is able to identify what works and what doesn't, and modify his programs accordingly. "The biggest factor by far is that the students can see and feel that they are part of an integrated rugby pathway," he explains. "These kids are inherently aspirational. When they are able to see the real outcomes that students before them are having in rugby, meet and touch their heroes, that's a crucial motivator for how they approach their own involvement."

There's more. "The provision of playing kit, for example, is vitally important. Not because it's free gear, but because they get to wear the Rebels colours and badge. They feel as if they belong to something real, like they are the Rebels Super Rugby and Super W players of the future. And from there, future Wallabies and Wallaroos."

It's plainly obvious that this is the critical link between the professional and community game that Australian rugby has been missing for too long. But, as things stand today, it has also led Orange into a world of pain. With education budgets stretched, Orange encountered principals who loved the concept, but who baulked at the expense. A solution was brokered with Rebels' chairman Paul Docherty, and Stephenson, whereby the Rebels would subsidise half of the cost, and more schools duly signed on.

All were uncomfortable that it should be left to a professional franchise to fund a schools development program that should fall under Rugby Australia and the state body. But, faced with the choice of mirroring what New South Wales and Sydney rugby did - turning their back on Western Sydney and leaving these schools open for rugby league to pick the eyes out of - or secure these schools for rugby, with Rugby Australia's knowledge, they proceeded.

Orange is reluctant to criticise hard-working and well-intentioned individuals working within the hierarchy, instead pointing to systematic failure and a lack of vision from the game's leaders. "It's like rugby development has become a slave to structure. This is the way we do things, because this is the way we've always done things," he says. "Our central and state bodies have become bogged down spreading themselves too thinly, in some cases even trying to charge schools to send development officers in. And the ones they do get into, the depth and quality of what they deliver is questionable, because there's no integration with the rest of the game, and in some cases, little understanding of the communities we're dealing with."

That arrangement set Orange onto a path where, the week before, he attended a meeting at which the appointed administrator for the Melbourne Rebels confirmed Academy Movement as an unsecured creditor. Orange is now owed tens of thousands of dollars for services delivered through his program, with little prospect of seeing it paid. It seems ridiculous that Orange, doing some of Rugby Australia and Rugby Victoria's job for them by developing rugby pathways on the ground, is left substantially out of pocket for doing so. But like everyone associated with the Rebels, Orange is more anxious about what things will look like for 2025 and beyond.

"I have another two schools looking closely at the program," he says. "There's capacity for another five, possibly up to ten more schools after that. But not while we're hindered by all this uncertainty. And not if we're unable to demonstrate a direct flow through to the Rebels."

His comments carry a stark warning. "It's clear what will happen if we walk away. Rugby league's approach isn't education based, so in my view, the kids are already disadvantaged. But they are walking into schools saying 'rugby is dead' and 'we are the pathway to a junior contract with the Storm'."

Should rugby fail to find a way to accommodate Orange and the Rebels, he has another option. Just yesterday he met with officials from Cricket Victoria who, unsurprisingly, were very receptive to how transferable Orange's model is for state schools with large, cricket loving, migrant enrolments.

"Going down that path would be so much easier for me. There's so much more money available in cricket, it's way easier to find coaches, and there's a much wider demographic."

With his Hawke's Bay blood running thick, it will take a lot to prise Orange out of rugby. But individuals like him, and the game itself, can only sustain so many hammer blows.

On his way to the offices of Cricket Victoria, Orange met briefly with Rugby Australia CEO Phil Waugh at a Melbourne CBD hotel. Waugh promises to reconvene during the weekend of Super Round. (That second meeting never eventuates).

With so many competing priorities no-one envies Waugh's task. Friday's announcement of an increase in funding to women's rugby of $3m was both welcome and necessary. But Rugby Australia's forward funding remains uncertain. It can't finalise a new broadcast deal without knowing how many teams it will have to play and in what competition. It doesn't know how many teams it can afford to have without a new broadcast deal. When it comes to Orange and to the Rebels, there is a sense of Waugh being in a race against time. If the Rebels are to be cast adrift, (and there are many within Rugby Australia and New South Wales and Queensland rugby for whom this is a welcome fait accompli), it might be best done before Waugh is forced to release the report commissioned into Australia's World Cup debacle.

Setting a huge multi-million-dollar budget blowout, including the best part of a million dollars splashed on psychologists, adding in an extravagant multi-million-dollar contract for Sydney Roosters outside back Joseph Suaalii, against what Orange could deliver for rugby with just a fraction of that money, would be a telling indictment on Rugby Australia.

For forty minutes the trial is a reality check for the Rebels. The Drua are big, fast and extremely well organised. Caned at the breakdown and in the penalty count, half-time arrives with the Rebels behind by 21-7. But in a rare case of players doing exactly what is requested of them by their coaches during a half-time spray, things are tipped on their head in the second half. When Lachie Anderson crosses in the corner with a couple of minutes remaining, the Rebels have recovered to lead 26-21. It's a second impressive trial win.

Even better, save for centre Matt Proctor feeling a tight hamstring, there are no injuries. Soon after, with the rugby crowd dispersing and the flow of 'Swifties' along the walkway next to the ground growing thicker by the minute, Kevin Foote stands in the middle of the pitch, already contemplating selection dilemmas for Monday. He smiles a wry smile. It's daunting, but it's a problem he's been looking forward to having.

Chapter Seventeen

20th February, 2024

Finally, after what feels like the longest pre-season on record, match week has arrived. In just three days the Rebels will be playing for competition points. For eighty minutes at least, the focus will be on rugby, not who owes how much to whom, and what is going to happen next year and beyond. It feels like a blessing.

No matter the switch to game mode, there is always room in a rugby team environment to enjoy a laugh. Video Analyst Jarod Rutley, affectionately known as J-Rod, begins the team meeting by rolling tape showing a US College Football coach, upset at things not going his way on the field, ripping off his headset and slamming it into the ground. He then rolls close-up film of yesterday's forward's session, where scrum coach Nick Stiles, unhappy with what he is seeing, grabs at the whistle hanging around his neck and, similarly, hurls it into the turf. The room erupts in laughter. Stiles, not knowing it was coming, turns fire-engine red but cops it on the chin. After all, it's nothing more than a sign of how committed he is to getting the detail right.

The serious stuff begins with Geoff Parling and Brad Harris leading a SWOT analysis on this weeks' opponent, the Brumbies. Every point made is supported by video: some from last year's matches against the Brumbies, and some from their recent trial matches.

"Look at how the breakdown is never over", says Parling. "Even when we think we've got the ball secured at the back, in they come again, repeated efforts, and here they are, knocking Hundy off the ball, all because we got lazy and thought we'd already done all the work."

"Watch for how they always have two sides to their attack," stresses Harris. Most sides will keep folding around, going the same way, but they're never afraid to switch the point, and look how quickly they do that. We must never go to sleep on the negative side."

"We have to stop their dominant carries," he continues. "That's where they get their momentum. We must have two on Robbie (Valetini). Every time."

For today's training run, two sides have been selected: the starting fifteen, and a 2nd fifteen, which includes the match day bench. That's 30 players in active match simulation, with the remaining squad members into skills and conditioning drills behind the dead ball area. Of itself, the 'train-on' group paints an informative picture. It contains players like Ryan Louwrens, Cabous Eloff, Pone Fa'amausili, Lukas Ripley and others who have been regulars in the match day 23 over the last two seasons but who, this week at least, are spare men. Any player not quite 100%, or in Louwrens' case, where three into two doesn't go, will have to wait their turn.

It's an impressive show of depth, but it doesn't come without cost. Kevin Foote recounts his sleepless night on Sunday, agonising over his choice at halfback. In the end, it's come down to a little bit of horses for courses. The Brumbies' efficiency hints at the potential for more kicking from the base than against different opponents. Jack Maunder's kicking skill set and organisational ability has won him the 9 shirt. Bobby Tuttle's energy and fizz, and his back-up goal kicking, will see him wear 21.

The only real disappointment is that Matt Proctor's hamstring tightness will prevent his debut. He is philosophical as he watches from the sideline. "I ran this morning and it doesn't feel too bad. Do everything right this week and I'm sure I'll be good for round two," he says.

The main training block is modified contact: enough to simulate a match, defensively and attacking, but pared back to ensure there are no unexpected, untimely injuries. Nevertheless, it's a heart stopping session for the coaching staff. In the space of ten minutes, Alex Mafi, Jordie Uelese and Taniela Tupou all go down in contact and stay down. Every one of them takes a moment to let a grimace wash over them, before carefully probing at their ankles. All three, in turn, slowly rise to their feet, prop on their 'good' leg, and push off gingerly. All three, after a few tentative steps, break out into a trot, then a run, before rejoining the action. The relief is palpable.

Off field, there is relief of sorts, too. With the administrator due to hand down its final report on March 4th - which could precipitate immediate liquidation - Federal Court Judge Catherine Button has granted a 60-day extension which will allow the Rebels' board to file an alternative proposal to creditors: known as a Deed of Company Arrangement (DOCA).

It's a critical turn, for a number of reasons. For one, it takes some heat out of the immediate situation, effectively buying an extra eight weeks where the media should have little new to report on, in turn allowing the club, the players and coaches, to focus on the first half of the season.

There's also the matter of the board members now being able to shore up their position. First order of business is to try to force Rugby Australia to the negotiating table, asking them to come good on the annual funding withheld, plus approximately $2m for salaries and income tax paid for Wallabies players while they were on national duty. The thinking is that if the quantum of the debt is reduced to a level where the ATO receives a part-payment it can live with, and a new payment plan is implemented for the balance, that might be enough to open things up for a 'white knight' or a consortium of funders, to step in.

That's a whole lot of 'what ifs and maybe's', but Judge Button identifies a key issue: "Directors raise that it would be more beneficial to extend the convening period rather than have the company go into liquidation because the proposal would (have the potential to) offer a better return to creditors than an immediate winding up."

It's the 'nothing to lose by having a look' option. Such a solution, should it be forthcoming, would be put to the vote of creditors: a ray of hope compared to the certainty of immediate liquidation.

Tellingly, when consulted by the administrators, Rugby Australia opposed the application for extension. A spokesperson says, "We didn't think it was in the best interests of the staff." That's a reference to the redundant staff not being able to access superannuation payments until the administration process is finalised and the club formally enters liquidation. Nobody involved wants staff entitlements to be withheld. But nobody associated with the club believes that is the real reason for the objection. Importantly, Rugby Australia has been prevented from tipping the Rebels straight into liquidation. It's an option many people inside the club believe the central administration would have taken.

Vivid battle lines have been drawn. The Rebels' board members are making it clear they will not roll over and own a debt they genuinely believe isn't theirs, solely, to own. In turn, Rugby Australia has made it clear they have neither the means nor the inclination to cover the Rebels' shortfall. As ever when it comes to Australian rugby, nothing is clean and simple.

Chapter Eighteen

23rd February, 2024

Being a Scot, it's highly possible renowned poet Robert Burns would have enjoyed rugby. Unfortunately, he never had the opportunity to find out; Rugby School's William Webb Ellis didn't pick up the ball and run with it until 1823, twenty-seven years after Burns' death.

Burns must have felt something in the water however. One of his most famous works *To a Mouse* contains the line: "The best laid schemes 'o mice an' men, Gang aft a-glay." It is as if Burns penned that line especially for the Rebels who, desperately keen to start well, over-commit too many players to a high, central kick chase, leaving space for the Brumbies to work the ball to speed merchant Corey Toole on the transition. The season is just three minutes and thirty seconds old and the Rebels are down by 0-7. Such are the best laid plans of mice and men.

It's too early for panic, but for some reason, things don't quite feel right. The line out - considered in-house to be an area of strength - never settles. Over-throws, under-throws, obstruction calls, the full works. Meanwhile, on the opposition throw, Burns' match report would have concluded that 'nary o fing're nail' was placed on the Brumbies' ball.

In the 16th minute, assistant coach Brad Harris' words from Tuesday are revisited. "Never go to sleep on the negative side." The Brumbies switch back to the blind side and flyhalf Noah Lolesio - in an impressive return to Super Rugby - finds himself one on one with Sam Talakai, and easily skins him on the outside. Less than a quarter of the match has gone, Toole now has two tries and the Rebels are chasing the game.

Like a racing greyhound hot on the tail of a mechanical lure, it's a futile chase. Rugby has largely become a matter of converting opportunities when inside the attacking 22, or 'red zone', and limiting the damage when the opposition duly gets their turn. Tonight the Rebels make sixteen separate visits to the attacking 22, for a measly sum total of three points. Four attacking lineouts are lost (and as many in other areas of the field), three penalties are conceded while in possession, there are five dropped balls, two wayward passes, one penalty kick cannons against an upright, and one is successful. Add on for good measure Carter Gordon kicking the ball dead, when there should have been another line-out opportunity from five metres out. No side is winning any rugby game with that kind of red zone conversion.

By full-time the score has blown out to 30-3, four tries to nil. It's a bitter pill for fans who, having endured an awful few weeks reading about the likely demise of professional rugby in Melbourne, desperately wanted something to cheer. It's an even more bitter blow for the coaches.

"We never saw this coming at all," says a visibly upset Foote, immediately after the match. "The prep's been good, we thought we had the boys calm and focused, but that level of execution… it's beyond disappointing."

All losing dressing rooms carry an unmistakeable pall. The weight of abject disappointment. The stench of defeat. This one is no exception.

The players are allowed a few minutes to reflect and consider their wounds before parents, partners and children are admitted. Nick Stiles momentarily parks his disappointment and outlines to everyone the importance of connection to family.

"I love having all the kids in here," he says. "Seeing guys that come to the club as 18-year-olds evolve into fathers. Obviously, things haven't gone our way tonight, but we all know we're better than that. And win or lose, one of the most important things we have, and what we value and appreciate more than anything, is the support the families provide. You allow this to happen."

Stiles then talks about history. The Rebels are a young club, but all long-standing traditions start somewhere. It has been determined that all players, past, present and future, will be issued with numbered caps. During the season, debutant players will receive theirs after their debut match, while existing players will have theirs presented in batches, as the season rolls out. The first two are both special; assistant coach Geoff Parling, who was also player #127, and Rob Leota, the first local player to become captain of the club.

The debutants follow: Lukhan Salakaia-Loto, Jack Maunder, Filipo Daugunu, Taniela Tupou and Jake Strachan; Rebels #198 to #202. By the time Brad Wilkin receives special mention for having played his 50th match, and the featured players drain a can of the sponsor's finest, the mood has lifted slightly. There are showers to be had, pizza and fruit to be grazed on, and hydration to be attended to.

For the coaches, a difficult weekend awaits. All will be poring over video, trying to identify what it was they missed. Tomorrow there will be conversations developing and, by Sunday, a series of meetings via zoom, as they reach consensus around what went wrong, what needs to be fixed, and what the work-ons will be for the new week.

Chapter Nineteen

26th February, 2024

"When I was a player, it would take me hours to get to sleep following a game. You'd get so wound up beforehand, then obviously there'd be the physical exertion, and then afterwards, the adrenaline would still be there and you'd be playing it all out in your head, over and over." Geoff Parling parks himself on a bench, a few minutes early for a line-out review meeting, and weighs up the differences between playing and coaching. "I actually sleep much better now that I'm a coach. Sometimes I'm so mentally drained, I find I drift off a lot easier."

He smiles a wry smile. "But not this weekend. On Friday night, the last time I remember rolling over and checking the clock, it was 5.07am."

The impact from Friday night's loss is felt most by Parling, whose specific area of responsibility, the line-out, failed dismally. He sets the tone for the coming meeting. "We know we have a good line-out. Last season it was one of the best in the competition. The worst thing we can do now is panic the guys. There'll be no major changes. But we have to learn fast."

The line-out forwards file in and huddle in chairs close to a whiteboard. Parling already has it filled with numbers and letters - a language the players inherently understand. To an outsider, it's an impenetrable code reminiscent of the work of Russell Crowe's John Nash, in the film, 'A Beautiful Mind'.

Parling's strategy is not to avoid what went wrong, but also to not dwell on it. "We had a chat, straight after the match. I didn't need to say too much, we all know where we went wrong," he says. "You need to be careful straight after a match. Not be too emotional with the players. You can do a lot of damage if you get that wrong."

The focus is squarely on the round two match against the Force. Which variations they will use throughout the week, to get their line-out success rate back into the 90% range. The defensive line-out gets a going over too. "We weren't alert enough," urges Parling. "At some point, we have to decide if we're going to put pressure on them, or we're just going to give them a free ride all match."

Examples roll off the tape. There is confusion: lifters and jumpers in the wrong slots, too much time chewed up deciding what to do while the Brumbies hookers simply fire the ball in to an unguarded jumper.

"I don't mind if we get to that point, if we're not getting a clear read, if you take a guess. That's okay, get up there and see what you can do. But don't just stand around watching, every time, coming up with nothing."

The main jumpers, Lukhan Salakaia-Loto and Josh Canham lean forward, nodding in agreement. Everyone wants their coach to sleep better, next weekend.

The rest of the forwards join the group. Brad Harris works through the technical aspects of Corey Toole's second try. Sam Talakai is the man who missed Noah Lolesio, but he is Morton Thiokol's faulty o-ring from the doomed Space Shuttle, Challenger - the part at the end of the chain that failed, but only as a result of a series of system and organisational failures beforehand.

Again, the tone is constructive. "This is what we talked about. Don't switch off on the negative side. This is what we didn't do. And, this is what happened as a result. It isn't us," implores Harris. "What we put out there isn't us! And we'll get it right."

Now it's Nick Stiles' turn: "Let me tell you, on Friday night, I don't think I've ever been so flat after a match. Ever. Saturday, I walked for miles, still kicking stones. Then, by Sunday night I was back in the fight."

He highlights some key scrums from the match. "Look at the correlation… all the good scrums, we get the front row loaded, punch through the back five, then snap with our knees. That's what we're looking for, every time."

Inevitably, he comes to the crucial scrum right on half-time, near the Brumbies line, with them just having gone down to 14 men, and the Rebels with all of the momentum. A try - which felt inevitable - would have seen them go into the sheds down only by 17-10. Instead, referee Angus Gardner penalised the Rebels for not pushing straight, leaving the half-time score 17-3: a totally different scenario.

"We had the ascendancy, I get it. The instinct is to hammer that home. But we were too anxious. Patience. A bit more patience."

Tim Sampson has a similar message for the backs. "We must back our systems. Stay in the moment. Once we fell behind we had too many players trying to solve things on their own. Playing outside of our systems is bullshit."

By the time the whole squad comes together, Harris has some good news to share. The forwards tackle success rate was 88%, with 10% of the tackles dominant. That's a good return. Very good. It shows the effort is there. Where the backs are concerned, 71% is too low, but again, the dominant tackle rate is up, at 16%. "That's excellent," he says. "We've got something to build off."

There are more stats. "Defenders beaten, 42, that's the highest in the competition across the whole round. Ruck wins, 96%, that's second in the comp. Rucks lost, 4%. These are very good numbers," says Harris. "We created opportunities."

Rob Taylor highlights the kick-offs. "Our pressure was good. We kicked off seven times and got the ball back four of those times. That's outstanding chase pressure."

Everybody knows there's a 'but' coming. Sampson takes over. "First eight line-outs, we got past three phases just once. Six of those line-outs, we never even got to first phase. It's one of our pillars: three phase completion is critical."

The players are shown a list of all of the negative outcomes that were under the Rebels' control. "Seven negative outcomes in the first 15 minutes. Second half… 18 negative outcomes that we controlled. That's not us," says Sampson, borrowing from Harris.

As ever, the language used is spare. Players don't tolerate waffle and the coaches can't risk their core message being fogged over. Every possible action has a code name: Grenade, Cannon, Rocket, Laser, Bullseye, Mortar, Grass and Jet for kicking. Core passing, running and pod options have names like Ace, King, Bungy, Tsunami, Bivy, Joker, Bridge, Hippo and Turbo. And - as they used to say on the K-tel adverts - there are many more.

The communication isn't all one way. Players step up and lead the team through explanations of what occurred and, briefed by the coaches beforehand, what the fixes are. There are lingering concerns around Australian rugby that Carter Gordon was scarred by his World Cup experience. Not in this room. He commands the centre of the gym and, like a seasoned professional, leads the team through what plays he will be running this week, and why. Alex Mafi and Lukhan Salakaia-Loto are forward voices. Calm, authoritative, constructive. And Jack Maunder, perched on a raised bench, steps up with a comment on his old Exeter teammate, Nic White, who will likely be starting for the Force on Friday night.

Maunder's contribution is a generous one. Kevin Foote has just informed him privately that he has gone from starting half-back to out of the team altogether. His face and body language paint a picture of obvious disappointment, but when the opportunity arises to contribute positively, he jumps in without hesitation. For a pasty young son of a butcher from Devon, the concept of Ubuntu fits easily.

There's a frank, open discussion about Brad Wilkin's decision in the first half, with the side down 14-0, attacking while holding penalty advantage, to deliberately knock the ball on, so as to automatically receive the penalty.

"I just felt like we needed to come away with something," he says. "Settle things down, take the three, at least get on the board, then come back down again."

He puts forward a strong case, but it's countered by Gordon and the video. "Look. The cross-kick to Kells is on."

Foote steps in to make a call on a team rule for the future. "We keep going. Play to score. We can always come back to the penalty. Nothing to lose by having a crack."

It's a frank, mature discussion. No tension or awkwardness, just a collective desire to learn from the match and improve things for next time.

Foote stays in control, this time highlighting two great plays by Filipo Daugunu.

"Look at what happens here," he says, more animated than usual. "We're not one of those teams that runs around celebrating nothing. Or does it for fake. But here's a guy who's new to the club, working his arse off turning the ball over on a second effort, and nobody comes in to congratulate him or give him a hug. Not one person."

He holds the moment to let that sink in.

"C'mon guys. We know it's things like that which give the team a lift. That's not us. Mates win!"

There's time for a break and a light snack before the team comes together again, and full attention is shifted to Friday's match against Force. In half a day the coaches have cleverly manoeuvred the team through the stages of grief, the retrospective imperative of acknowledging what went wrong, into the first flickers of optimism and anticipation that comes with looking towards a new, beatable opponent. All carefully and deliberately managed. All without destroying confidence or belief.

The team to play the Force is highlighted on screen. It serves as another line ruled under last week and a signpost for the new week, albeit Foote is still carrying the weight of the one-on-one meetings he squeezed in during the morning, with the de-selected players.

"It's so difficult, having those conversations," he says. "Of course, they never agree, but I take them through some video, and I explain the reasons for the selection and… you know, they're professional players, they just have to get on with it. Sometimes they haven't done much wrong, it might just be more about horses for courses. Also, that's the thing about having a deep squad. We've always got alternative options if we think that's the way to go this week."

If Stan commentator and ex-Wallaby great Tim Horan had his way, Foote would be selecting the team on 'hardness'. Speaking on Stan's 'Rugby Heaven', Horan labels the Rebels' side "poor" and the forward pack "as soft as I've seen them". Former Wallaby Cameron Shepherd is on the same panel and adds for good measure, how he was "shocked" at the difference between the Rebels and Brumbies.

That's the thing about a disappointing loss. You get a chance to redeem yourself in seven days, but in the meantime you have to cop whatever criticism comes your way. Fair or unfair, informed or uninformed, it doesn't matter. If you're not doing the business on the field, explanations just look like excuses.

The team files out of the gym to begin preparation for the afternoon's training run. With every hour, they put more distance between themselves and the Brumbies' match, and draw closer to the Force match. Rugby media are a fickle bunch. Bandwagons are made for jumping on and off. They'll turn quickly enough. But only as long as the team delivers what they are capable of.

Chapter Twenty

1st March, 2024

For most coaches and captains, post-match press conferences are something typically something to be endured rather than embraced. A necessary contractual obligation. With TV broadcast coverage now dominating the immediate post-match, by the time coaches arrive for the official press conference, they have already been put through the wringer out on the field. But the requirement remains, because of the need to reach fans who may not have subscription TV, or do but who missed the coverage.

Press conferences in Melbourne have their own distinctive flavour, particularly for visiting teams who, upon arrival, invariably find an almost empty theatre. The reaction of Blues coach Leon McDonald and captain Tom Robinson a couple of years prior, says it all: an incredulous Robinson asking, "Is this a fucking stitch up?" while scanning the empty room for hidden cameras, like he'd been set up as a mark on the old TV classic *Candid Camera*.

That's all a function of the mainstream sports media outlets, Nine (ex-Fairfax), News Corporation and the ABC having long dropped off covering Rebels' matches. It seems that these days, rugby only rates a mention for its off-field woes, not for coverage of the competition itself.

Press conferences are also a lesson in Body Language 101. Rare is the coach whose face and demeanour doesn't betray his words: win or lose. Often, questions and answers feel superfluous. Train the camera on the coach for thirty seconds and you learn all you need to know about what happened in the game and what's in store for next week, no questions asked.

Kevin Foote and Rob Leota take their seats in front of the cameras and prove the point. The shift in Foote's body language from last week to this is a full 180 degrees. The Rebels have just rattled up 29 unanswered points in the second half to defeat the Force, 48-34. By no means a perfect performance, with the same line-out jitters from round one evident in the first half, the final quarter finally saw the team find its 'right' tempo, and run away with the match. It's a much-needed bonus point win, but even more important, it means the team now has the confidence to take the same game style forward into the following weeks.

Leota reflects on a key moment - his side down by 24-12 on the stroke of half-time, with the feed to an attacking 5m scrum. It's an identical scenario to that of a week before, when the Rebels, over anxious, desperate to stay in touch, were penalised for not pushing straight. This time, despite several nervous re-sets, they hold their nerve. Off a rock-solid platform, Carter Gordon runs hard from the open side to the blind and Andrew Kellaway, enjoying a splendid game from fullback, does the rest. So, what was different about this week?

"With our front row, I knew all I had to do was ask the question, 'I need this scrum, can you give it to me?'," Leota says. "In that moment, as a pack, we just knew they were going to break. We just had to keep going, keep going, and we were able to get that try for Kells in the corner, and then I was just telling the forward pack, especially the front row, 'that's your try'."

Asked about the situation surrounding the club, Foote's main message is to thank fans who have been coming to support the Rebels for 14 years, and to acknowledge the board, who, "have been smashed over the last couple of months, but jeez, these are people who have invested so heavily into the club... they've put their own money into the club... they're hurting, and so from everyone's perspective, I've spoken a lot about galvanising fans, supporters, the players, but we do feel like every one of these wins means that much more for people."

The noise and buzz in the changing room amplifies that story. Everybody loves a win. Foote presents Matt Proctor with his debut cap (Rebel #203), before the Leota leads a rousing rendition of the team song. "The Rebels are having a party" rings out loud and strong. Taniela Tupou laps up the excitement despite having to lip synch his way through, not yet having learned it properly. Perhaps he'd used all his words up earlier, telling the Stan commentary team in a 2nd half sideline interview: "I'm fucked".

With the players and families dispersing, Foote turns his attention to next week's match against Moana Pasifika. "They were impressive last week. Well organised. They're always physical. They've lost their two best backs from last year (Levi Aumua and Timoci Tavatavanawai) but they've recruited well, they've got fitter... we'll need to be smart about how we go about things."

Moana Pasifika are listed for the early game tomorrow, against the Fijian Drua, but Foote won't be at the ground.

"I'll be out at Moorabbin (the Rebels 'A' team is playing the Western Force 'A' team). It's an important game for us, to get some game time into some of the boys, like Jack (Maunder)… Joostey (Nick Jooste), he never got on the park tonight… and I'm so excited to see young Judah (Saumaisue). His potential…"

Foote tails off his sentence, shaking his head. If the Rebels don't go forward into 2025 it's the lost opportunity to bring young talent like Saumaisue through that will hurt him as much as anything.

"We've got the women playing afterwards. I'll stay out there and support them, so by the time I get home… it's better if I find a quiet place and watch Moana on TV, on my own."

Unusually, there is only one board member present in the rooms. With the Rebel's licence having been handed back to Rugby Australia, strictly speaking there is no longer a board, although with the club under voluntary administration, the directors joint and severally liable for the club's debt, and those same individuals fully invested in being part of the Rebels' future, they remain very much in the picture.

Their absence is down to the dispute between Rugby Australia and the Rebels directors escalating. A brief of a concise statement that has been prepared for the administrator, designed to flag a potential claim against RA with respect to commitments made to them for ongoing funding, plus an additional $2m paid to cover the wages of players while they were on Wallabies duty: a total of $8m. As a result, director and Rugby Victoria president Neil Hay, is barred from attending a summit between RA and franchise officials. With the club in the hands of Rugby Australia, and the Rebels board members now 'persona non grata' as a result of their action, individuals have chosen to keep their distance.

The Federal Court allowing the Rebel's directors 60 days in which to act prior to the end of the administration period, highlights how there are multiple purposes to the statement. It is a signal to the court and to creditors that there is another side to the story. It's also designed to tie the historic debt to the prospect of keeping the club alive into 2025 and beyond. A leverage play that seeks to force Rugby Australia to come to the negotiation table: something they have been unwilling to do since late last year.

The directors believe there are incentives for Rugby Australia to talk. Should the matter not be resolved and Rugby Australia choose to defend a court action, there is potential for disclosure of dirty linen that might reflect poorly on the organisation, its board and executives. Worse, should they elect to fight and lose, there are other franchises waiting in line behind the Rebels, who will have precedent to themselves seek similar amounts withheld from them.

It's a longshot, but it feels like a pathway to the future. Everything on the table, past, present and future, with the 'least worst' option for Rugby Australia being to hand the Rebels' licence to a new ownership group, with the Victorian state government, major creditors and old board members all party to a negotiated settlement with respect to the historic debt.

Super Round, the third held in Melbourne, is widely considered to be a success; at least on the field, where all six matches are highly entertaining, logging a combined total of 58 tries. All Black coaches Scott Robertson and Jason Ryan are highly visible throughout, dressed for a beach bar-b-que, relaxed and joking with fans, enjoying the rugby on offer. Meanwhile, new Wallabies coach Joe Schmidt is more circumspect, taking in the action from a private box, trying to formulate which players might press their claim for closer inspection. Disappointingly for the headline hunters, there is no repeat of last year, when coach Eddie Jones sat in the stands with an open notebook containing a list of names, which was snapped from behind his shoulder by a budding, amateur paparazzi.

The most dramatic match is saved until last, where the Hurricanes - down to 14 men after a red card to Jordie Barrett - eke out a 33-33 draw against the Reds, before finding the winning try in the 6th minute of extra-time. That result, coming on top of a convincing win the night before by the Waratahs over perennial champion the Crusaders, hints at a 'closing of the gap' that is much desired on both sides of the Tasman - albeit that it is only round two, too soon to be drawing any definitive conclusions.

What is conclusive is the media and fan reaction from elsewhere in Australia and New Zealand about the turnout. Around 10,500-11,000 attend each day: not a great look in a 30,000-seat stadium. For many commentators, like Auckland-based sports journalist Dylan Cleaver, it's conclusive evidence that "Melbourne is NOT a rugby town."

Brisbane breakfast radio host and ex-Wallaby, Greg Martin, didn't even wait for the event to begin before putting the boot in, telling 'The Platform': "I'm going to apologise before the games start. I'm sorry. I'm sorry you've all had to come to Melbourne for magic round (sic)."

Alternative venues are tossed around like confetti. Queenstown, Wellington, Gold Coast, Perth, Fiji and more. None of that discussion addresses the commercial reality that Super Round can only exist if the travelling teams that forgo a home game to do so, are suitably compensated for the lost gate and provision to sponsors. 'Visit Victoria', an arm of the Victorian state government, has been prepared to underwrite those costs when nobody else has. It is hard to find anybody who doesn't think that rotating the event around various host locations is a good idea. But as ever, when it comes to rugby in the region, it comes down to money and who is prepared to pay.

As demonstrated in rugby league and AFL, these types of combined rounds are designed to work as 'destination events', where fans travel from interstate and overseas to make a big weekend of it, soaking up the football and whatever the host city has to offer. The attendance across the weekend is on a par with that of 2023. It seems pertinent to ask, 'what has happened in Australian rugby since then that might positively influence sentiment around the sport and motivate more fans to travel to attend, to join the local audience and make the event bigger than last year?'

Changed? In the year since, Australian rugby politics has been as dysfunctional and divided as ever. Rugby Australia CEO Andy Marinos was pushed out, followed later in the year by the exit of chairman Hamish McLennan. The Wallabies World Cup campaign was an unmitigated disaster, which was followed by coach Eddie Jones jumping ship to Japan. On both sides of the Tasman, there is constant chatter in the press and on-line rugby forums about how broken Super Rugby is. With rents and interest rates soaring, economic conditions for individuals and families in Australia are trying. And the local franchise, the Rebels, are in voluntary administration, now controlled by a parent organisation that gives every indication they would like them shut down. With all of those factors in play, the notion that fans will be more inclined than a year ago to roll up in their thousands, seems fanciful.

If that's not concerning enough, what's even more worrisome is how bereft of answers those running the game appear to be.

On the Saturday of Super Round, executives from Rugby Australia, NZ Rugby, player union representatives and the various franchise CEO's attend a meeting, to discuss pressing issues relating to the competition. Privately, some CEO's emerge shellshocked by the absence of any conclusive forward strategy. New Super Rugby Commission chairman Kevin Molloy speaks eloquently about plans to improve marketing and promotion, but this only serves to highlight the lack of strategic purpose and direction underpinning the competition. There is little more than familiar thought bubbles and straw clutching. Re-admit Argentina. Align better with Japan. Shift Moana Pasifika to Melbourne. It is only a year since NZ Rugby produced its own 'Aupiki Report', which countenanced a stand-alone elite professional competition with invitations extended to just two Australian sides. Rugby Australia, potentially heading to court with one of its franchises, can't be sure to what extent it can afford to stay in.

Anyone who believes this is all about Melbourne - patchy crowds at Super Round, multiple franchises weighed down by debt, how many teams in Super Rugby - misses the point. The Melbourne Rebels are a symptom. A canary in the coal mine. Super Rugby has been in a downward spiral for some years. What is at stake is the future of professional rugby in the region.

The meetings continue into the new week; this time a 'summit' for Australia's leading stakeholders. In a following press release, CEO Phil Waugh states: "This runway presents a once-in-a-generation opportunity to set the game up for the future, and it is important that as a collective we have a common understanding of where Australian rugby is at - this summit represents the first step in rebuilding the game together."

The comments of two CEO's catch the eye. David Canham, CEO of the Queensland Reds says; "We have identified an agreed process to move the game forward together, but importantly we are now at the doorstep of a transformational opportunity to deliver sustained success on and off the field." Paul Doorn, CEO of the NSW Waratahs, adds; The summit set a clear direction for what we need to achieve success at every level."

It is wholly ironic that the summit, which is making decisions on the future direction and pathway for rugby in Australia, is held in Melbourne. The only professional franchise without a senior rugby official present at the meeting, the only franchise without input into the future of professional rugby in Australia, is the Melbourne Rebels.

Chapter Twenty-One

4th March, 2024

In her role as Player Development Manager for the Rebels, Moana Leilua falls into the same category as Kevin Foote and Nick Stiles: torn between having to deal with her own personal uncertainties and needing to provide a leadership role for others in the club.

"It's not easy, but because my role is to provide support to players, I've really had to put to the side my own self-care. Otherwise I wouldn't be able to do what the players need me to do," she explains. "In one sense I'm lucky because I'm employed by RUPA (each Super Rugby franchise plus the Australian Sevens program is allocated a development manager), so compared to the Rebels' staff, I'm a bit more protected. Then again, if the club doesn't go forward, obviously my role here becomes redundant."

Like many of the players and coaches, Leilua moved to Melbourne just to take up the role. "It might sound weird coming from a Samoan New Zealander, but I've got a real heart for Australian rugby. I love the code, I want to contribute and be a part of it. Like everyone, I've got no idea what I'll be doing on the 1st July, but I know I don't want my time in the game here in Melbourne, to be over."

Leilua's path into this role started as a netball player in South Auckland transitioning into playing rugby in 2014. She enjoyed it so much she volunteered as the Counties sevens' team manager for two years, before graduation to manager of the Counties Steelers NPC side for four seasons.

"There was a real focus there on Pasifika and Māori players, so when I found out about the opportunity with the Rebels, and learning more about the Melbourne rugby community and how the Rebels were beginning to engage more in that community, there seemed to be an obvious fit."

"My job isn't all about culture and cultural awareness though," she explains. "That's just one of the pillars. Life skills, financial management, careers and education, wellbeing, personal integrity: I work with the players in all of these areas. For example, there's a huge emphasis on keeping players active outside of rugby, and at the moment we have almost twenty players in university education or on work placements, which I facilitate."

Leilua is also part of the club's welfare committee, along with Nick Stiles and the medical staff. Coupled with RUPA providing access to clinical psychological support, and services around things like gambling addiction, what makes all of this work is how it is embedded into the club.

"Footey really gets it," says Leilua. "The club isn't just about rugby. It's about connection with each other, with our families and with the community. Everyone looking out for each other. Being part of something bigger. The rugby aspect - performances on the field - flows from that."

Taking family to the nth degree, Leilua's role was expanded to include management of the club's homestay program - where young players new to Melbourne who don't have family, are housed with families of board members and supporters of the club. There is also a creche on home match days, where two babysitters are provided for the players at the club for the players who are young dads, so that their partners are able to relax and watch the game. "This has been a terrific initiative," she says. "We're the only club in Australia that does this."

Leilua's family responsibilities don't end there. "Post-match, I get an update from Bryn (club doctor Bryn Savill) and it's my task to advise the families about any serious injuries and keep them updated."

Below the serious injuries are the regular wellness assessments, as players check-in with Katherine Rottier around soreness, fatigue and state of mind. It's a simple traffic light system, with Leilua watching for orange and red indicators. "That can be where I become a touch point, and while I'm supposed to clock off, there are times when players contact me at odd hours just looking for some reinforcement of support on a matter. I always respond and often, it's not so much about what I might say, but more the fact that there is somebody available for them, that is important."

It's not a surprise to Leilua, that there is a motherhood aspect to the role. "Obviously, the boys all need to feel safe talking to me. And when they open up about something, I have a duty to maintain confidences. But if I feel that there is an issue or a potential response or action from the player that is potentially going to harm them or the club, then I'll counsel them around what I believe is the appropriate way to deal with things. Sometimes, matters need to be brought into the open, other times they are better dealt with confidentially."

What about the rewards that come with the job? Leilua enthusiastically lists them: "When we have laggards or guys reticent about starting a course, who finally do so - to see how motivated some of the post-graduate study guys are, and to see guys develop as people. That's a challenge for me too, in dealing with a young player like, say, Mason Gordon, who, through high school, academy, then the Rebels, his whole identity is rugby. Versus a player like Matt Gibbon, who was an ex-tradie who had a life prior to rugby, so my interactions with them are different."

She's not supposed to have favourites, but Gibbon is one of Leilua's 'special' players. "I've seen Gibbo transition from single man to getting married and now being a new dad, and watched him grow into that role, and it's been a real delight, seeing him become the person he is today."

On the education side, she's also proud of how Rebels' players took out the RUPA education award in 2021 (Ross Haylett-Petty) and 2022 (Michael Wells), and how both of them were highly supportive of helping get some of the Pacific Islander boys into courses and becoming very important role models. "Kells (Andrew Kellaway) is now in that similar role, doing a great job as RUPA player director. Which is extra special for me, because he'd come across to New Zealand and played a season with the Steelers, so he was the only person I knew when I first came here."

Looking towards the future, regardless of what happens to the Rebels, Leilua isn't going to be sitting idle. She played a role with club management and the board in making representations to the state government, speaking at a formal event in the grounds of Parliament House, and also met with government representatives alongside Jimmy Orange and Academy Movement graduate Leafi Talataina, to garner support from the education department for the academic and rugby pathways provided by Orange's program.

That dovetailed nicely into her selection in 2023 for the World Rugby Capgemini Women in Rugby Scholarship program, through which she received mentor support and funding for study. "That's been awesome," she explains. "Firstly, I attended a summit (self-funded) in Paris during last year's World Cup. My mentor, Susan Kearney, sits on the World Rugby Council and has been a wonderful advisor. And next month, in April, I begin my course with the Australian Institute of Company Directors. Longer term, I'm interested in board level governance of rugby, and really excited about moving into executive leadership, in particular making an authentic impact in the Pasifika diaspora."

That's all for the future however. What really matters is the now; playing her part in getting the team - and herself - through to the end of the competition and, hopefully, beyond.

"The situation is very real," she explains. "So many players made careful decisions to come from the UK and elsewhere, to join the Rebels. They'd heard about our program, they were excited, and they wanted to be here. So, to have this unfold like it has, has been an awful shock for everyone. What's helped is that we're now playing rugby, so that helps take minds away from the off-field negativity. But even so, there's still a lot of nervousness around; you can't help but feel it."

Leilua picks up on another point, not understood outside the club bubble. "This is a high-octane, high-performance environment. It's very unusual to be in that situation without having somebody in the leadership role. And specifically, Baden. In some ways still, it doesn't feel real. I was in his office earlier today and I realised that I still call it Bado's office: like we all do!"

Leilua speaks for many when she shares her concerns for the future, if the Rebels franchise is terminated. "The ripple effect of losing the Rebels will definitely impact upon the rugby community - which is largely my community. Nothing good can come of such a decision. That said, whatever happens, the fight to establish and sustain rugby in Melbourne and Victoria will continue, and if I can be a little bit selfish about it, that's why I'd like to remain in Australian rugby. It feels like we're only just getting started."

Chapter Twenty-Two

5th March, 2024

Normally at this time of year, General Manager of Rugby Nick Stiles, is elbows-deep into negotiating and finalising player contracts. With nothing to offer players beyond the 30th June (the same applies to his own contract), and the Rebels and Rugby Victoria senior representatives excluded from Rugby Australia's summit, his phone has stopped ringing. It seems that player agents are only interested in talking to him when there is a transaction to be had.

Instead, Stiles is today manning the bar-b-que, cooking a tasty stir-fry of beef mince, vegetables and rice for the player's lunch. And trying to bring to an end a week-long quest to be authorised to source and purchase strapping tape for the team.

"Obviously, all expenditure needs to be approved by Rugby Australia. But because, since we went into VA, they haven't provided anybody on the ground here in Melbourne, it's been a hell of a task to keep a lot of the basic things ticking over," he says. "I've got my wife looking sideways at me because of purchases I've had to put on our own credit card, worried about not getting reimbursed. And it gets very tiring having to explain to bean counters, non-rugby people, why we need to buy certain things."

Stiles' frustration is clearly evident. "I've got someone in Sydney pushing back at me, asking where all the tape we got last time went. We had three teams playing on the weekend - the Rebels, the 'A' team and the women's team. That'll do it. And now we're one day away from travelling to New Zealand for a match, and we don't have enough strapping tape."

He expands further; "We'd already taken actions to reduce costs wherever we could, to become more self-sufficient. For example, instead of doing player lunches at Edwins (the cafe located within the stadium precinct) we decided we'd purchase ingredients and do most of the food prep ourselves."

Club nutritionist Alexandra Parr smiles ruefully. Working at the club on a part-time basis, in concert with her private practice, she notes how her role has changed. "It's still my responsibility to plan the meal programs, and to ensure the player's protein intakes are kept up, but I find that more and more of my job is walking the aisles at Coles on Swan Street, doing the grocery shopping."

Stiles points to other changes since the beginning of the voluntary administration period. "One of the big things is that without a CEO, and without RA dropping anyone in to replace Baden, that leadership vacuum starts to manifest itself in certain ways. We've already lost some of that connection between the high-performance team and the commercial team. I mean, we're all still here in the same building, and we're all still united behind the Rebels, but Baden and a couple of the administrators, they were really the glue that bound everyone together, just through their communication, and their roles straddling both departments."

Stiles acknowledges the importance of his role, to try to fill that leadership void, with one frustrated face for behind his office door, and another public face in front of staff. But just two weeks into the competition, with no indication as to how things are going to fall beyond June 30th, there's already significant fraying at the edges.

"It's tough for everyone," he says. "I'm proud of how everybody is knuckling down, everyone has been totally professional. But we just don't know what we're dealing with. And it can't stay like that for too long. Something will have to give."

One thing that has already given is flanker Brad Wilkin's hamstring - a nasty tear, low down, near the insertion behind the knee. Finishing off his stir fry, Wilkin jokes about the cause being due to not playing golf during the week (a keen golfer, his brother is PGA Professional Fraser Wilkin). But behind the humour and bravado is a devastated player.

"It's not a regular hamstring tear," he explains. "Because of how and where it's torn, I'm looking at surgery, then an extended rehab. If things go well, best case is I'll be available again for the very end of the season. I actually had the same injury, back in 2018, when I was with the Waratahs. Because of my age, the advice then was to let it heal naturally, but this time, we think the best option is for a more complete repair via surgery, and to cross fingers hoping it takes and there's no complications as I move into recovery and rehab."

And then, the kicker. "What's different this time too, is that there's no avoiding our situation. If I'd been signed to a longer contract, as we were ready to do, then it's not quite so harrowing. I'd have the security of knowing I could get it right and there'd always be next year. But right now, it's not a good time to be injured. If it turns out everybody has to go and seek contracts elsewhere, that only just adds to the stress and disappointment."

Matt Proctor is the other player with a hamstring problem. After a session of stretching and light exercise in the gym, he's more hopeful of being available sooner than later, albeit he won't be rushed back in, given his breakdown during the Force match.

For the players in the match-day 23, it is Brad Harris who leads today's team meeting with the theme for the week; 'Shut the front door!' That message is a testament to Moana Pasifika's physicality, and 'in-your face' approach, on both sides of the ball. "Everything this week comes down to just three things," Harris urges. "Work-rate, physicality and discipline. Fall down on any one of those things and we're in for a world of pain. Get them all right, then happy days."

He rules off the meeting with an important observation. "As a club, we've been historically poor at getting repeat wins. Guys maybe getting too comfortable with themselves. Good sides don't rest on their wins, they build on them."

Chapter Twenty-Three

8th March, 2024

In 2009, visiting Springboks coach Pieter de Villiers caused a ruckus that rippled across the Waikato region of New Zealand, when he warned of his players suffering from hotel fatigue because, "There's nothing to do in Hamilton."

Keeping the players occupied in Hamilton is an unexpected challenge for the Rebels, with the game against Moana Pasifika transferred at late notice, to the river city's FMG Stadium. Moana's regular home ground in Auckland, Mt Smart Stadium is hosting the NZ Warriors' round one NRL match; Eden Park a concert by US performer Pink; and the intended venue, North Harbour Stadium, has been determined unfit for play due to issues with the playing surface.

Fighting against Hamilton's dubious reputation, the Rebels players bravely try to keep themselves busy. Bobby Tuttle is one of the early risers: "I room with Kells, which goes back a long way, from when we were in the Australian schoolboys. We went for a walk at 7.30am, then ended up at a favourite coffee shop of ours, Kopi Cafe. The staff there are terrifically friendly, and they have a bit of fun with the designs on the top of the coffee. They know we're rugby players, but even so, it's a bit of an eye-opener to have your coffee come out with a penis on it! After that we chilled in our room for a bit before meeting downstairs for a team walk at 10.30am."

The team walk is not a Friday morning shopping expedition, but a chance for the players to connect and, in lieu of a captain's run the day before, stop at a couple of open, grassed areas to reinforce key objectives for the match.

"We were back at the hotel by the middle of the day," Tuttle continues. "Some of the boys like to take a nap but Kells and I decided to watch *The Hobbit*. Being in Hamilton, not far from Hobbiton where it was all filmed, it felt like the right thing to do. Then, before we knew it, it was 3.30pm, which is the start of strapping time and the pre-match meal."

At 5.30pm a charter bus is waiting in the forecourt of the Novotel Tainui Hotel, and at 6pm sharp the players are seated in a room underneath the main grandstand, ready for Kevin Foote's pre-match address. Their match jerseys are adorned with black armbands, acknowledging the passing of the wife of Mark Fraser, volunteer embosser of the club playing strip since match one in 2011, and also the death midweek, of chairman Paul Docherty's mother.

"The greatest challenge in rugby is to come to New Zealand and win," Foote says. It's a powerful opening, only partly qualified by the fact that Moana are not one of the New Zealand's traditional franchises or provinces. "This is the place where rugby is religion. No matter who we play. They all have the same rugby DNA," he continues.

The mood is intense, but not over the top. The days of a coach whipping players into a hate-filled, face-slapping frenzy, are long gone.

"To become the greatest Rebels team of all time we have to do things differently. Win in New Zealand. Win week after week. And we do that through our character and hard work. We know that, right? Mates win. I love seeing how you guys care for each other, off the field. Those connections… what we've been speaking about since the start of pre-season. Watching all of that come together. Mates win."

Foote's voice ramps up in urgency. "Character. How important is character? We're about to run out into an empty stadium. Acknowledge that now. That means we bring the energy ourselves. We feed off each other. Vaiolini… his brothers and sisters are here from Auckland. How proud are they of him? How proud are we that he's starting tonight? Get alongside him."

With that, Foote and the coaches exit, leaving the players to find the right level of individual and collective excitement, for their on-field warm-up.

Outside, overhead and ground conditions are perfect for rugby. Sky NZ's three-man expert panel steps into their work on the sideline. It's quite the collection of rugby IP: ex-All Blacks Jeff Wilson, Aaron Cruden and James Parsons, with Mils Muliaina floating around for good measure. Oh, and ex-All Black greats Tana Umaga and Sir Bryan Williams present in their capacity as Moana Pasifika head coach and patron, respectively.

Beyond that, the crowd thins out noticeably. Around 400 people are in attendance, hardly surprising given the venue switch to Hamilton. Sensibly, stadium management confines fans to one side of the ground only, although because it's the same side as cameras, TV screens at home are filled with rows and rows of empty seats. Understandable, yes. But it's an awful look for the game.

Soon after kick-off, captain Rob Leota busts up the middle of the park, but a chopping tackle jars the side of his knee. Losing the skipper early isn't in the script.

The Rebels' set piece however is strong, and that dominance delivers three first-half tries: Andrew Kellaway and Ryan Louwrens crossing out wide, and Vaiolini Ekuasi bouncing off a 5m scrum and crashing over to the delight of his family.

This Moana Pasifika side is a different beast from last year, however. Noticeably fitter, they hang tough, and by the 59th minute they have recovered to lead 20-19. All the momentum is their way.

The situation demands cool-headed, authoritative leadership, and it's Lukhan Salakaia-Loto who provides it, demanding his side plays through its strength at scrum and line-out maul drive. That scrum power brings a try to Lachie Anderson, coming in close, off his wing, to reap the benefits of a huge shove.

Carter Gordon's conversion miss keeps Moana Pasifika in the hunt, and with seven minutes left, they mount a promising attack on the Rebels' line. But the two plays that follow ice the match: a scrum penalty to the Rebels, then, after the kick to touch, another penalty from a solidly constructed line-out drive. Gordon's second kick is a beauty - in those two plays the Rebels have gone 80m, not only to relieve pressure, but to set up the match-sealing try to Glen Vaihu. Like Ekuasi, Vaihu has family present, not just in the crowd but on the pitch. Cousin Tomasi Maka is making his Super Rugby debut off the bench for Moana Pasifika. Vaihu's proud Aunt hangs over the front fence, still beaming twenty minutes after the final siren.

The match finishes 29-23. It's another bonus point win. For tonight at least, the Rebels sit atop the ladder.

Inside the changing room, there's a curious vibe. To a man, the coaches are delighted. They got the result they came for, and the team showed character and resolve when they were placed under pressure. But for the players, while nobody is downplaying the win, the overriding feeling is one of quiet satisfaction and relief more than unbridled joy.

Pointing to different corners of the changing room, coach Foote seizes upon the player's reaction. "I love this from the players. They know we can play better. They're already thinking about next week."

What they're not thinking about is food. Multiple baking trays containing enough cheese toasties and chicken tenders to feed a village, lay on a bench, untouched. Their provision is well-intentioned and appreciated, albeit they were probably at their best around the time the second-half front row replacements were made. More out of courtesy than hunger, Tim Sampson bravely takes on a piece of chicken. He quickly switches to the jelly snakes. It's a small thing, but it feels like an opportunity to pare back a little of Super Rugby's operational cost.

Foote and his coaching team now have an interesting puzzle to mull over. Last year, the side captured the hearts of fans by adopting what was at times, close to a 'run at all costs' policy. Two things have happened this year: the definition of 'fearless' has been refined so as to draw a line between what is fearless and reckless, and the scrum has developed to become one of the best in the competition.

Back at the team hotel, Brad Harris acknowledges the conundrum. "There's a trade-off, for sure. We're fit, we want to play up tempo, all good sides play to move the ball into space. But when your scrum is going so well, you have to take advantage of that. To what extent that shapes our game moving forward, we'll have to look very closely at it."

They'll also have to look quickly. The next night, not long after the Rebels arrive back in Melbourne, their next opponent, the Reds, stuns the competition by beating the Chiefs, 25-19.

It's a strikingly impressive performance. Combative at the breakdown, inventive in attack, connected in defence. Once the season gathers momentum, things move very quickly. The Rebels will need a strong week on the training track to be ready for the Queenslanders.

Chapter Twenty-Four

15th March, 2024

As it happens, it's a patchy week on the training track. Loads of energy and some quality from the so-called 'A' team, but a few niggles preventing a few of the starting team training at full steam. Not enough to keep anyone out of Friday night's match, but an impediment when it comes to running combinations in attack and defence.

Off-field, it's worse than patchy. Highly damaging, in fact. Filipo Daugunu is owed around $7,000 for expenses incurred in his relocation to Melbourne, and he's not happy about it. It's standard practice for players to meet those costs and have them reimbursed via an expense claim, but because Daugunu's expenses are from the period prior to the club entering voluntary administration, and Rugby Australia is responsible only for debt incurred post-voluntary administration, Daugunu's status is effectively that of an unsecured creditor.

It's the greyest of grey areas. The player's Collective Bargaining Agreement (CBA) provides for Rugby Australia picking up the contracts of all players in the event of the failure of a franchise, and the Rebels' players have indeed received a verbal assurance from Rugby Australia that all existing contracts will be honoured. But Rugby Australia has deemed that non-salary, incidental expenses belong in a different bucket. And because there's a war waging over who is responsible for the club's debt, and a number of other players have pre-voluntary administration debts (mostly in the form of small superannuation payments due), Rugby Australia is wary of creating a precedent by paying Daugunu what he is owed, and opening the floodgates to others.

It's not the news Daugunu and his agent, Damien McGregor-Lowndes, want to hear. Nor Stiles, who becomes buried in the middle of talks back and forth. On Wednesday he and Moana Leilua meet with Daugunu, where it becomes apparent that if payment is not made, or the provision of a cast-iron guarantee of payment with a firm date attached isn't forthcoming, Daugunu is at risk of withdrawing from Friday night's match.

It is Rugby Australia's new Head of High Performance, Peter Horne, who comes up with a neat solution - to provide Daugunu with an "advance" rather than reimbursement. This keeps Rugby Australia clean with respect to pre- voluntary administration debt, provides Daugunu with his money, and buys time for the necessary accounting to be righted, once there is clarity on the Rebels' financial position.

It's still not enough. Negotiations drift into Thursday and then into Friday. Game day. McGregor-Lowndes and Daugunu aren't for shifting. Their message is, 'reimburse the expenses claim without variation or strings attached, or risk him withdrawing from the match'. In response, Stiles makes the obvious point that whatever Daugunu's argument with Rugby Australia is, it is the team who will be hurt by his actions in pulling out.

At around 4.45pm - one hour before the players are required to assemble for the match - Stiles' in-box pings again. All his efforts have been in vain. McGregor-Lowndes officially informs the club, via email, that because of concerns for Daugunu's mental health, his client is unfit and unavailable for tonight's match.

At 6.00pm the playing squad wander into the middle of AAMI Stadium and gather in a tight circle. They have just been informed by Kevin Foote that Daugunu won't be playing, with utility back Nick Jooste named as the late replacement. He will play at 12, with David Feliuai shifting out a place to 13.

It's an awful predicament for Foote. The culture he has installed around his team demands that there is no bullshitting or obfuscating: everyone deserves and needs to know the truth of the situation. At the same time, he never anticipated beginning a team meeting before such an important match by informing the team that one of their teammates has opted out of playing.

There is no choice but for everyone to park the matter and keep focus on the Reds. The early meeting time is a result of the Rebels' schedule containing so many Friday night matches, necessitating a change to their regular training schedule. With the player's CBA providing for a day-off during the week, full training days are now held on Monday, Tuesday and Wednesday, with Thursday, instead of Wednesday, becoming the free day. As a result, there is no opportunity for the players to conduct a 'captain's run', typically held at the match venue, to assist players with their mental preparation and provide positive imagery and familiarity with the venue.

In lieu, meeting early mirrors a practice employed effectively by the Crusaders. The players amble up the field, stopping to gather in zones - defensive, midfield and attacking - where the team leaders talk through what they will be looking to achieve in each. As captain, Rob Leota's is an important voice, Lukhan Salakaia-Loto too, but the person providing the tactical direction, and the dominant voice, is fly-half Carter Gordon.

Two hours later, barely anyone has the breath to utter a word. It is half-time and the Rebels have been run off their feet by an at times brilliant, Reds outfit. The score is 33-7, a result of the Reds dominating possession by 70%-30% and making the most of it, through lightning quick recycling and a supremely confident - and well executed - short passing game.

The Rebels' try is a beauty, to Andrew Kellaway - his 4th of the season - from a well worked move off first phase from an attacking scrum, but it's the five conceded at the other end that are of utmost concern. It's not like the Reds have brought anything unexpected, but it's one thing knowing about it and another thing altogether, to slow down the speed of the Reds' recycle and give their defence an opportunity to re-set.

Two factors are identified at half-time. Much of the possession disparity is due to soft turnovers. To turn pressure back onto the Reds, the Rebels need to play with more vigorous and purpose in attack, and retain possession in the process. In defence, the first-up tackling needs to be far more purposeful. More double tackles, more impact in the collision area.

He's far from the Lone Ranger, but Taniela Tupou offers little presence and is replaced before half-time, along with his propping partner, Matt Gibbon. Other changes follow at the break; Foote desperate to inject players who can match the Reds' speed and intensity.

For the next twenty minutes, it works. The Rebels find their tempo and two of their best, replacements Isaac Aedo-Kailea and Tuaina Taii Tualima, are rewarded with storming tries. There is a glitch when winger Glenn Vaihu compounds a rare Kellaway error and gifts a simple try to Josh Flook, but entering the final quarter down 38-26, there are faint flickers that the impossible might even be possible.

It's not to be. Chasing the game, the Rebels are done on the turnover and fast transition, and limp into the sheds, well beaten by 53-26.

In the rooms, with families gathered around as is now custom, Jooste sports a nasty black eye - cruel reward for his manful effort as the late replacement. Stiles speaks about the path tonight's two debutants have taken to become Super Rugby players. Both have battled the hard way, through club rugby: hooker Ethan Dobbins in Brisbane, and loose forward Maciu Nabolakasi in Melbourne's Dewar Shield. Both have earned their stripes through sheer hard work, and quality of performance when provided with an opportunity. Dobbins receives cap #204, Nabolaksi #205, and each of them speaks humbly about their journeys and their gratefulness to families and coaches for their constant support.

It is halfback Ryan Louwrens however, acknowledged for his 50th Super Rugby match for the Rebels, who unwittingly hits on what is lurking behind the eyes of some of his teammates and high-performance staff.

"I love this club," he exclaims, to rousing applause. But, without Stephenson's voice and presence as CEO, without board members present, without the colleagues who were laid off, and with those who remain facing an uncertain future, there is an overriding sense that this is no longer a club at all, rather a shell with the Rebels' brand atop it.

That shell is now little more than this team. A team that is, as evidenced by Daugunu's actions, fraying at the edges.

Salakaia-Loto can feel it too, quietly reflecting on the events of the day. He's hard on himself for spilling a couple of balls when running into heavy contact, but it was his line out steal that helped switch momentum after half-time. Just as he has been all season, he was again one of his side's best.

"We have to get better," he says. "Right from the start. It shouldn't take a rev up from the coaches at half-time. We're good enough to play like that right through the game."

He looks across at Foote and acknowledges some tough selection decisions ahead. "Maybe we have to change things up a bit. I'm really excited about the energy we got from the bench players."

Salakaia-Loto hasn't been there as long, but like Louwrens, he obviously cares deeply about the club. He ponders for a bit longer, before he is the last player to leave. "Hard work. We go again next week. We have to work harder."

Unsurprisingly, players always disperse more quickly after a loss. With the room almost empty, Foote is tapped on the shoulder by Reds' coach Les

Kiss who, despite his own players now ready and waiting on their team bus, has slipped in to have a quick word.

It's typical of the empathy and understanding professional coaches have for the job and for each other. They all know how narrow the line is between penthouse and outhouse. How injury or an unforeseen event, can mean the difference between looking like a genius or a dunce. An event like a player pulling out of a match unexpectedly. Kiss is happy to take the win. His side is playing as well as any in the competition. But he also knows that tonight wasn't a fair fight, and his words to Foote are respectful and appreciated.

Last men standing, Foote and Stiles grab a beer. It's been a hell of a last few days.

"I'm not sure where we go from here," says Stiles about Daugunu. "They've made their position clear. It seems that his mental health is only going to be improved by being paid the money. And because they didn't take what was put on the table, and RA isn't going to suddenly change tack, it's hard to see what his path back into the team is."

Stiles' use of "they" is instructive. Neither he or Foote believes it is Daugunu himself who is pulling the strings.

"After training on Wednesday, Filipo was laughing and joking, and he and a few boys stayed out on the field playing soccer," says Foote. "Nothing wrong with his mental health there."

"It's really hard to accept demands being made on the club, when Filipo's manager knows that we are not in control of the finances," adds Stiles. "My relationship with Damien goes back years. He's also Sambo's (Tim Sampson's) manager. We should be fine. But really, you'd have to strongly question the advice Filipo is getting. We know he's happy and settled here. It's crazy that he didn't play. And now we have a much bigger problem."

Stiles is referring to the concerns expressed by Stephenson just prior to his departure. That with a vacuum of leadership and experience, and no firm forward direction for the club, there would be cracks appear, that would inevitably manifest themselves in team performance. It's only round four, but feedback from players indicates that managers are now openly canvassing options for next season. And through his manager, Daugunu has broken trust with the coaching group and the team.

"He probably doesn't even realise it, but he could be the first domino to fall, the one that could send the club into free fall," says Stiles. "It's really hitting home now. The team we've built, the environment where players want to come here to be part of something special… the fabric of that, it's all being peeled away."

Foote joins in. "We always knew that Kells would be leaving. But Josh Kemeny, he's a new Wallaby, with everything to play for. Him leaving for the UK, it shows just how little confidence the players have in Australian rugby. And now, with every day the situation is left hanging, another piece gets chipped away. It feels unfair. On us, on the players, on the supporters."

That's another thing Stephenson reinforced before he left. The absence of context. People outside of the organisation don't know or don't understand how the feeling of uncertainty impacts on a club. Not just in the moment, but in how it compounds into tangible damage, which requires time to rebuild and recover from, before any new forward push can be made. The Rebels have lived on that precipice twice already, in 2017 when, ultimately, the Force were cut, and in 2020, when the team made a desperate last-gasp dash to leave Victoria before being locked down, playing out the season living out of suitcases on the NSW Central Coast.

If it was just those two events in isolation, perhaps things would be manageable. But a third time? What is clear is how important it is for success to have as many pieces as possible in place, both within the club's control, and outside. Australian rugby is like a garden hose. Despite the majority of young football talent being lured to the NRL or AFL, there is still plenty of water available at the source. But there are so many holes and leak points across the game, what comes out of the other end is barely a trickle. Those holes have names; pathways, coaching, fan engagement, vision, structure, strategic foresight, governance, culture and, as always, finances.

In that context, the last thing the Rebels and Australian rugby needs is commission-driven player managers stepping into a void left by Rugby Australia, understandably working in their self-interest, but in the process, collectively destroying the values and respectful relationships that exist between players and clubs.

Chapter Twenty-Five

19th March, 2024

Three months after Rugby Australia stopped engaging with the Rebels over their finances and operations, the Rebels directors finally have the meeting they've been requesting. Albeit it's a different meeting now than one they would have been having before Xmas. Instead of working together as partners on a cash-flow projection and debt management plan, they are now antagonists.

Representing the directors are board members Paul Docherty, Tim North KC and Georgia Widdup, plus legal advisor Marcus Avery. (In a piece of irony, that will play out in explosive circumstances, Avery is ex PwC Australia, an ex-colleague of the appointed administrator, Martin Ford). Also present is the Rebels' ace-in-the-hole, Widdup's father, Leigh Clifford.

At 76 years old, with a 37-year career at Rio Tinto, including a stint as CEO, before serving as chairman of Qantas from 2007-2018, Clifford is not a man to be messed with. On October 29th 2011, in a dispute with engineers, pilots and baggage handlers, Qantas grounded its entire fleet, resuming service two days later, only after the full bench of Fair Work Australia ordered the airline and the unions back to work. The following year, in 2012, Fair Work Australia would go on to reject key union demands around pay and contract worker restriction demands. With such a significant national event on his CV, it's hard to imagine Clifford being intimidated in skirmishes with Rugby Australia.

Rugby Australia is represented by Phil Waugh, ex CFO, now COO, Richard Gardham, board members Brett Godfrey and Karen Penrose, lawyer Joseph Scarcella from Australian corporate law firm Johnson Winter Slattery, and representatives from their advisors, Deloitte. As it happens, Godfrey and Clifford have been adversaries before, if briefly - Godfrey a co-founder of Virgin Australia before exiting the airline in 2010.

North frames the meeting, outlining what the directors view as three points of risk for Rugby Australia should they not agree to the terms that will form part of their upcoming Deed of Company Arrangement (DOCA).

The first concerns the way salaries are structured for Wallabies players, where the franchises are, in effect, reimbursed for wages paid to players while they are on duty with a national team. What the directors believe hasn't been accounted for is the split of PAYG tax owing to the ATO for those players for those periods; an amount calculated by the Rebels to be well in excess of $2m.

The second point relates to language used by Rugby Australia with respect to their relationship with the franchises, and undertakings made previously with respect to an expected $300m funding injection from a private equity partner. In their own words, Rugby Australia repeatedly describes these five relationships as partnerships. At a meeting held in conjunction with the launch of the 2027 World Cup, attended by representatives from all five franchises and prospective private equity investor Silver Lake (fresh from their NZ$200m capital investment into New Zealand rugby, and ahead of their $62.5m additional raise in December), then, in the reflected glow of the sails of a Sydney Opera House lit up in celebratory green and gold, CEO Andy Marinos and chief operating officer Adam Fulsham stepped the franchises through how the anticipated A$300m raise would be distributed. One third was to be set aside in a future fund, one third to go to the development of grass roots rugby, and the remaining third to fix the state and franchise balance sheets.

"This is your balance sheet," they exhorted, emphasising the strength and nature of the partnership model.

Yet seemingly now, when it suits Rugby Australia, with the value equation for a private equity investor tipped on its head, with no $300m deal consummated, with the game nationally facing a substantial debt, the Rebels' directors, unlike the Waratahs who have been folded into the tent, now find Rugby Australia's understanding of 'partnership' to mean something very different.

In media reports accompanying revelations of the Rebels' financial plight, one prominent narrative is that Rugby Australia was unaware of the extent of the problem. The Deloitte representative confirms that via meetings held in 2023, there was in fact full visibility of the Rebels' finances. The Rebels' directors consider that if Rugby Australia board members happened to be individually unaware, this is an internal communication matter.

There is discussion around the 2017 partnership agreement between Rugby Australia and Visit Victoria, the tourism arm of the Victorian state government. With Rugby Australia desperately short of funds, the deal made to take ownership of the Rebels' licence from then owner Andrew Cox provided for a payment of $16.5m from Visit Victoria to Rugby Australia to cover the period 2017-2025, contingent upon receiving hosting rights for Bledisloe Cup matches and the guaranteed ongoing presence in Super Rugby of the Rebels. North reminds the meeting that should the Rebels be excluded from Super Rugby in 2025, a clause in the agreement provides for a penalty payment, from Rugby Australia to Visit Victoria (reducing over the term of the agreement but said to be well in excess of $1m).

Surprisingly to the Rebels camp, this seems to be news to some people on the other side. (Later, Rugby Australia would claim that the because the Rebels did not formally extend an option, the requirement to retain the Rebels expired at the end of 2023. What isn't explained is why, if that was the case, the Rebels weren't excluded from the 2024 competition).

What North is effectively outlining is that, whatever the amount Rugby Australia expects to save from cutting the Rebels, that very act puts them in danger of triggering or crystallising substantial losses.

Discussion swings back and forth - bravado and brinkmanship, frustration and foxing, restatements of rights and righteousness. The original meeting folds into a second, new meeting, this time without advisors present.

At the heart of the discussion is the amount of detail Rebels directors intend to put into the DOCA, in around two weeks' time. Unlike what is in the press - a simplistic narrative that the Rebels' directors are threatening action against Rugby Australia only as a desperate measure to save their own houses - the twist in the tale is that the DOCA will contain a forward solution for rugby in the state. One the directors hope and believe will be very difficult for Rugby Australia to ignore.

Upon exiting the meeting, Docherty, North, Widdup and Clifford are cautiously optimistic. Fellow board members are duly updated. If Rugby Australia has a plan to cull the Rebels from Super Rugby, it feels like it is one that has arisen out of circumstance, almost accidentally, as opposed to being strategically devised and capable of being delivered with precision.

North calls Baden Stephenson at his home on the Sunshine Coast. He's loath to get ahead of things, but he's optimistic enough to talk to Stephenson about what should happen after they get their licence back. There might still be a chance to keep the gang together.

Chapter Twenty-Six

22nd March, 2024

So much for that idea.

Johnson Winter Slattery lawyer Joseph Scarcella's nickname is 'Scud'. A letter from Scarcella, acting for Rugby Australia, which is delivered to the Rebels' directors on the Friday, three days after the Sydney meetings, lands with the full force of a dozen scud missiles. At its heart it states how, for various fundamental reasons which are unspecified, Rugby Australia is not prepared to engage of participate in any form of deed of company arrangement with the current Rebels' directors.

For the directors, it's a stunning missive. As unexpected as it is unfathomable.

It's also a wake-up call. Those closely involved with the club have always wanted to believe that Rugby Australia wanted to do the right thing. But now there can be no doubt or pretence around Rugby Australia wanting to save the Rebels. Instead, it's open warfare.

"Perhaps we're guilty of being naive," says director, Owain Stone. "When Phil Waugh got up and spoke at the sponsor launch, it was just what everyone was looking for. And it was received extremely positively. Now… it's so hard to reconcile that evening with this action."

Stone pauses and allows himself the indulgence of looking into the future. "Even if the Rebels survive, it will feel like a pyrrhic victory. The Rebels would be around because Rugby Australia failed to exterminate us, not because they want us."

Stone also makes it clear that the Rebels' position is not contingent on the current directors staying on. "It's not like we're being selfish or are in this for the money," he explains. "We get tickets to the chairman's club, yes. But that's the extent of it. Every away game I've ever attended, I pay for it myself. Tickets, travel, accommodation, the lot. We do this, all of it, because we love the game and we want to see it flourish in Victoria. I'm an active rugby referee. The narrative that the directors are somehow in this for the money is complete nonsense. It costs us. Some of the directors have pumped enormous sums of their own money into this club. And all of us… if for the Rebels to move forward we have to stand aside, then that's something we'll happily do."

The directors struggle to make sense of Rugby Australia's position. Research commissioned by the governing body has identified the western, northern and south-eastern corridors of outer Melbourne as the highest growth opportunity locations in Australia for rugby. Why leave this open for rugby league to take a stranglehold, just as it happened in western Sydney? Have no lessons been learned?

Stone repeats how, in October, when Rugby Australia pushed their preferred centralisation model onto the franchises, and the Waratahs immediately took it up, the Rebels made it clear that they were open to doing the same. This to the point where legal documents were requested of Rugby Australia with, subject to board approval, a view to proceeding.

Nobody is quite sure what changed.

With the private equity play having evaporated, and an $80m facility with Pacific Equity Partners put in place instead, some directors believe that Deloitte and/or CFO Richard Gardham simply found another solution that was cheaper than keeping the Rebels. "Liquidate them and wait for (Rebels board member) Lindsey Cattermole to write a cheque for the debt", says one director, sarcastically.

Other directors believe that it wasn't until the latter part of 2023, following Hamish McLennan's exit, that the full extent of Rugby Australia's dire financial position was realised. The Waratahs. The Rebels. The Brumbies. Three substantial debt traps. The Force back in, just three years after being culled because the game couldn't afford five professional teams. Too many mouths to feed. A massive overspend on the failed World Cup mission. Sponsors exiting. With a new broadcast deal in the offing, but widespread negativity surrounding the game in Australia impinging on the value of that, there is no surety on the revenue side. In such an environment, with inexperienced CEO Waugh lacking political capital, they believe Gardham's voice will have carried increasing weight. At every opportunity, reduce expenses. Austerity. Immediately and forward.

Others point to McLennan's exit and the subsequent void in strategic business acumen. "Whatever McLennan's failings around personality and management style, at least he provided strategic depth and direction", says one director, ruefully.

Whatever the reason, if the letter is some kind of tactic, or it's a final 'see you in court' middle finger, the view of the directors is that it doesn't really matter. What is now important is that they push on with the DOCA, garner the support of the administrator and the creditors, and go from there.

Before that happens, there is a hiccup with the administrator. To date, the administration has been handled by Martin Ford and Stephen Longley from PwC Australia's Melbourne office. Evidently, there is history between Ford and the Rebels director's legal advisor Marcus Avery, which relates back to a disciplinary matter when both were at the same firm. A text message from Ford to Longley which refers to Avery in explicitly unflattering terms is inadvertently sent to Avery. With PwC in the midst of well-publicised integrity and cultural issues, a situation where an administrator is referring to the legal representative of the main party involved in such a manner, is untenable. Ford is bumped off the job and Longley is now the administrator in charge.

None of this is Rugby Australia's doing, but for those observing, the situation feels entirely apt. Where Rugby Australia is concerned, this whole episode is fast degenerating from chaos to farce.

Chaos is the only way to describe what unfolds at Palmerston North's Central Energy Trust Arena, later that night. The rugby pitch is ringed by an unattractive dirt speedway track, and the Hurricanes are operating at full throttle, opening up a 33-0 lead before the Rebels are finally able to mount any kind of sustained attack. Angelo Smith scores just before half-time, but the Rebels are scattered in the dirt-brown dust, going into the break 33-7 down.

The second half is better but, with the game long lost, not in any serious, constructive sense. For the second week in a row, the Rebels invite pressure upon themselves through skill errors, and ineffective first-up tackling, which only serves to pile more stress onto their defensive line, as the impressive Hurricanes get their fast recycle game working.

The match finishes 54-28, the only real bright spot being the first appearance (complete with debut try) of Mason Gordon, and a touching presentation of his cap by his older brother Carter, in the sheds afterwards. The younger Gordon, 'Moose' to his teammates, becomes Rebel #206.

Before the team leaves New Zealand, events catch up with them. In the Tuesday meetings at Rugby Australia headquarters, both parties agreed that it would be counterproductive to brief media of ongoing negotiations, and pledged not to do so. Within two hours of Scarcella's letter being received by the Rebel's directors, there is an article posted on-line on the sports and rugby website, *The Roar*, by Perth-based Mark Drummond, entitled "The Rebels aren't going down without a fight - and they might drag Rugby Australia down with them".

The piece speculates about how the Rebels are about to "lob a Molotov cocktail into Rugby Australia HQ", and that they have been "holding a gun to the head of RA", implying a legal response by the Rebels to Rugby Australia's decision to turn their back on negotiations and the DOCA.

That's news to coach Kevin Foote. On the two-hour bus ride from Palmerston North to Wellington airport, his mind is racing with thoughts about what he can do to get his side to start better, and to minimise their error rate. Instead, there is chatter on the bus, from players who are reading the article on their phones.

Players ask Foote what he knows. "Are the club's directors really prepared to take down the whole game in order to save themselves? Is that what all of this has come to?"

It's an easy question for Foote to answer - he knows nothing about it. What he does know is that anybody who thinks all of this off-field drama isn't having an impact of the team's psyche and state of mind, and their performance, has no idea what they're talking about.

Chapter Twenty-Seven

25th March, 2024

At 1.30pm, after a morning full of unit review meetings and light gym work, the squad hits the training track. For a side that has, just a couple of days ago, had 54 points put on them, and been force fed media headlines around talks with Rugby Australia having escalated into a civil war for the code, the mood is remarkably upbeat and energetic.

Perhaps that has something to do with the coaching team shifting the focus. In four out of five matches this season the Rebels have been blown away early. There simply cannot be a repeat, and with the Waratahs on a short week, travelling from Fiji, having played almost 90 minutes in stifling heat and humidity, there is fortune resting with the Rebels that they simply must take advantage of.

To realise that edge, the coaching group decides to switch up the training detail. Instead of starting with separate forwards and backs units, following warm ups, the match day and reserve side go straight into match simulation, at full pace from the get go.

Under a pleasantly warm sun, the players relish the opportunity to get stuck in. Ball movement - for the most part - is clean and accurate. If only all of this form could be carried into match day, rather than just some of it.

There is just one sour moment: a sharp, shrill whistle brings proceedings to a halt at a midfield ruck set-up. Attack coach Tim Sampson steps in over the top of a tackled player who is laying on the ground with the ball at his belly. He's angry. "We've just come out of a game where we got pushed off our own ball at the breakdown… we've talked about it all morning… and here we are, the ball sitting here waiting for the opposition to help themselves while you guys are just standing around with your hands on your cocks!"

The next breakdown sees the timely arrival of two cleaners.

With the scheduled time up, the players split into unit groups. At the city end of the field, Nick Stiles oversees a scrum drill, where on one side packs a tight-head prop with a lock and flanker behind him, and on the other, a hooker and loose-head prop, with one lock behind them.

Stiles calls the 'crouch' and 'bind', then, after the weight goes on, on 'set', and he is satisfied with the work going in, calls each mini-scrum over.

"It's a drill I like because it forces the tight-head to stay straight throughout the push," he explains later. "If he has any slight tendency to angle in, he'll be immediately exposed by the weight from the other side spinning him around. Similarly, on the other side, the drill promotes connection between the loose-head and the hooker. Any softening in that connection will be exposed by the tight-head boring straight in between them."

Players are rotated in and out, each scrimmage accompanied by shouts of support from the other players ringed around, as if cheering on an arm-wrestle at a pub.

It's not where it ends however, Stiles adding more forwards until there is eight versus eight, exhorting all of them to find the right body height then maintain it as the pressure of each scrum ramps up.

"That's good work guys," he says at the end of an intense, but short, session. "We go again in the morning."

A few weeks into the season, there are signs of attrition beginning to emerge. Alex Mafi doesn't train, after being replaced against the Hurricanes with an ankle injury. Scans haven't shown up anything, and while he's a little ginger, he should be eligible for selection.

Josh Kemeny observes training from the sideline, riding an exercise bike. He too, will train tomorrow and hopes to strip fit for Friday night in Sydney. Josh Canham comes to the sideline mid-session, having taken a knock to a knee that was already sore from last week. He insists he's okay but physio Katherine Rottier keeps him away from contact, instructing him to gently walk things off. Taniela Tupou raises a scare, rushing over to Stiles to ask permission to be excused from the first scrum. In his case it's not because of injury, but for an urgent toilet stop.

"That's one way to lose weight," quips Stiles.

Matt Proctor is back into full training, but won't be risked this week. His eyes light up at the prospect of his return match being against the Fijian Drua.

Andrew Kellaway is absent altogether; broken ribs suffered in Palmerston North will see him out until at least round eight against the Highlanders. There's a slim chance he could be ready a week earlier, but Kevin Foote's wry smile spells out the obvious.

"If you're coming back from broken ribs, I don't think the Drua is the match for that," he says.

Kellaway is a significant loss but it also represents a potential opportunity; either for Mason Gordon to build on his promising debut performance, or for sevens speedster Darby Lancaster to debut. Given what an asset the speed of Corey Toole has become for the Brumbies, everyone associated with the team is keen to see what the hard-working and likeable Lancaster can do.

The rehab group includes Brad Wilkin, who has this morning received clearance from his specialist to begin to up his gym and cycling/walking load. As the players head towards the showers, Wilkin duly rides off on his e-bike, wearing a black, German WWII-style helmet with his long, ginger mane splaying out the back. He looks for all money, not like a professional rugby player, but a foundation member of the AAMI Park chapter of the Headhunters bikie club.

Against the tide, there is one important 'in' for this week. Filipo Daugunu seeks out Foote before training, to express his regret and remorse at his decision to withdraw from the match against the Reds. He assures his coach that nothing like that will ever happen again.

It's a sensible and predictable outcome: one the coaches welcome with open arms, albeit with some wonderment at the way Daugunu's teammates clap and cheer as if celebrating the return of a lost hero. For the coaches, in their time as players, a teammate pulling out before a match in that fashion would have found a way back impossible. None of their head coaches would ever have countenanced such behaviour.

All of this coaching group are younger than 50. Yet today, they are made to feel like old men, reminded of the generation gap between themselves and today's players.

Chapter Twenty-Eight

28th March, 2024

In need of a circuit breaker, a couple of days away from the small, windowless box underneath AAMI Stadium that serves as his office, is just what the doctor ordered for Nick Stiles. He hops out of a cab on Sydney's Moore Park Road, and strolls into Rugby Australia HQ. It should be friendly territory but he feels like he's entering the lion's den.

Inside, he's immediately struck by how the cavernous foyer feels like a homage - not to Australian rugby, but to New South Wales and the Waratahs. With the Waratahs now firmly under Rugby Australia's controlling hand, and CEO Phil Waugh reminding a University of Queensland rugby lunch audience last week how the vast majority of Australia's professional rugby players come from New South Wales and Queensland, and that resource allocation moving forward will reflect this, it's not altogether surprising. It's another reminder of where the Rebels - and the advancement of rugby in Victoria - sit in the pecking order.

Stiles is here to meet with Peter Horne, newly appointed Director of High-Performance Rugby, and Toby Duncan, National Head of Team Contracting. But because of the unresolved situation between Rugby Australia and the Rebels, out of necessity, it's a meeting full of 'what ifs?' and hypotheticals.

Player agents and overseas clubs are not just circling the Rebels, waiting to pounce, but are brazenly gnawing at their flesh. Horne's objective is to keep players who are coming off contract, in Australia. At the same time, he knows that if the Rebels fold, five into four doesn't go. He can't keep everyone and he wants to hear from Stiles, his opinion on where the best talent resides on his list.

Stiles isn't enthusiastic about being asked which of his children he's prepared to put up for adoption. "I get it," he says, "we all have an obligation to do what is best for our players. Obviously, I want everyone to stay at the Rebels. We've worked incredibly hard to build our playing list, and high-performance staff. If there's a chance of us going forward into next year and beyond, I'd be crazy to help usher people out the door, and then be faced with building it all up from scratch again."

"On the other hand," he continues, "if it looks like we aren't going to survive, I don't want to see anyone miss out on an opportunity elsewhere. There are positions coming up with the Wallabies, for high performance and coaching staff. All our guys want to stick together as Rebels, but I couldn't have it on my conscience if I held information back, or got in the way of their career advancement."

It's a heavy bind, a responsibility that Stiles accepts, but doesn't pretend to relish. "After three years, this is pretty much my list. It's been built around the trusting relationships I've developed with players. And now, with a lot of the stuff that is being played out being around financial matters and governance - an area where the players have little understanding - they're looking to me even more to keep them educated and informed."

Stiles also empathises with Horne and Duncan. "They're operating in a vacuum as well. As soon as we put some detail into the discussion, like 'with four teams, is the salary cap going to increase?', or 'what are the programs and systems in place?' it was clear that they had no idea. That's not their fault, there was no sense of them withholding information from me, they simply didn't know. And it was just as obvious that the reason they didn't know, wasn't because people above them were deliberately keeping them in the dark, but because Rugby Australia doesn't actually have a plan. There might be people there who have decided they want the Rebels gone, but they don't have a plan to be able to execute that cleanly. And they certainly don't appear to have a plan for what happens after that."

The timing is clearly of major concern to Stiles. "We're in that critical window now," he notes. "Player signings have been held off, not just at the Rebels but at all the clubs. But the pressure is building. From Japan, from France, from the UK. The agents have been holding off but they have to offer their players certainty. I'd say we have two weeks, three max, before off-contract players start to disappear. And then… we think we have a problem today… that *really* becomes a problem for the game here."

Formalities completed, Stiles decides to clear his head by tackling the renowned Coogee to Bondi walk. With the help of clear skies above, and positivity coming from the directors, he finds a happy place.

Until his phone rings.

One of the high-performance team informs him that the playing group has been approached during the week by Rugby Australia, via RUPA and team representative Andrew Kellaway, regarding the superannuation amounts owing that remain outstanding as a result of the administration. (Kellaway, having graduated with a Bachelor of Business (Finance), works part-time as a research intern for Triple Eight Capital, the investment company co-founded by Roscoe Widdup, husband of board member Georgia Widdup).

Of themselves, none of the individual superannuation amounts owed are substantial, nevertheless, nobody on any side of the dispute is comfortable with players and staff being unsecured creditors of the Rebels. With the next creditor's meeting due before the end of April, and Rugby Australia's emergent position increasingly to try to force the Rebels into liquidation, matters will hinge around a creditor's vote to accept or not, the DOCA soon to be put forward by the directors. The offer put to the players is that Rugby Australia will pay all of their superannuation entitlement immediately, (rather than have this caught up in the administration and potential liquidation), in return for the players transferring their votes to Rugby Australia, for them to take to the creditors meeting, and presumably use to vote against the DOCA.

Stiles is flabbergasted. And angry. For one, the player's contracts provide for Rugby Australia to pay such outstanding entitlements anyway, without them needing to give up any individual voting rights. Someone is trying to pull the wool over the player's eyes. From where Stiles sits, it feels like Rugby Australia brazenly attempting to weaken the Rebels' position by going at the players. Divide and conquer. It's the day before a match. Which just happens to be against Rugby Australia's own franchise, the Waratahs.

It's yet another wildfire Stiles and Foote have to stamp on before it has a chance to take hold. Some players are drawn to the idea of receiving the money they are owed, sooner. Others are confused.

Stiles stands on the famous Bondi pathway, looking straight across one of the most iconic panoramas in Australia, but without even noticing it. He can scarcely believe what he has been told. Thankfully, he is assured by senior players that the group remains solid with the club.

As it happens, there's another thing that is bothering Stiles. Yesterday, before travelling to Sydney, Phil Waugh reached out to request a meeting with all staff, next Thursday, via zoom. Given the lack of engagement from Rugby Australia officials since going into administration, this doesn't feel like good news.

"What is the meeting about?" Stiles asks.

Waugh insists that there is nothing for staff to be fearful of, just that there is no particular topic.

"Why on the Thursday? The day before a game?" asks Stiles, sick of every week's preparation being compromised by late, off-field drama.

"No reason," says Waugh.

Meeting invites are duly received via email by staff. Well, many of the staff. Six high-performance staffers discover they're not on the distribution list. Anxiety levels rise again; what does this mean for their futures?

Stiles hits the phone. "What is going on?" he demands to know.

"Sorry, admin error," he is told. "Working off an old list."

It is hardly enough to lift the mood around the office, but Stiles has been around the traps long enough to know that, when it comes to Rugby Australia and a choice between conspiracy and stuff-up, stuff-up is typically a raging hot favourite. At the same time, he's frustrated because not everything that has happened is as accidental as it seems.

"Take the salary cap," he says. "There's a lot of misinformation and speculation out there about reckless spending on players being a reason for the Rebels' debt. The fact is, all player contracts are tripartite agreements where Rugby Australia is a party and has full visibility. All payroll goes through RA. Any extra payments or variations that might be made are all signed off by RA. All franchises operate under the same system with the same level of scrutiny. There are mechanisms within the cap for variations around length of service, marquee players and so on, and the fact is, when you look at player wages in totality, including RA's international top ups, the Force and the Rebels are always the lowest spending franchises."

"A lot of the damaging stuff that's out there, that could have been knocked on the head straight away by a simple statement from RA, clarifying the cap and the player salary system, and confirming that we're 100% compliant. But instead of doing that they've been happy to let that misinformation fester. All because it suits their narrative or strategy to paint us as bad guys. And that's incredibly disappointing."

Friday night's match at Allianz Stadium is, for much of the eighty minutes, an exercise in frustration. Having focused on turning around the amount of possession lost last week against the Hurricanes, player after player proceeds to spill the ball - in contact and in open space. On top, the early season line-out wobbles have returned. The Waratahs, off a short week returning from a punishing extra-time loss in Lautoka, are ripe for the taking. If only the Rebels can hold things together for long enough to take advantage.

Halfback Ryan Louwrens takes matters into his own hands, tapping and running - a chaos play that freakishly opens up a try for Lachie Anderson. Shortly before half-time, Carter Gordon chases down a flying Dylan Pietsch to prevent what appears to be a certain try at the other end. It's inspirational. And, in the context of a close match, crucial.

In the second half, the Rebels find a way forward through their scrum, and eventually the tries come: to debutant Darby Lancaster (Rebel #207), a delighted Taniela Tupou, then, to finish matters off at the end, Filipo Daugunu. Final score, 28-21.

Asked afterwards about the high error count, Foote, without going into any detail around the turmoil attached to the superannuation payment proposal, describes how it's been "an emotional week".

Delighted to get the win, he's already thinking about how to dial down that emotion and pressure, to get his players to relax more and play rugby, and draw instead on the character they showed to secure the win. 'Fast, fearless, resolute' remains the mantra. If only they can get a clean run at it.

There's one more sting in the tail. Matches between the Waratahs and Rebels are played for the Weary Dunlop Shield: Dunlop a renowned surgeon, decorated war veteran and prisoner of war, was the first Victorian player to represent the Wallabies. It's a trophy that holds special significance for the Rebels, one that aligns perfectly with the values Foote strives to install in his players. It seems that those values, and the same respect for the shield, are not in evidence at the Waratahs. Last year, as holders, the Waratahs neglected to bring the shield to Melbourne with them. (The match was won by the Rebels and the shield had to be transported afterwards).

This time around, the shield is on display at the ground, but nothing has been put in place to present it to the winning side. As the Waratahs file off the ground and the Sydney crowd disperses into the night, captain Rob Leota wanders across to silently collect the shield before gathering his team around for a photograph.

Chapter Twenty-Nine

2nd April, 2024

Anyone aspiring to be a professional rugby physio should not to expect to spend their mornings sleeping in. Head of medical, Katherine Rottier and her team of Kristian Waller and Simon Lumb, are on deck at 7.30am, conducting the daily ritual known as physio screening.

It's a routine check through of newly injured players, those who might be on the borderline of returning and anyone the physio or high-performance teams believe isn't quite operating at 100% and have a watch on.

On a typical morning, there might be eight or nine players undergoing screening. Yesterday during Monday's training, prop Matt Gibbon picked up a knock to his calf. This morning he's put through a physical inspection, and after a brief chat, it is agreed that he will sit out today's training session. Gibbon is confident he'll be fit for this Friday night, but the sensible precaution is to hold him back and reassess things tomorrow morning.

Rottier, an experienced physio of 18 years standing, including two years with the Chiefs and two-and-a-half years with the NZ Sevens, has seen it all a thousand times before. "Players invariably downplay their injuries," she says. "At first, they're mostly looking for reinforcement from us that they haven't done anything too serious, that will keep them out for too long, but after that, once they start to feel like things are on the improve, it's only natural they want to get back as soon as possible. Our job is to be dispassionate. Of course, the players want to play. The coaches want them to be available. But they also need to know the players will be at their best over the full eighty minutes. Anything less than that, then it becomes too risky for the team."

It's clear there's a complexity to Rottier's position that isn't immediately obvious to anyone looking from the outside. "This role really tests your analysis and decision-making skills," she says. "On top of that, I have a management element with my staff and the doctors, and obviously, with everything that's going on this year, that's quite challenging. I enrolled in a 'Women in Management' course which I found useful, and as part of that they encourage you to connect with a mentor in the workplace. So, Moana (Leilua) has been really supportive and Stilesy as well; nothing is too much. The real benefit though, is being able to have career progression in terms of management, while still being able to remain hands on."

Where a void exists is around the formal, co-ordinated approach similar to what is in place amongst coaches and S & C staff around the country. "That led a few of us to organise a 'What's App' group for physios and medical staff at the franchises, where we can share information or reach out for assistance or advice on matters. Which I did when Brad (Wilkin) hurt his hamstring, asking for opinion around surgery versus management for that particular grade of injury. That group must have triggered something, because the Wallabies physio, Kieran Cleary, has just set up another group, we've just had our first meeting, and with Peter Horne coming in as high-performance head, all of that feels like a positive step forward."

There's an extra edge around Rebels HQ this week. With successive home matches against two sides occupying the same section of the points table - the Drua and the Highlanders - everyone knows the next fortnight will be season defining.

Lachie Anderson, sporting a new Grace Jones look with ten stitches across his right eyebrow, will sit out this week as part of the concussion return-to-play protocol. He knows exactly what's at stake.

"It's massive. They're both eight-point games," he says.

Win both, and in the process, stunt the progress of two sides competing for the same finals spots, and the team will go to their bye week within touching distance of cementing their first ever finals series in a full Super Rugby competition. Lose one or both, and the second half of the season, with matches against three more New Zealand sides looming, becomes an entirely different proposition.

Nick Stiles has the forwards huddled in close. It's no surprise to anyone to find that the scrum has been deemed their pathway to success against the Drua. He rolls video, one clip after another. Scrum penalties won against the Drua in the pre-season trial match. Scrum penalties conceded by the Drua against the Force, last weekend.

"See what happens when you stay low and long against these guys? They stand up!" Stiles exhorts. "It doesn't mean we go overboard on the push and fall asleep. We know Frank (Drua halfback, Frank Lomani) is going to take off. Eyes open at all times. We keep our shape and we keep the effort on."

Brad Harris expands on the same theme - Lomani's unpredictability and speed off the mark. "The Drua have scored six tries this year from quick tap and runs. That's easily first in the comp. It's another set piece for them. What does that mean? It means that if you're penalised, don't concede quick access to the ball. Nothing silly, but hang on to the ball. We need to buy four, five, six seconds. Everyone else, get square, and get back ten. We have to be urgent."

Harris pinpoints another Drua strength, supported by a graph showing when their tries are scored.

"They power surge. Look how many back -to -back tries they score. One followed immediately by another. They feed off positive emotion. Know that when we get scored against they will come in waves. If they score, take that time to connect. Embrace it. Then when we kick off, take that power surge away from them by muscling up.

Team instructions are interspersed with messages for individuals. A slide features Wilkin, in chef mode, offering a full rack of bar-b-que ribs for the player who makes the best clean-out in the match.

In the 45 minutes before training starts, the physio room becomes a hive of activity. This is Rottier's office and there is no question that the players respect that boundary. But it's also a safe space for them; a place where, having built up personal relationships with physios during countless strapping and massage sessions, they are able to express themselves more freely than they might to one of the coaches.

As Baden Stephenson says, "If I ever wanted to know the mood of the club, get a handle on what's really going on with the players, that's where I'd go. The physio room." In that respect, Rottier is upfront about how the situation surrounding the club impacts upon the demeanour of players. "Everyone's got a lot more used to it now, so we've all kind of figured out how to deal with things. My staff all have young families so we've been very upfront about talking the truth about dealing with the uncertainty or how the future might look, and if anyone needs to secure a new position somewhere else, how they'd be fully supported. With the players, mostly they deal with it through black humour. Which is fine if that's what we need to get through it. But because we get groups of players in here on match days and training days, everyone is very conscious about staying focused on the rugby, and so that kind of thing isn't spoken about. On non-training days, or with the rehab group, where the pace might be a bit slower and there's more time, that's more where those deeper conversations are happening and the concerns are being expressed."

Comparing this Rebels group with the New Zealand players she worked with, Rottier observes how; "Everyone talks about differences in performance and perhaps conditioning between New Zealand and Australia, but one key difference I would point to is how the players here at the Rebels - and I don't know what it's like in the other states - have a much lower sense of entitlement. One way that manifests itself is in how players here commit to rehab. If we need them to come in, even if that's a designated day off, they'll gladly do it, and not only that, they tend to hang around the club, around the environment, for much longer. Whereas in New Zealand, I'd find it almost impossible to get a player to come in if they were entitled to that designated day off. I'm sure some of that is because in New Zealand your team is on the news every night, whereas here it's a very different mentality. That's good in some ways, because I don't think it's always healthy to put young sportspeople up on pedestals, but on the other hand, that lack of publicity for rugby here in Melbourne, definitely isn't helpful."

When it comes to game day, there is a set order for players so that they have certainty around their preparation and aren't forced to stand around waiting, but on training days, it's first in, best dressed.

"We have our regulars," says Rottier. "Some players can't put a boot on without being strapped first. Others reserve it for game day only, and other players again, we hardly ever see them unless they have an injury. And then, there are all the idiosyncrasies - some players firm, some soft, some haggling over the music."

This morning it's U2's *Beautiful Day* that fills the small, windowless room, causing an upbeat Lukhan Salakaia-Loto to proclaim that it is indeed a beautiful day and this training session will be the best of the year.

On the adjacent bed, Pone Fa'amausili stands to have his knee strapped, while Taniela Tupou parks himself on the end of it. More than 250kgs of prime Rebel beef is quite a test, but the bed manufacturer, Metron, passes with flying colours.

As it happens, Salakaia-Loto is off the mark - coach Foote is disappointed with a number of loose aspects of the training session.

"Some of the things we're getting wrong in games; accuracy around handling, line-out… the precision still isn't there, he says, mildly annoyed."

The session is busier for the physios than they would have liked. With the eye of a hawk, Rottier spots young squad member Timma Fainga'anuku cop a stray knee to the head at a ruck, and momentarily stumble. It's not much, but it's enough for her to pull him off immediately, and have him enter concussion protocols. Due to fly later in the day to Brisbane, to play in club rugby over the weekend, Fainga'anuku is disappointed to know he won't be going anywhere.

Darby Lancaster pulls up a little proppy, feeling at a groin. He'll shower and have lunch, then undergo a post-training exam.

At least he gets to have lunch. Rottier misses out, called into a meeting with Luke Vella, Taniela Tupou and two gentlemen who arrived earlier in the morning to observe training.

New Wallabies coach Joe Schmidt keeps a respectful distance from proceedings. Of slight build, his status and reputation provide him with undeniable presence. In tow is renowned scrum guru Mike Cron, who has this morning been announced as the new Wallabies scrum coach. Having flown in last night from Christchurch, from where he will continue to live and commute, Cron divulges how he relishes the opportunity to work with a group of players in Australia who, while not short of talent, have considerable upside.

Schmidt is not there to read the riot act to Tupou, but to get across where Australia's star prop's body and mind are at. Loaded up with huge amounts of game-time at the Queensland Reds, Tupou suffered a leg injury at the World Cup - a setback which has seen him off the pace fitness wise, compared to his teammates. A niggling wrist injury has only compounded matters, and while there has been improvement over the last couple of weeks, through appearances in a limited bench role, Tupou is still playing through pain.

Rottier and Vella are there to provide support to their player and candour to Schmidt about where they see things. It turns out they're hardly needed. Tupou speaks honestly about his ailments and impediments, and convincingly about what he wants to provide for the Wallabies and how he intends to go about getting there.

Like boarding schoolboys summonsed to the headmaster's office, a mini-procession of other players also make their way in to sit with Schmidt. The meetings are brief - of the 'keep up the good work' or 'I'd like to see more of x and y' variety as opposed to anything too deep and meaningful. For most of the players, especially inside centre David Feliuai, the real value comes with just knowing that they are on the radar. Players who aren't called in get a message about where they stand, as well.

Schmidt's final meeting isn't with a player, but with Rebel's assistant coach Geoff Parling. It's essentially a final job interview, with line-out coach the remaining piece of the Wallabies coaching puzzle to be filled.

As Parling sits in a room selling his wares to Schmidt, there is another arrival in the office - Taylor Whyte, an Irishman who connected with the club in 2023 as an unpaid intern, doing the rounds before he returns to his homeland.

He's a popular visitor, copping handshakes, backslaps and well-wishes all around the office. Popular because the staff are happy to see him alive.

In December, with pre-season in full swing, in an effort to inject energy into team-building activities, Parling arranged for staff to race-off in a Bronco, complete with Stawell Gift-like handicaps, for the players to watch, laugh at, and bet on. Whyte, slight and lean, was one of the favoured runners, but finished out of the money, out of breath and distressed.

By the next day, Whyte was in the emergency department at the Alfred Hospital, suffering from an enlarged spleen - an infection in his heart pumping tainted blood around his body. An extended stay in hospital followed, leading to open-heart surgery in January, where he had two valves replaced.

Since the event, Parling has copped plenty of ribbing, stretching to accusations of attempted murder. Stiles points across to the meeting room. "Geoff's in there now, trying to tell Joe Schmidt, because Taylor had an unknown pre-existing heart condition and it was uncovered because of the Bronco, how he saved a man's life."

Schmidt is evidently persuaded by Parling's life-saving capabilities. Two weeks later, the Englishman turned Melbournian is confirmed as the new Wallabies' line-out coach.

Chapter Thirty

3rd April, 2024

It was US General Douglas MacArthur, who once said, "One cannot wage war under present conditions without the support of public opinion, which is tremendously molded (sic) by the press and other forms of propaganda."

To date, in the battle between the Rebels' directors and Rugby Australia over the future of the franchise and ownership of the clubs' debts and obligations, it is Rugby Australia which has understood the need to win the propaganda war and control the narrative. It's a simple, persuasive story: $22m of debt and growing, an unsustainable financial model into the future, Australian rugby lacking the talent and financial capacity to sustain five professional sides, Melbourne not being true rugby heartland, the Rebels' directors interested only in saving their own backsides.

The director's position is more nuanced - something that doesn't easily lend itself to headlines and grabs catchy enough to swing public opinion to their side. But change has been in the wind, ex-chairman Paul Docherty indicating behind the scenes: "We are coming with a solution. And it will be awesome and inspiring."

Aware how desperate staff and players are for something positive to latch on to, the directors engage a public relations consultant and the fightback begins with a press release that is immediately picked up by all major news and rugby news outlets:

PLAN FOR NEW MELBOURNE REBELS HOME IN CITY'S WEST

The Wyndham Regional Football Facility

A private equity-backed consortium is in the final stages of high-level talks to move the Melbourne Rebels women's and men's professional rugby club to Melbourne's fast- growing western suburbs.

Under the innovative masterplan, the Melbourne Rebels would negotiate a deal with Western Melbourne Group which would see them sharing the Wyndham Regional Football Facility in Tarneit with the Western United Women's and Men's A-League teams.

Led by Leigh Clifford, the former Chair of Qantas and former CEO of Rio Tinto, the consortium he has assembled are all a part of the Melbourne business community that see the benefit of keeping professional women's and men's rugby in Victoria, but equally see the benefit of their first of its kind business model for Super Rugby, based out in the West of Melbourne.

The Melbourne Rebels consortium is well on the way to raising $20-$30 million from private equity to invest in the Rebels over a number of years.

The Federal Government and Wyndham City Council have been briefed on the plan over recent months.

There are obvious synergies and cost efficiencies between the sporting codes which would see both Western United and the Melbourne Rebels share a community-based facility and growth strategy. Wyndham is home to one of the largest Pasifika communities and already has a large Rugby Union fan base in the West of Melbourne.

The deal will include playing games in the recently opened 5000 capacity stadium and the 15,000-capacity stadium which is anticipated to be ready for the 2026/27 A-League Season and the 2027 Rugby World Cup.

The broader precinct owned by Western Melbourne Group in partnership with Wyndham City Council, features a 1000+ residential estate and over 100,000sqm of commercial land, which is earmarked to be the centrepiece of Wyndham's Riverdale town centre and proposed Oakbank PSP.

Jason Sourasis, the Chairman of Western Melbourne Group, the parent company of the Western United Football Club, said: "The Western Melbourne Group's vision has always been to host Multi Sports and create a vibrant city underpinned by sports, education, health and wellness.

"We are proud to have created only the second rectangular stadium in Victoria that is built for both men and women and is already A-League and Rugby Union compliant. There are obvious synergies hosting both Western United and the Melbourne Rebels and naturally, we are keen to explore those opportunities," said Mr Sourasis, who is also Executive Chairman of Western United FC.

"Our first Women's A-League game at Tarneit last month was a great success and this Saturday the 6th of April we take another huge step with the first Men's A-League game at the facility. The growth of both our organisations will come from connecting with the local community and providing a precinct that the region can be proud to call their own.

"We welcome the opportunity to continue to achieve that connection in close collaboration with the Melbourne Rebels women's and men's teams."

Consortium spokesperson and current Melbourne Rebels Director Georgia Widdup said the move to Tarneit "would be the game-changer that the Melbourne Rebels and the sport of rugby desperately needs in Victoria".

"We have an exciting vision and a detailed, common-sense plan to grow the sport of rugby in the fastest growing municipality in Australia," Ms Widdup said.

"The Rebels are committed to the women's game, the Pasifika community and important programs for the western region's youth and this move will enable us to significantly expand these critical areas."

The Rebels club was placed into voluntary administration earlier this year and is restructuring for a bright future for the game, in one of the fastest growing rugby corridors in the country.

"The Tarneit Masterplan is a new financial model for our club, teams, our players and our fans that is sustainable and embraces our future, not our past," said Ms Widdup.

"This is an opportunity to grow rugby's grassroots supporter base and attract significant new private investment to make the game sustainable into the future," she said.

"We are passionate about keeping rugby in Victoria but we realise for the Rebels and the sport generally to thrive we need to innovate and be smarter."

"We are also impressed by the vision of the facility and future of the precinct in respect to a core focus on the women's game. As the first Super Rugby Club to pay its professional women players in Australia, we are focussed on continuing to develop the women's game and we believe this provides us that opportunity to once again lead the sport".

Rugby Union in Victoria has seen major expansion over the last decade throughout some of the fastest growing Pasifika communities in the country; through its growth in

State school curriculum programs; and through its community Clubs that have embraced diversity and the women's game in a leadership capacity.

"Rugby's investment through the State Government in the North at our State Centre of Excellence at La Trobe where women will be based for training and high-performance, our investment in Clubs in the South East, and now our ground-breaking professional model in the West of the city, make rugby a game for all," said Ms Widdup.

"Combined with the greatest sporting facilities in Australia in AAMI Park, Marvel Stadium and the MCG, we intend to continue to bring rugby to all of the Victorian community, and we look forward to being an integral part of the innovation and work that Jason and the Western Melbourne Group are doing in the West of Melbourne."

Fan responses on social media forums are overwhelmingly positive. Tim Sampson identifies a shift in mood at the Rebels' office; "It's really been tough, so this news has come at just the right time. I've sensed players and staff becoming increasingly unsettled. There's not a lot of trust when it comes to RA, so we won't be getting too far ahead of ourselves. But no doubt, this is big news. It will be interesting to what see Phil Waugh's mood is, in tomorrow's meeting."

Chapter Thirty-One

5th April, 2024

Sampson and the rest of the staff don't have long to wait to find out. Waugh connects via zoom and, according to many on the call, spends the next thirty minutes practising the art of talking while saying very little. He apologises for not having visited and spoken to staff for a while (since the club entered voluntary administration he hasn't spoken to staff at all until today), and offers empathy for their situation.

Asked about timing around decisions on the franchise's future, Waugh puts the broadcasters in the frame. Negotiations for a new broadcast deal for season 2026 and beyond are ongoing. But until they are finalised, until Rugby Australia knows what its revenue base will be, it isn't in a position to commit to the Rebels.

No specific time-frame is offered, but with staff contracts set to expire on June 30th, there is little confidence that a long-term broadcast deal will be in place any time soon - certainly quickly enough to provide a level of comfort for staff sufficient to prevent them from having to seek jobs elsewhere.

Nick Stiles laughs off the convenient use of broadcasters as the controlling factor. "As if all of this is on the broadcaster's shoulders? Who is actually running the game in Australia? Where is the strategy for the future of the game? Wait for a TV network to tell us what they want? Really?"

Around the office, heads nod in agreement. It's hard to imagine Nine/Stan or any other interested bidder arguing for a reduction from twelve teams to 11, thus reducing the weekly content from six matches to five. And if the plan is to replace the Rebels with a development side from Argentina - as has been mooted in New Zealand media - it's impossible to imagine an Australian network paying more for that than for a presence in the Melbourne market.

For staff, the outcome of the call is nothing more than continued frustration. Another week slipping by without any clarity about the future, another week with off-field matters infringing on match preparation.

Baden Stephenson couldn't count the number of times he has walked up the steep pinch that is the player's tunnel at AAMI Stadium. But this is the first time he's done it as anything other than Rebels CEO. Having just accepted a position as interim General Manager Rugby for the Fijian Drua and, upon his return to Melbourne after being terminated seven weeks ago, standing near the edge of the pitch, watching the Rebels Super W team playing the Reds, Stephenson harbours mixed emotions.

"It's nice to be able to come along and not have to look nervously around the crowd, counting numbers in my head, stressing about how much the night might be costing the club," he says. "On the other hand, obviously I'm still very invested. You don't switch off all of that work and attachment, just like that. I'm desperately keen to see what happens and that there's a good outcome for the club and all of the people involved."

To illustrate the point, the previous evening, he joined the Fijian Drua coaching staff for dinner, then afterwards, caught up with his ex-chairman Paul Docherty. "The best thing I can do now is get stuck in and do a good job for Fiji, there's a lot of great people in their program, and while I've got a couple of trips home I can use, I'm going to live there. That's the only way to do the job justice," he says.

It seems that everyone wants a word or a moment to shake Stephenson's hand. As a result, he sees less of the women's match than he planned. The Rebels - with just a single win in their seven years of Super W existence - miss a late penalty goal attempt and fall agonisingly short, 17-15.

The main match follows what is now a familiar path, with the Rebels once again conceding a sizeable early lead. In the shadows of half-time, they find themselves down by 20-8. Brad Harris' instructions from Tuesday prove prophetic, Drua halfback Frank Lomani taps and runs a quick penalty and, with the Rebels' defence in disarray, scores what becomes their seventh try in similar circumstances this season.

The final play of the half is critical. The Drua lose a player to the bin for a high shot on Carter Gordon, and Jordan Uelese wriggles over for a try following a line out maul. At 20-15 down, things don't seem quite so tenuous.

With no time to waste, halftime runs like a well-oiled machine. The players split into two groups: backs and forwards, with videotape from the first half already loaded by the analysts, ready for the coaches to use.

The physio team query incoming players about who might need attention. Glen Vaihu reaches for some deep heat, but it is only Taniela Tupou, feeling a little tightness in a hamstring after sitting for 40 minutes on the bench, who needs a rub down. Kristian Waller works on him on the ground, adjacent to the forward's huddle.

Once the players are settled, debut skipper Sam Talakai gets first shot. "Keep to our structures," he says, calmly and authoritatively. "We know they'll fold if we keep working hard for each other. We go as a team, not as individuals."

Geoff Parling is insistent that the team doesn't get loose. "If we've got advantage, don't run away from them. Latch tight and take them to a dark place."

The line-out is functioning efficiently but Angelo Smith wants more pressure placed on the Drua throw.

"We know where they're throwing it. Just listen to their calls," he says.

"They're in Fijian," comes a reply.

"Yeah, that's easy," says Smith, momentarily forgetting that he's Fijian and it's not so simple for the rest of the pack.

The group erupts in laughter.

Stiles steps in to seize the moment. "See, that's what this group means to each other. We're in the middle of a dog-fight and we're laughing at jokes together! Let's take that with us." Stiles also reinforces the main theme. "Stay on them. We build pressure through our scrum and maul dominance."

Brad Harris takes his turn. Three tries have been conceded but, for the most part, the Drua's dangerous runners have been cut off at the source. "There's been some great defensive pressure applied boys. Keep that going! And I love how you've taken their power surge away. Our pressure from those kick-offs was excellent."

The backs join the forwards and, with Kevin Foote pacing back and forth in the background, Tim Sampson takes over. "We need to stay tighter and more connected in attack. A couple of times there, we got too spread out. That's too easy to defend, and it exposes the receiver."

A cry comes from near the doorway. "Ninety seconds!"

Foote paces a little more before he steps in with the final words. It's a classic example of how recency theory works. The contribution of every coach is important, but wherever there is an excess of information, people tend to remember more the first thing they are told (primacy), and the last thing (recency). He chooses his words carefully, not adding anything new that might confuse or muddy what has already been said. It's the tone that is important. His is the voice of authority. Firm, urgent, trusting. Win, lose or draw, the players leave the room in no doubt about what it is they must do to come out on top.

A man to the good, the Rebels surge from the kick-off, adding tries to Glen Vaihu and Maciu Nabolakasi to the one scored by Uelese: that's 21 points piled on in the sin bin period.

By the time the front row replacements are made, the Rebels pack is well on top. The dominant scrum is a reliable source of penalties, enabling Gordon to kick for territory, and Josh Canham to add to his remarkable line-out work - 16 individual wins on the night.

The Drua have indeed been taken to a dark place, nevertheless it is a shock to all inside the stadium when a frustrated Lomani lashes out at Canham with an ugly, elbow to the back of the head.

Referee Damon Murphy has no option but to send Lomani - an ex-Rebel - from the field. (Canham would go on to receive 20 stitches after the match and miss the following week in concussion return-to-play protocols). The action, a '12 to 6' downwards chop, is deemed so dangerous it's banned in the UFC - a sport where the purpose is to batter the opponent into submission. SANZAAR's response is to issue Lomani with a six-week suspension.

Incredibly, replacement hooker Jone Koroiduadua also enters the red card shame file, delivering an ugly head butt which - fortunately - grazes Alex Mafi's lip when he could easily have split it open and done serious damage. (His sanction is a mere two weeks, astonishing most observers and triggering a social media storm).

After a dominant second half, the match ends 41-20. Kat Rottier and Waller convene on the sideline then again in the rooms, pinching themselves that, given expectations around the physical nature of the Fijian players, this has been their quietest night all year. Aside from Canham and some minor attention to Uelese in the first half, it's been a stress-free night for the medical team. Yes, there will be sore bodies tomorrow, but already, they know that come Monday morning they will have a smaller number of players than usual in the physio room, seeking attention.

Media obligations out of the way, Foote leads the celebrations in the rooms, singling out the contribution of Harris, coaching for the first time against his old club. Foote also acknowledges and introduces his mother, visiting from Johannesburg. This is her first visit to AAMI, her first time seeing her son's team play. In baseball terms, she's batting 1.000.

In amongst all of the red card ruckus, it's been a strange, almost surreal night. A raft of cameras, coaches demanding discipline, and a focus on preventing head injury has all but eliminated thuggery from the game. Yet tonight, there's a sense from people of, even just for a moment, stepping back in time, to an age when differences were created, then settled, on the field, by whatever means, fair and foul. Foote is as non-plussed as anyone: shocked at the actions of the two players involved, and how close his own players came to serious injury; upset at how such actions hurt the integrity and reputation of rugby, yet empathetic and understanding of how disappointed his counterpart, Mick Byrne, will be at being let down by his own men.

News also begins to filter through on social media, of a dispute between Lomani, after he came from the field, and a Rebels fan, seated behind the Drua bench. It's isn't clear what exactly was said, but a clip from a spectator's phone carries audio of accusations of racism, and shows the fan leaving, at the request of a security officer. (SANZAAR launched an investigation on the Monday following the match, and just over a week later announced that it had failed to substantiate what had occurred).

The bye round means that not all teams have played an equal number of matches. But for tonight at least, the Rebels sit 4th on the ladder; a position they have never held, this far into a season.

Chapter Thirty-Two

8th April, 2024

Ex-Liverpool great Graeme Souness. Cricketer Kevin Pietersen. Judy Murray, mother of dual Olympic Gold medallist and multiple grand slam winner, Andy. David Campese. And many more. You don't need to go far to find voices critical of contemporary sportspeople; 'Too soft, mollycoddled, unable to think for themselves' among the complaints.

In a related vein, any rugby player on the wrong side of fifty will recall their coach gathering the team in a tight circle moments before leaving the changing room, initiating a twenty-second burst of rapid-fire high knee raises, hands slapping against thighs, studs rapping the floor, the skipper shouting to be heard over the cacophony, screaming "we hate these c*nts", before the team manager would swing the door open and dispatch their platoon, with all of their pent-up electricity in tow, out into battle.

These were the days where ideas around confronting fear and embracing collective, military-style toughness reigned supreme. Inherently masculine and aggressive, overlaid with the need for conformity. Where, within the prescribed models of team behaviour, sportspeople were expected to find for themselves, the mental strength required to sufficiently motivate them to overcome challenges.

As Rebels' team psychologist Andrew Waterson explains, sports psychology has come a long way. "Psychology historically has been based on a deficit model: ie, there's something wrong with someone, they need to be fixed. But sports psychology has moved on to a strength-based model, where we recognise that these guys are already high-functioning athletes, and our job is to help them thrive in what is a challenging environment. That derives from what are well-established psychological theories about how our brains need to function in order for us to be creative, open and free. If we have fear, the task for the brain isn't to function and thrive, but to seek safety. Obviously, in high-performance sport, that's sub-optimal."

A psychologist holding a doctorate in sports performance, Waterson's career boasts associations with NZ Rowing and work with Olympic snow sports, as well as being attached to the Melbourne Demons in their 2021 AFL premiership winning year. For season 2024, he has become a regular at the Rebels, four hours per week, every Monday.

"In 2022, coming out of the second COVID season, I started seeing some Rebels players in my private practice," he explains. "I later got to meet Kevin and we spent a lot of time talking about how psychology can affect a program and how it can be used to have a positive effect. We aligned around placing an emphasis on psychological safety and creating an environment where people are able to function at their best. From there, I became available to the team on a consistent basis."

"What I discovered was that Kevin had this idea of a 'high challenge, high care' environment, and what I did that was swap that around so that care came first before challenge. And to be fair, the only reason he presented challenge first was because he knew he already had the high care element in place. Why that order or emphasis is essential is because it's that what allows you to have those really difficult, challenging discussions you need to have as a team, or a leadership group, or as individuals."

Waterson expands on the theme: "The reality is, the players are going into combat. Compared to a lot of other sports I've observed, when you stand in a rugby changing room, just before the players go out, it's dead quiet, and there is stress, because the players know they're about to face an intense physical battle. So we need to establish a firm 'high care' base from where they can go to that space. If the players feel connected to the group, then that enables them to be physically and psychologically fearless. The next psychological challenge that flows from that is that because the players are exposed - they've been encouraged to give their all and show everyone what they've got, and if they don't meet that challenge they might be embarrassed if they fail - in order for them to feel comfortable enough to take risks, it's critical we establish strong connections across the whole group."

Anyone who has ever blitzed the questions on 'Who Wants to be a Millionaire' from the comfort and safety of their sofa, but can't bear the thought of going on national TV and risking the eternal humiliation and shame that bombing the $100 question would bring, can relate to what Waterson is saying.

"For me, that's the art of successful coaching, and it's what I've seen with Kevin. He has great ability to connect with his players, which provides them with the freedom and licence to go out and try things. In pro sport there's both a physical consequence and a psychological consequence attached to failure. Damaged bodies. Public and media criticism. But if the player knows that whatever happens, within the four walls of the team environment they'll be respected and cared for, they'll be better placed to go out and perform to their best."

Waterson describes how the season has progressed so far. "We began with a group program: red, white and blue groups, based on age and experience, what sort of mental skills we thought each group of players might need, their ability and capacity to be aware of and regulate their emotions. And with the younger guys, we had to put more work into them, getting them to better identify and understand their values."

"As the season has advanced, we're now into more individual sessions. Sometimes this need is flagged by the coaches, but as I become more woven into the fabric of the place, players seek me out and it's a more natural exchange," he says.

And what about the additional challenges that have emerged this year? "The biggest factor is the lack of predictability. People like to know what is coming in their future and that's been taken away from these guys. At the start, it wasn't dissimilar to COVID: i.e. norms had changed and predictability had gone. But the big difference here is that COVID affected everybody, and during COVID, even though sport was disrupted, there was never a question around 'are we ever going to play sport again?' Here, the question is, 'are we even going to exist?' That's a massive difference, and it's been extremely challenging for everyone."

"So, as the season has gone on, a lot of my work has been around allowing the discussions about the 'what if's'. To acknowledge the situation and pay it respect. But then, it's really important to shift the focus to things that matter on a daily basis, like performing in the next match or training session, or being the best husband or father they can be."

Waterson explains how there's been an element of everyone learning on the run, due to the uniqueness of the predicament. Nevertheless, he is impressed by what he has seen. "I couldn't be more complimentary of Kevin and how he and the coaches have handled this," he says. "The expectation on them as leaders is high. And they've got their own personal challenges to deal with. Faced with the nature and scale of the challenges it would have been easy and understandable for them to avoid things or put the cue in the rack, but that hasn't happened."

He concludes by illustrating how that outcome is a reflection of the strength of the culture. "All of the coaches genuinely care about every player and every staff member. And importantly, it's the same in reverse. Watching on, I can actually see the parts increasingly starting to work together, see the cogs matching up. See the common understanding: 'We're all here for the same shared purpose, to make this team better'."

After a couple of one-on-one player meetings, Waterson's work for today is done. Successive victories have the team in a good frame of mind, and in good position to claim a third, on Saturday night against the Highlanders. Before then however, focus shifts to another team, who are in search of their first win.

Chapter Thirty-Three

9th April, 2024

One team with a shorter history than the Rebels is the Rebels' Super W side. Born out of what had been a Rugby Victoria rep selection, the women first played under a Rebels banner in 2017, prior to the Super W competition starting a year later.

"There was no competition as such in those days," explains Meretiana Robinson, captain of that inaugural team. "We used to travel to a tournament, which wasn't ideal because you had these shortened games in close succession, and if anyone picked up an injury then that was pretty much it, they missed the whole season."

Since retired, Robinson is now the Women's and Girls Co-ordinator for Rugby Victoria, and while she is happy that gains have been made, and is realistic about the financial realities that constrain faster progress, she remains frustrated at how opportunities to promote and develop the women's game in Australia have been spurned.

"I look at all the hype around the Matildas - and good luck to them for what they've done - and also around women's State of Origin and NRL, and I can't help but think that we had an opportunity to own that space. When our girls won the gold medal in Rio in 2016 (for rugby 7's), there was so much excitement, not just from rugby people, but from young girls looking to follow star players like Charlotte Caslick and emulate them. But for whatever reason, we never kicked on from that, we never figured out a way to maintain the interest levels or link that sevens success to the whole women's game. And now, in terms of professionalism, the public interest, the ability to attract athletes to our sport… we've been left far behind. And for the girls who are in the sport, not only is that disappointing to see us being dominated by other sports, there's also a feeling that this is just another example of a lack of equity shown to the women's game over the men."

For the players who have chosen to make a go of women's rugby, Robinson provides a picture of the imposts placed upon them; "The girls are forced to balance full-time work, full-time study, full-time parenthood and the demands of trying to be an elite athlete. What we miss are a lot of the things that happen off the field, the 'one-percenters', the reviews and the analysis. Recovery is compromised. Training at night, players travelling long distances, means that many of them are eating late then having to get up early and go to work, so there's an issue around getting the right amount of sleep. That feeds into conflict around expectations of players about what it means to be a professional athlete, and people's expectations of them as professional athletes, but the players not actually having the tools to meet all those expectations."

"COVID obviously messed things up as well. Instead of a competition there was a training hub and a tournament in Coffs Harbour, although I wasn't able to attend because I got appendicitis and was recovering from surgery. So, it was very difficult to get momentum, until things shifted and in 2022, we were taken over by the Rebels and became the first club where the women were paid to play. It wasn't a lot of money but it was very exciting because it signalled that we were important and on the radar. In my case, it enabled me to cut some work hours and invest that into training, without taking a drop in income, so I know myself and other girls, really appreciated that move."

In Melbourne over the weekend with the Fijian Drua, ex-CEO Baden Stephenson provides some of the background; "At the end-of-season Super W Awards function in November 2021 at Bells Hotel, a monumental decision was made. I noticed (directors) Lyndsey Cattermole and Paul Docherty deep in conversation during a break between awards. Docs approached me and said, 'this is not good enough; we have to stand up for our female athletes and do something after they had to give up work, shifts and take holidays to participate in the Super W competition. Lyndsey and I have pledged our financial support, what do you think about being the first Club to pay our females players?' As soon as I smiled he didn't hesitate; 'I want you to get up there and announce that we are going to be the first Super W team to pay our players starting next year'!"

"The announcement was met with raucous applause, tears, cheers, emotion and relief," Stephenson continues. "When I asked who else is going to make a commitment to our Super W team, hands went up, people yelled out 'I'm in' and many were nodding to say how could we not? With $150,000 committed at the event the Melbourne Rebels sent out a press release the following day. The leadership and initiative shown that night was the first step in professionalism and equality for women's rugby in Australia. I remember captain Mel Kawa was beside herself, saying that she'd dreamed of this moment all of her career. It was a special night that just happened; it wasn't planned. It was a brave decision but one that demonstrated love for our people and the club's vision of changing people lives through rugby union."

"This was a legacy decision by the Melbourne Rebels that we believe ultimately changed the conversation for women's rugby in Australia. At the time we were driving the strategy of 'One Club' and this decision sent a very clear message internally and externally that our women players needed to be elevated, supported and loved. And it's fair to say, the initial reaction from Rugby Australia and the other Super Rugby franchises was far from supportive."

That reluctance, or financial inability to elevate women's rugby across Australia means that for the players, progress since 2022 has been frustratingly slow. "Basically, the Rebels women don't have a home," explains Robinson. "There's no tangible home base where they can associate. No changing room with their names on a locker. They're not allowed on Gosch's Paddock to train, that's restricted to the Storm and the Rebels men only. Instead, trainings are shifted around the city - currently they're at Powerhouse Juniors in Newport - which for many girls, depending on where they work and live, is problematic."

"I'm privileged because I'm in the office and I can see and understand how much people like Stilesy and Bado have been trying to change things for the better. The care is there, the passion is there and the support from the Rebels' staff is terrific. And so I communicate that to the girls. One of the things Bado was working on was to establish more of a 'one club' feel. But now, with everything that's going on this year, everyone is flat out just trying to keep their shit together and their head above water, so that whole club idea has been lost. I mean, when you look at the redundancies, no CEO, everyone in limbo... there's not really any club as such. There's a men's team, a women's team and a few staff. But it's not a club any more, it's a shell."

Robinson describes other things that have been lost. "There was a social media campaign developed by Annika Jamieson, 'Rebel Like Her', which was fantastic. But since her contract was terminated, nobody is doing that work now. And Rugby Australia doesn't drive a social media platform that promotes women's rugby."

It is apparent that the same uncertainty that hangs over the men's program applies to the women. "We're hearing nothing from Rugby Australia. That's in general, about what type of competition there will be moving forward, whether it extends from five matches a year to a home and away series, or whatever. But also, with respect to the Rebels specifically, not one person has spoken to the girls. Everybody is totally in the dark about where we stand. Personally, it feels to me that there is a world where, even if the Rebels are shut down, the Super W team could continue. Because we're not much of a cost and we're already used to scrapping around, that's how it was before we can under the Rebels' umbrella. But really, somebody should be talking to us."

What about the role of the player's association? Robinson sighs. "There was a 'tick-a-box' at the start of the season, but once the competition was confirmed, the players got their contracts and the season started, that's been the last of it. It's my belief that the player's association should advocate more strongly on behalf of women players, asking important questions of Rugby Australia and getting them answered. But unfortunately, this hasn't happened."

Robinson takes a moment to reflect on how that issue is common across sports. "Look at the AFLW. Despite all the money and resources that sport has, they can't get it right. The women players there have many of the same issues and problems we have."

Robinson is speaking to the conflicted circumstances player's associations face, relying on the largesse of the respective sporting bodies for their very existence. "It's like they do a good job around the mechanics of contracts and so on, but on the more difficult issues, when we really need strong advocacy, they go missing because they can't afford to upset the people who fund their existence."

So, what are the things that can be done? "One of the biggest issues here in Victoria is that because we're not a traditional rugby state and participation numbers are lower than New South Wales and Queensland, for anyone who has talent, it's not hard for them to stand out. So, some girls, they can put minimal effort into training and skills development, and still be a high performer. That means that we see girls come through into Super W not really understanding what it takes for them to take the step up into a more professional setting. To match those bigger states and perform at their level. For many girls, it's hard for us to drive the attitude change that is necessary for the light to go off and to align that with performance expectations. And then, even if we're able to establish the right drive and attitude, because some of the girls are conflicted with work and so on, there are always forces working against that forward ambition."

Robinson explains further; "Really, I think we need a youth girl's high-performance academy. That way we can set performance expectations with young girls before they've learned anything else. There are already school programs producing girls who are suitable for this; Jimmy Orange's schools, Fountain Gate, and Grange has an excellent S & C program running for girls. And other than providing an aspirational target, this piece really has little to do with the Rebels; whatever happens with them, this is something Rugby Victoria can manage. I know this is something Stilesy and Jaime Fernandez (Rugby Australia Women's High-Performance Manager) are supportive of, an elite program for the best girls. For example, we've got a couple of 16-year-old players who are absolute guns, but if we don't look after them, don't show them a realistic pathway into Super W and beyond, then we'll lose them. Even now, these girls are fending off offers from rugby league."

On Saturday night the magic finally happens. Following a heartbreaking 17-15 loss to the Reds the previous week, the Rebels women knock over the 2022 and 2023 champions, the Fijian Drua, by 34-21. It's just the second win in their history. It's not only the scoreline that impresses, but the manner in which they play. Tiarah Minns dominates the line-out, fly-half Cassie Siataga carries strongly and kicks like a dream, captain Mel Kawa seemingly tackles everything that moves. Tries are scored in close and out wide. There can be no doubt, the Rebels' Super W team is evolving rapidly.

But just when improvement should be being built upon, after just five matches, the women are effectively cut off at the knees. Having missed the finals, it is already season over. Rugby Australia has a multitude of challenges to overcome and problems to solve. And so little money with which to assist. But unless it wants to hand everything over to rugby league, the provision of a meaningful season for elite women players must be right at the top of the list.

Chapter Thirty-Four

13th April, 2024

Final messages delivered, the coaching team leaves the players to their own devices; a final ninety seconds to collect thoughts, calm heart rates and ensure their fingers and hands are sticky before they take the field. Transfer to the AAMI Stadium coaches box is a via a walk along an underground concourse - where short but polite handshakes are exchanged with Clark Dermody and the Highlanders coaching group - through a narrow corridor into a public foyer and lift, (which has been held for the coaches), up two levels, before a sharp right turn upon exit takes them straight into the home coaches' box.

Like well-rehearsed airline pilots, the four coaches immediately take their assigned seats. Analysts John Batina and Jarrod Rutley are already perched in the row behind. A moment is taken to 'cross-check', to ensure comms are working, there is a last round of 'good luck', before an atmosphere of calm, controlled tension is broken by the sharp, shrill blast of referee Paul Williams' whistle. Take-off.

For anyone new to the box, the extent to which the feed from the referee's mic fills the room is immediately disarming. It is as if the coaches are transported to the field of play; unable to communicate themselves with the officials, nevertheless fully connected to the match in terms of what pictures the referee is receiving and giving, able to plan their responses accordingly.

Weeks of slow starts have been a growing source of frustration for the coaches. This time, the Rebels maintain possession early and in one lengthy, continuous phase, irresistibly impose themselves on the Highlanders' line, where halfback Ryan Louwrens has an easy pick up and dive over. The four coaches react in identical manner; a short burst of delighted satisfaction, immediately followed by calm consideration of what follows next. In a year where most sides have struggled to exit cleanly after scoring points, this will provide a good indicator as to what state of mind the side is in.

Each coach has their own computer screen, able to be customised to suit. At an early stoppage Geoff Parling takes in a close-up of a line out, while next to him, Tim Sampson scans over a wider shot, checking backline alignment.

"Can I get a clip of that line out breach for half-time, please?" barks Brad Harris, to the analysts. As always, requests are made courteously, but firmly enough to ensure they are heard and actioned.

A scrum penalty goes against the Rebels and Kevin Foote leans straight into the internal comms network; "Rob (Taylor), get a message to the refs. Their tight-head is pancaking, it's not up to Gibbo to hold him up."

Soon after, Jordan Uelese delivers a second successive poor throw. This time it's Parling with an urgent instruction; "Message to Lukhan. Revert to a simple call to the front. Settle things down for a bit."

Down at ground level, multiple staff are wired in to the box. Katherine Rottier patrols the far side of the ground, club doctor Bryn Savill and Rob Taylor the near side, with Luke Vella roving. Usually, Nick Stiles is stationed near the reserves bench, but tonight, with the Super W team having completed their final match, and already into the first stage of what will be a hearty celebration in a function room on the eastern side of the ground, he's covering multiple bases.

Up higher, with eyes over the ground, the coaches are able to get messages onto the field via whoever is closest to the play at a given point. In that respect what might first appear to be odd - a physio requesting a tactical change on the field, or admonishing a player - isn't odd at all. Players know the staff are conduits and exactly where the messages are coming from.

As for how much of the coaches' instruction actually has an influence? For the referees, Foote acknowledges not much at all. "I mean, Stilesy will be down there, chipping away at the fourth official and the touchie, and we'll have our frustrations heard too, but most of it is after the event. It's not like it's going to change anything that's happened. At the same time, the refs are human, if they feel like they might have got something wrong, if there's a picture they're not a hundred percent clear about, they talk at half-time, they re-set too, just like the players. If there's a chance that we can influence one factor in the game that can help a decision swing our way, then of course we'll try to do that."

To be most effective, it is important that the coaches retain focus on what they can control, rather than slip into reactions based on refereeing decisions. Nevertheless, some of that is inevitable, and it is standard fare for referees to lurch suddenly from hero to villain as the game unfolds.

On the stroke of half-time, a deft flick-on from Andrew Kellaway puts Darby Lancaster into space down the left-hand touchline. Despite being stopped just short of the line, Lancaster has the presence of mind to release the ball, quickly regain his feet then collect it again and dive over the line.

It's a crucial score. Celebrations in the box are kept short by the need to rush back downstairs for the half-time talk, but as the coaches rise off their chairs the voice of the TMO cuts through, asking Williams to check a potential knock-on in the lead up.

"Oh, fuck off!" rings a chorus of voices.

It's a faintly comical sight; bodies half-way out the door, eyes peeled down onto referee Williams, waiting for his judgment. He takes one look at the big screen, watches Lancaster place the ball and regather, and advises his TMO that he's happy with the action. In a flash, Williams is in the good books, the lift is filled and the group is on their way downstairs. Nobody sees Carter Gordon nail the sideline conversion for a 26-10 half-time lead.

The messaging at half-time is kept simple. A rough patch just before half-time saw the side get loose; players transferring pressure backwards, a loss of focus bringing with it basic errors. The players are urged to revert to basics; punch forward, support each other and, if the support option isn't clear, not to be afraid to go to ground and recycle.

The second half begins badly. The scrum concedes a penalty and all of the computer screens freeze. Rutley is immediately up and about, trying to resolve the issue. A re-set restores the live feed but everything is running slowly - too slowly, too far behind the play - to be of much use to the coaches. It frustrating and inconvenient, but there is no choice but to park things for now. Midfield defence is more the immediate concern.

"We have to keep pushing up higher on the inside," yells Harris.

"When they step back on the inside they should be getting hit!" echoes Foote.

Despite the half-time messaging, the Rebels are still too loose with the ball. Foote again directs an instruction to Taylor. "We have to go to ground. Get tighter."

Sampson is concerned at the number of loose transfers in contact that have again crept in. "Carry and latch," he says, frustrated by the player's inability to do something that, from the box, looks clear and obvious.

Folau Fakatava scores for the visitors, and with the lead narrowed to 26-17, Foote puts it to the rest of the group; "We need energy. Angelo for Tuaina? What are we thinking?"

A couple of minutes later, Foote asks again. "Are we happy to go with Angelo?"

Lock Angelo Smith is duly hustled off the bench. Foote relays the instruction to Taylor, who is alongside Smith as he waits to come on. "Do the simple things well. Tight carries."

A bust and hand-off from Taniela Tupou paves the way for a thrilling try to Carter Gordon. When Gordon follows up soon after, a second try from a quick tap, the tension in the box eases.

Just for a moment.

Defending a 'three-try' bonus point and a 5m line out, Lukhan Salakaia-Loto attacks the Highlander's throw, leaping high to tip the ball onto the Rebels side. Foote immediately realises something is wrong; Salakaia-Loto is slow to get up and get back onside. Other eyes are on replacement half-back Jack Maunder who gets his ball placement at the back of the Rebels ruck all wrong. Instead of picking the ball out at his leisure and clearing his line, Maunder can only watch as Ethan de Groot gratefully pinches what is deemed a live ball, and scores. In a horrible few seconds the bonus point is gone and - although nobody knows it yet - so is the season for the Rebels best-performed forward.

The game is safe, but there is still a chance for the Rebels to steal back the bonus point. It comes out of nowhere; Gordon makes a crunching tackle in mid-field, jolting the ball loose for Lancaster, running onto it at speed, to bend over and, without breaking stride, pick it up off his shoelaces. From there, it's an easy 50m run in for the speedster to complete an impressive hat-trick and frank a 47-31 win. Minutes later, it will come as no surprise to find the Stan commentary team, kicking into their post-match coverage, all over Lancaster like a rash.

Aware that he doesn't want to give the Highlanders a final opportunity, Gordon tries to run the clock down with the conversion, but Williams insists that there will be a restart regardless. It doesn't matter. Kellaway, as he has done all night, leaps high to collect the ball cleanly, and Gordon pumps it over the touchline, triggering a series of satisfied high-fives in the box.

It's a happy, quietly contented ride back down to ground level. Brad Wilkin, observing in the box for the first time, notes how quickly time has flown by; the intensity of the coaching process during the match ensures that, just as for players, things unfold rapidly. Opinions must be formed in a hurry and decisions made decisively and quickly; in some cases almost instinctively.

Exiting the lift, the remaining walk to the rooms is a chance for the coaches to level out emotionally. The box is a hot-bed of extremes; sudden highs offset by lows that, while brief, can be very low. Players cop it for failings much harder and heavier than the message that will be communicated to them later, in person. It's nothing personal, just a combination of the nature of the sport, a reflection of how modern players accept and response to criticism, and an illustration of what is at stake. Reputations. Careers. And in this case, the future of the club.

The three-match block everyone has been locked into is over. From a possible 15 ladder points, the Rebels have snared 14. It's a satisfying situation in which to send everyone off to enjoy the bye week. With the dressing rooms emptied, staff wander around the internal stadium walkway to gather back in their kitchen, to share beer, corn chips and any cold pizza the players have left behind. Realisation kicks in that whatever happens in the bye week, the Rebels can't be knocked out of the top four. It's a modest celebration but an authentic one. Everyone knows there are tougher times ahead; a more difficult second half schedule, and continuing job instability. But mostly, the vibe in the room is underpinned not just by the win and the ladder position, but by the expectation of what lies ahead in the next few days; a chance for everyone to relax, recharge and re-unite with family.

Chapter Thirty-Five

22nd April, 2024

After Melbourne's first cold snap of the year, the mood on post-bye Monday is as bright as the welcome morning sun. Dispersing in all directions - some to family interstate, a few to a short golfing break on the NSW Central Coast, and others no further than their sofa and the local coffee shop - most of the squad reported back in on Friday, save for those players required for Hospitals Cup club duty in Brisbane.

Of that cohort, the Wests Bulldogs players have a spring in their step; a third successive win has them atop the ladder. More important is the competitive game time provided to players like Ethan Dobbins, Cabous Eloff, Mason Gordon, David and Glenn Vaihu, Divad Palu and, most notably Daniel Maiava, whose rampaging ball-running headlines a weekend highlights reel put together for today's team meeting, by analyst Jarrod Rutley.

List management just below the regular match day 23 is a constant challenge for Kevin Foote and Luke Vella, who have to determine which players are required as immediate back-up and can't be risked, and which players need game time. Nick Stiles has the task of liaising with clubs to ensure that spots are available, and that every club is treated respectfully and never feels that the Rebels are taking them for granted.

"It helps that we have forged this strong relationship with Wests in Brisbane," Stiles says, noting the number of Rebels players aligned with the Bulldogs. "It's not just about getting our squad players game time, but the cohesion element that comes with them playing alongside each other at the same club. Obviously, we don't have the luxury of having a second team or junior team, but this is the next best thing. By the time they're ready to come into Super Rugby, they're able to do so alongside teammates in the same position, who they're familiar with."

The Friday session has cleared the decks for the new week to be fully focussed on the coming match against the Crusaders. For Kevin Foote, it allowed him to tick off four things; park the successful three-week block and move forward, acknowledge Brad Harris' 50th birthday, ditto Geoff Parling's appointment as Wallabies line out coach, and update the group on Lukhan Salakaia-Loto's status. It's good news/bad news; an operation to insert a plate in his foot seems to have gone well but, at best, it's an 8-week injury. As always, these things present an opportunity to other players and Josh Canham, Tuaina Taii Tualima and Angelo Smith are charged with stepping up. There's also a private word for promising youngster Luke Callan. "He's raw," says Foote, "but he's a real trench-fighter and scrapper. He's showing us he has what it takes for this level."

With Sunday a long travel day for the Crusaders - all the way from Perth to Christchurch - and with wounds to lick following their 37-15 defeat by the Force, the Rebels are keen to take advantage of their longer, less interrupted preparation time.

"That's clearly a benefit for us this week, so we're lucky in that respect," says Foote. "But across a season, it balances out. We'll get a short week, with travel, against a side that has an extra day to prepare. It's just the nature of the competition."

It's also hard to figure out if the Crusaders slumping to their seventh loss is a blessing or a curse. Will they lack confidence, or are they now a week closer to a win; particularly with Scott Barrett and David Havili scheduled to return from injury?

At the end of the day those suppositions don't count for anything. All the coaches can do is to prepare the team to the best of their ability. Parling and Stiles address the forwards in the gym, while Harris, Taylor, Sampson and Foote sit with the backs, inside their dressing room.

Every player is already aware of the danger Sevu Reece provides but, just in case, Harris runs some clips. "Obviously, he's got the ability to go around us, but nine times out of ten he likes to jink and come back inside. Filipo, Proc, David… what's critical is that after the ball has gone past you, we maintain our line up on the inside. We know he's going to step, don't give him that space to step into."

Next is something borrowed from the Waratahs, who have already beaten the Crusaders twice this year. Harris again talks over the video; "Look at the work Jake Gordon does off the ball. It's crucial. We're going to do the same. Apply a lot of defensive pressure off 9. Try to force their 10 to play early. It's not Mounga. Whether it's Hohepa or one of their young guys, they're not used to it. Make them rush a decision, force a mistake."

Foote jumps in. "It also shows the importance of slowing down their ball. We get to defend on our terms, not be reactive to what they're doing."

Sampson takes the floor and the emphasis switches to attack. He demonstrates how Levi Aumua is used as a destructive runner (again, news to nobody), but shows how, in defence, he has a tendency to bite inwards. This, combined with their wingers liking to rush up and crowd the outside channel, creates a seam for the centres, fullback or swinging winger to run into; something the Force did to great effect against them.

Kick return is another focus. "The Crusaders are a big kicking team and don't mind a kicking duel," Sampson continues, quoting over 1,000 kick metres from them this season. "Not just long ones, but if it's dewy, they like to slip grass kicks in behind. Work hard off the ball, get back to support the catcher and clear the ball out of the area quickly." Video shows the Crusaders flooding the contest and forcing turnovers as a result of that pressure. "That's why they go to their grenade (contestable kick from halfback) so often," he continues. "Wait for a catcher to become isolated or make a poor decision, and then, bang! Let's take that away from them."

Andrew Kellaway chimes in; "On the longer kicks, we'll have opportunities on the return, but only if we're smart about it. On those returns, we need our centres on the edges, giving us extra options."

The two groups merge in the gym. There's time for joke of the week, this time delivered by strength and conditioning coach Jared Hoare, referencing bananas and condoms. It draws raucous laughter plus an observation that perhaps it was just as well HR Manager was one of the positions made redundant by Rugby Australia.

The serious business is kick-started by Rob Taylor, demonstrating how the Crusaders send two hunters on their long kick-offs; one targeting the catcher and the other infield, looking to deny an easy pass to a running number 8 on the return. The forwards are also brought into the kicking duel discussion, Taylor stressing the importance of them working hard on the Crusader's kicks to target the defensive 10m line as a marker they need to get back to.

Carter Gordon explains why; "If me or one of the guys on the run back, if we can get over the 40m line with forward momentum, then that's where we can create exciting attack from; play Rebels rugby. But if the forwards don't work back hard enough or far enough, then we risk getting tackled behind the gain line without support, and putting ourselves in a vulnerable position. Which really forces us to keep kicking it back to them."

With the ball, Taylor wants to see the kickers squeeze the Crusaders into their defensive corners. "They don't mind kicking the ball out towards halfway and going to a line-out. That suits us, we can build play off that. But they key is to shorten their exit kick. Don't give them an easy out."

A reminder of how fickle statistics can be follows. In eight matches the Crusaders have conceded 25 tries, equal third best, which belies their last place on the ladder. Yet Parling highlights their 224 tackles missed; the worst in the competition. "Many of those are in the tight five," he says. That's where our opportunity is. Make them work in close. Make them fall off our runners. Remember, the Tahs and the Force won the collisions. And they won the game."

Team directions ruled off, Foote holds the leadership group back for a moment, getting their buy-in for how he wants things unfold on the pitch in the training session to follow. There's no dissent, just an all-round eagerness to get outside in the sun and rip in. Within the hour, that's exactly what they're doing.

Chapter Thirty-Six

24th April, 2024

No team has dominated Super Rugby like the Crusaders. Their honours board boasts 14 full-competition wins plus two more in the COVID-enforced New Zealand regional competitions. But after eight completed rounds this season, the Crusaders have won just one match and sit dead last on the ladder. By the time the Rebels arrive in town, there is the blood in the Avon river.

Since their 37-15 loss to the Western Force on the weekend, Crusaders CEO Colin Mansbridge has been busy fending off New Zealand media, all looking to stamp their take on the flailing franchise and, for some, to claim the scalp of coach Rob Penney. Mansbridge isn't about to throw the baby out with the bathwater. "It's well known that we're advocates of the work of Gain Line Analytics and big believers in cohesion factors around Team Work Index (TWI). Obviously, we got to a point with Razor (coach, Scott Robertson) picking up the All Blacks job, and key leaders like Sam Whitelock and Richie Mounga finishing up, where we knew those indicators were coming off and we were going to be in for a couple of more difficult seasons while newer players developed and we rebuilt that cohesion. Particularly if we picked up injuries to some key players, which we have. Now obviously, we weren't planning to be running last, but on the other hand, I don't think things are quite as dire as what some people believe them to be."

From the press and social media reaction, it's almost like nearly three decades of success has been wiped from people's memories in an instant. "To be frank, we expect that from our local supporters," says Mansbridge. "They're used to winning and I understand they're not going to tolerate much of a turn back, so that's fair enough and we get that. But with some of the media and people from other parts of the country, it does feel like some people have been waiting for this moment."

Made of sturdy 'mainland' stock, Mansbridge attended St Kevins College in Oamaru, before playing club rugby for Dunedin, and in 1983, making two appearances for Otago at prop. In his second match he received a serious head injury, which led to him having the best part of two-three seasons out of the game. He then resurfaced at the Belfast club in Christchurch and ended up playing for Canterbury 'B', which happened to be coached by Wayne Smith; on his way to establishing himself as one of the game's great coaches. On the commercial side, Mansbridge worked his way through the graduate scheme with BNZ (Bank of New Zealand) to executive management as Head of Mortgages. A few different appointments later, in 2018 he ended up in the top job at the Crusaders.

Mansbridge is at pains to point out that the Crusaders' renowned cultural elements are a legacy of what was built in the first phase of the professionalism, from 1995-1997. "What I've done, I like to think of it as 'adding a coat of paint'. Reinforcing if you like, the concept of values; making sure that people feel like they belong, whether they be people within the club or in the community. The other thing I'm strong on is the concept of servant/leadership, where the leaders serve the people they lead - not servitude or servile - instead of how some organisations operate, which is kind of the opposite. My role is to ask people to be better, at the same time as supporting them to be better. It's also important that everyone checks their egos at the door, so that full focus is on supporting the team to perform better."

Mansbridge's comments reflect an emphasis on the development and nurturing of a 'softer' culture than one that might exist at an organisation where there is an over-emphasis on performance. "Absolutely," he says. "You have to have your talent identification and pathway development systems in place, but what is most important is how we ensure we actually live that culture. There's not really any 'secret sauce' but perhaps where other organisations might recognise these factors and talk about them, and paste lots of keywords around the walls, we're more intent on ensuring that we do it, as opposed to talk about doing it."

Mansbridge also acknowledges how the franchise was made stronger as a result of having to share in, and overcome, some remarkable adversity. "Obviously there was the 2011 earthquake, and what that did to the city, and how the club found itself becoming a beacon of hope for suffering people, as the team travelled right around the world continuing to play, only just falling short in the final against the Reds. We've also been through the Pike River mining disaster, then after the Mosque attack in 2019, we were forced to undergo a deep examination of who we were. The word "crusader" was actually used by the terrorist attacker. That placed a lot of pressure on us. A knight on a horse with a sword... is that really who we are? So that generated a better understanding of our meaning; crusading not for battle but crusading for causes. Crusading with heart."

The franchise CEO's regularly talk to each other to exchange ideas, to examine the state of the game and the competition. They travel with their teams and so develop a fair idea of what goes on in other franchises. Mansbridge identifies many of the same values and cultural elements at play with the Rebels. "The best teams are the ones where individuals play for something bigger than themselves. For family, for community. The Rebels are still a fairly new franchise and when it was all launched I think there was an element of positioning themselves in a certain sector of the sports and commercial market that's already very crowded. That was what it was, but in this second iteration of the Rebels if you like, now coming out of COVID, I think they're doing much better at recognising where their sustainable bedrock of support lies and making a better connection to that, aligning junior pathways to that and accepting the obligation they have to the rugby community to be everyone's team. There's still issues around overcoming scheduling, around their physical location and the distance from where a lot of the supporter base lives, and that's why it was encouraging to hear the new consortium talk about establishing a base in western Melbourne, right near where a lot of rugby communities are, and where many of the schools have new rugby programs. With respect to growth and long-term sustainability of the club, that's a real positive."

Mansbridge also believes that media and fans give too much weighting to crowd figures as a measure of franchise success. "Match day attendances are down in New Zealand as well as Australia, and there are a lot of reasons for that, some of them nothing to do with rugby, and there's things that we're trying to do to arrest that. But what people don't talk about so much is that for the 2024 season to date, TV viewership numbers are up, by a decent amount (around 11%). The following for the game is still there, more so if we're able to provide a compelling competition, which this year, with the Australian teams winning more games against New Zealand teams, we're doing. So, to bring that back to the Rebels, while it's never good to see empty or gappy stands, I think what's more important is that they're building something with a far more solid base. Expectations have been growing, they're seeing home-grown players coming through which in turn motivates the next lot of players, and now, under what is an enormous amount of pressure, they're winning more games."

Mansbridge laughs because he dearly wants to see the Rebels' winning run of three come to an end on Friday night. "They can start winning again next week, if they like," he chuckles. "But in all seriousness, their results this year aren't surprising to me. They've been able to galvanise under pressure. If you have the right people in your organisation, and provide the right value systems, then they'll develop and deliver, even under external pressure."

As for where it all ends up, Mansbridge doesn't pretend to know where to start looking. New Zealand has its own internal struggles around adoption of the recommendations of a comprehensive internal review, which he'd like to see resolved as a matter of urgency. "One thing I do know is that when it comes to rugby, New Zealand and Australia are vitally important to each other. Rugby is a truly international game, we can go anywhere around the world and people understand and recognise who we are; the Reds are doing that next season for example. What would be dangerous for Australian rugby I believe, is to be intoxicated by what AFL and NRL does, as essentially domestic sports, and try to mirror that. If they're not careful, turning inwards, playing in a local competition, particularly if it isn't authentically connected to the pacific region, will only see them (Australian rugby) competing against much wealthier sports in an arena where they have no hope of winning. That's a red water versus blue water scenario, one that I don't think makes any sense."

What makes more sense is the confirmation of one of rugby's core tenets that follows on Friday night; winning rugby begins and ends up front. The Crusaders' forward pack, welcoming back captain Scott Barrett after a six-week absence, wipes the floor with the Rebels, paving the way for a 39-0 shut-out. 'Comprehensive' doesn't even begin to describe what is a composed, ruthless dismemberment. The Rebels' scrum is shunted backwards, their line-out picked off, their few ball runners manhandled by a home side overdue to deliver a statement performance. Only once in 80 minutes are the Rebels able to mount an attack in the red zone; Josh Kemeny spilling the ball when reaching over bodies for the try-line.

At no time do the Rebels players drop their bundle, defending stoutly under the onslaught. But, coming on top of the Blues 46-7 demolition of the

Brumbies a week before, the match is a sobering reminder that when the best New Zealand sides set their minds to it, there remains a class, power and set piece difference between them and the Australian franchises.

To rub salt into the wound, the return flight to Melbourne departs Christchurch at 6.30am on Saturday morning. The positive is that the players will be home early and will get two full nights in their own beds before fronting again for training on Sunday. Even so, when you've just had your backside handed to you on a platter, a 4am call feels like a brutally harsh post-script.

Chapter Thirty-Seven

30th April, 2024

Sometimes the pain and consequences of a loss linger for days. This can be a result of high expectations not being met, or perhaps the complexities and hidden reasons for the defeat taking time to reveal themselves. This isn't one of those times. The nature of the 39-0 loss to the Crusaders - so wholly comprehensive at the set piece that no constructive attack was able to be mounted - means that there is nothing to dwell on.

"It was a pretty quick review for me," says Tim Sampson, effectively made redundant as attack coach. "A couple of small things around some carries and some decision making, but basically nothing to take out of the game. We got past four phases once, and that was in the 70th minute!"

Geoff Parling has a similar tale to tell. "We only had seven dominant carries in the whole match. Seven! We average four to five times more. That's the lowest I've ever seen."

Brad Harris highlights a clip from a ruck. "See there - one guy on the ball competing, and four guys, two on either side, just standing there, all trying to talk the referee into blowing a penalty. No wonder we weren't in the hunt, we forgot we had to work."

Kevin Foote is more specific about decision making. "Our scrum is getting hammered, the penalty count is massively against us, then we finally get a free kick and, what do we do? We call another scrum? That is crazy."

It's a trigger for Foote to shift focus back onto the 'fearless' principle. Not to become passive, not to be sucked into the style of game the opposition wants to play. "When things weren't going our way in Sydney, Hundy tapped and ran and made a try because of it, and then we were on our way. We can't be silly against the Blues, but we have to be smart. Move the ball away from their big guys. Not wait around to be dragged into playing the game on their terms."

Foote is also aware that, after nine rounds, the Rebels are the only Australian side not to have produced a 'statement match' against one of the top New Zealand teams. "The Force beat the Crusaders, the Waratahs beat them twice, the Reds beat the Chiefs, and now the Brumbies have beaten the Hurricanes. No disrespect to the Highlanders, but until we stand up against one of these other teams, it doesn't matter where we are on the ladder… we should be hurting that the other Australian franchises have got a result against a top side, and we haven't."

In front of the whole squad, Foote highlights the Brumbies' reaction to their big loss in Auckland. "It's all in the mind. See how they lifted their intensity. On the training field and then taking that into the match against the Hurricanes. Cutting down their space. Competing like dogs. Making their tackles count."

He then makes it personal. "I understand that, as players, you're embarrassed. We all are. It's a humility check. We're guilty of getting ahead of ourselves. So, we're going to change the process for today. Smaller groups. More accountability. No hiding, no sulking. The coaches are going to speak to you individually about your games. Then, when we come together it will be at high intensity. Everyone, right from now, we must be totally engaged."

Before the senior players contribute, Parling underlines a key message. "We don't limp into the finals. We're better than that. We're in position to push into the finals if we prepare and play to our ability. But it starts with our preparation and our intensity."

It's an easy trigger for Lukhan Salakaia-Loto and Sam Talakai to pick up on. Salakaia-Loto talks authoritatively about preparation and professionalism and how against the good teams, when the spotlight shines it exposes where each individual is really at. "Commit to the standards we set," he urges.

Talakai follows. "It's time to stop talking. There's a lot going on but the message is simple: 'get over your shit'."

Within half an hour, the players, along with the rest of the high-performance staff, are back in the gym for another meeting - this one with RUPA, to address the latest off-field developments. If the first team meeting served to frame the week, this second one frames the season. How, day after day, coaching efforts are compromised by players and staff constantly being reminded about the unpleasantness of the off-field situation, and of the uncertainty around their futures.

Nick Stiles leads off, stepping the players through a timeline for the end of the administration process, the upcoming creditors vote with respect to the DOCA lodged by the directors, and what will happen after that, should it be accepted or rejected. There was confusion around players voting as creditors at the meeting, but Stiles confirms - via the administrator - that only three players who are owed money for relocation and health expenses incurred prior to the club entering administration, are entitled to vote.

"Looking ahead, with the vote to take place on Friday - match day - even though it's a disruption to our preparation today, I felt it was far better to get this done now, so as to clear the decks for the rest of the week," Stiles explains, before thanking RUPA boss Justin Harrison for attending.

Harrison makes it clear that RUPA is supportive of the DOCA being voted through on Friday and the Rebels continuing in Super Rugby. "The DOCA is good news," he says. "A significant step forward."

Player representative Andrew Kellaway jumps in. "Bobby (James Tuttle) and I met with representatives from the proposed new consortium early this morning. They explained to us what is happening around their proposal. No doubts, it's real."

Under questioning, Harrison outlines how Rugby Australia has not engaged with RUPA despite numerous requests for information having been out to them. "We've asked for various things, and put a number of questions, for example, "help us understand why the Waratahs were allowed to avoid voluntary administration but that wasn't the case for the Rebels?' But nothing. Obviously, we'll continue to push them." Harrison's voice tails off, his frustration evident.

For their part, Rugby Australia has not been inactive. A media statement released on the 25th April emphatically reaffirmed its position with respect to the administrators report. In every respect, it's scathing of the Melbourne Rebels Rugby Union (MRRU) directors, in part stating;

"The Administrator's report suggests that MRRU and its former directors have been trading while insolvent since at least 2018. Given the seriousness of the conduct of the MRRU directors, the Administrator has made a report to ASIC."

"RA has complied with all its contractual obligations to MRRU. This includes the payment of all funding (which is subject to an agreement signed under authority by two MRRU directors on behalf of the MRRU Board) and also paying all applicable PAYG amounts to MRRU, who misused these funds and did not pay them to the ATO, which was the intended purpose."

"Despite multiple requests from RA, the MRRU directors have failed to provide any viable proposal or business plan regarding the future of the Melbourne Rebels."

Five days after the statement was released, one of those MRRU directors, Gary Gray, remains non-plussed about Rugby Australia's aggressive approach. "I really don't understand it," he says. "They clearly want to maintain their stance in public that this is all about us acting irresponsibility, trading insolvent, misusing funds and so on. Don't get me wrong, it's hurtful to be accused of those things. And maybe they think they can scare us away, or persuade the creditors vote against the DOCA. But at the end of the day, just because we've chosen not to argue in public, doesn't mean that it's true. How could a business supposedly trading insolvent in 2018, with its revenue in subsequent years decreasing because of the grant money being withheld, with all of the extra costs associated with COVID… thus the trading situation getting worse… how could it possibly still be trading in 2024? You can't just continue on running an insolvent operation for six declining years. It can't happen, someone would shut you down. Unless of course, you're not operating as independently as what is being made out. What all this means is that the potential end game will be for things to play out in court. And if so, that's where the truth will come out," Gray concludes.

An hour after the completion of the player's meeting, Foote knocks down two *Codral* tablets, grumpy at the arrival of a cold, and the continuing distractions and compromises to the season. "Things are starting to fray, I can feel it. It's just like what we went through at the Force. The last thing I wanted today was this meeting; we're playing the Blues on Friday. But the lesson from the Force was that when the players were instructed on how to vote on what to do, without being properly informed, there was an acrimonious split. So we know we can't stand up there and tell the players what to do, or direct them. Instead, we have to just give them the information, and be open and transparent with them, and trust them to figure it out. Even so, it's such an effort to hold things together."

Foote reiterates how Andrew Kellaway's signing with the Waratahs for 2025 was expected, and while Josh Kemeny's departure wasn't, it's an understandable career move, and has little or nothing to do with the current situation. "But I know there's a couple of other players who have signed elsewhere," Foote says. "And they won't come out and say, but of course everybody finds out. And one of those guys played poorly on Friday night. So, it doesn't take much for the rest of the group to tag him as having checked out." Foote shakes his head in frustration. "I don't actually think that's true. I know he's trying. But it just leaves a bad taste hanging across the group. And then, say we get another one, then the whole thing unravels a bit more. And we're powerless to stop it."

Of all the challenges, frustrations and impediments that rugby coaches face, perhaps the single most thing they fear is loss of control. Every coach knows that they can never control all of the variables, such is the nature of competitive sport. But the fewer factors careering in the background, random or introduced from the outside, generating a momentum of their own, the better life is for a coach. Right now, Foote feels as if his grasp on the controls is weakening by the day. And he knows that's a bad place to be.

Chapter Thirty-Eight

3rd May, 2024

By Friday afternoon, Foote's mood has turned for the better. A meeting of creditors has just approved the Deed of Company Arrangement (DOCA) as recommended by the administrator. For now at least, the club has avoided being forced into liquidation. Things are still hanging by a thread, but staff are noticeably buoyed by the prospect of receiving 100% of the entitlements owed to them and - dare they dream - the possibility of a lifeline into 2025.

It's also game day, an opportunity to block out the noise and for everyone to focus on what they love; playing rugby. In three hours the Rebels will be taking on the Blues, a competition powerhouse who this season have gone up another notch under new, hard-nosed coach, Vern Cotter. The visitors boast impressive strike power across the park; two outstanding wingers in Mark Telea and Caleb Clarke, and a forward pack full of hard, big bodies who are relishing the more physical and direct approach prescribed by their coach.

The afternoon before a match can be a difficult time for coaches. "There's little more we can do to influence tonight's outcome," Foote explains. "We leave the players alone. Our responsibility to them is to provide positive body language. Set the tone that way." He affords himself a smile, noting how, with the DOCA passing, it's not difficult today to greet arriving players with a smile and a warm handshake.

The assistant coaches fill their afternoon getting ahead on their preparation for next week's match against the Reds. For Foote, it's an opportunity for a Ju-jitsu session; "I get nervy on game day. Much worse than when I was a player. The physical aspect helps keep some of that nervousness at bay, and it also gives me some time to think through my pre-match address."

With Rugby Australia having voted against the DOCA, Geoff Parling cops plenty of stick, variously dubbed 'the mole' and a 'double agent', in light of his recent Wallabies appointment. It's all good humoured, nevertheless there is incredulity across all of the staff at the way in which, in a zoom meeting a week ago, Rugby Australia CEO Phil Waugh told staff how happy he was that the DOCA would ensure they receive 100% of entitlements owed to them in a timely manner, yet here was Rugby Australia this afternoon, voting against that DOCA, to try to send the club into liquidation, ensuring that they wouldn't.

At 5pm, Tim Sampson and Rob Taylor give the Reds preparation away and take in the start of the Hurricanes versus Waratahs match from Wellington. The Canes fire out of the blocks, and at 26-0, they're keeping pace with the clock. No vicarious joy is taken from the Waratah's plight; after all this is somewhere they have been themselves, as recently as round five, in Palmerston North.

By half-time, Nick Stiles has left the office to meet and host a group of sponsors. Gradually, players and coaches make their way around to the home dressing room. The physio team are already into player rub-downs, while team manager Will Nicholson, assistant manager Denver Murnane, and nutritionist Alexandra Parr have everything laid out, ready-in-waiting; warm-up kit, match kit and a selection of fruit, jelly snakes, light sandwiches, supplements and fluids for the players to graze on.

With respect to timing, nothing is left to chance, with the schedule pushed beforehand to every person's phone, and plastered onto the changing room walls for good measure. Nicholson is the off-field timekeeper, while Luke Vella manages things once the on-field warm-up begins.

"To be honest, by this time of the season, everything is pretty much running like clockwork," says Vella. "My job in this space isn't to be innovative. Routine is the player's friend. No dramas, just get everyone onto the field on time, work through our routines with good intensity, stick to the timings, and have the team ready to go come kick-off."

After some low-key set piece walk throughs, the players move en masse to the theatre. It's now 6.25pm, just over an hour before kick-off. Foote begins with a visualisation drill, asking the players to picture what success looks like, post-game. This late in the piece, it's all mental. "We are an unbelievable rugby team when our heads are right," he exhorts.

The lights drop and the players watch video of ex-Crusaders and Blues halfback Bryn Hall, appearing on a New Zealand rugby panel show, disparaging the Rebels. Foote swings in to action; "Three things. *Mindset*;

there's been excellent intensity all week; *Possession*; we go forward first but we know they concede 99% of their line breaks out wide, so we will hold the ball and we will keep the pressure on them there; and *Defence*; we must be first to set, they will try to blast through us, so we must get up and get set in tight. Every time."

Another clip rolls, the same one used earlier in the season from the last home match against the Blues, where Reece Hodge and Carter Gordon break out from their own goal-line and, an unbroken stream of phases later, Andrew Kellaway scores at the other end. Booming over the top is rapper Jay Rock and his repeated refrain; 'Win, win, win'.

By contrast, the entrance into the changing rooms five minutes later of referee Angus Gardner, feels markedly more understated. The forward pack gathers around him and decline his invitation to raise any matters of concern. "In that case," Gardner says, "with the scrum, I want to see the brake foot out, and stay out, and if there's any movement at all, I won't be calling 'set'. It's the same message to them, I'm asking for patience. As for the line-out, when you walk in, walk right up to the gap. If you stop short, I'll pull you up. It has to be a fair contest."

Patience is also the key word at half-time, as Kellaway stresses to the backs. "They don't like playing out of their own half. We're doing a great job of keeping them locked in there. Just keep doing the same thing."

The Rebels trail 11-12, but they have enjoyed by far the better of the opening forty minutes, maintaining possession for long patches, and applying intense pressure on the Blues at line-out and in general play. The only major negative is the loss of both centres - David Feliuai (concussion) and Matt Proctor (shoulder) - in the same phase of play. Nick Jooste and Jake Strachan have filled in impressively all season, and are already well in this match; albeit it's never a good thing to be forced into injury replacements in the first half.

Foote sits the whole team around him and repeats the visualisation drill; "think about hugging your mate at the end of the game." He expresses his delight at his player's mentality. "We're dictating the tempo. They hate it. But we have to stay one step ahead of them, we know they're going to come at us. Be ready."

Unfortunately, as tends to happen in rugby, the possession imbalance levels out after the break. Without as much ball, the Rebels can't assume the same level of control. By the end, the Blues have scored the same try four times; big, powerful forwards burrowing over the try line after repeated bashing at the door. By contrast, in multiple identical situations at the other end, the Rebels come within inches, but ultimately come up empty. The final score blows out late, to 38-11. It feels harsh, not a true reflection, but that difference in scoring ability and defence in the 'p-zone' is a telling indicator of the difference between an elite, top-of-the-table team and a good, middle-range one.

After interviews, handshakes and acknowledgement of fans around the fence, Foote and Rob Leota gather the team together inside the dressing room. There are thanks for a whole-hearted effort during the week. "We'll cop the disappointment, but come in again on Sunday and build again for Queensland," says the skipper.

Both are required for a mandated after-match press conference; an anachronism given the extent to which the broadcaster Stan has developed their on-field post-match coverage, but required for fans who access the rugby.com.au and overseas websites. As ever, Foote is probed about the off-field dramas, and today's DOCA vote. He focuses on the human side, talking about the severe stress placed on staff and players – many of whom have young families and whose livelihoods and careers are at stake – throughout this year. He references Waugh's comments in the zoom meeting and the impact Rugby Australia saying one thing and doing the opposite, has on all of the staff.

Walking out of the theatre, Foote's frustration is evident. "What am I supposed to say?" he asks. "All I can do is tell the truth."

With schedules tight and away teams usually keen to get back to their hotel and into recovery, there's not a lot of opportunity these days for fraternising after a match. Nevertheless, Blues' assistant coaches Craig McGrath and Paul Tito find themselves amongst friends, sharing a beer in the Rebel's rooms (McGrath is an ex-Rebel assistant coach, while Tito served under Sampson at the Force). They confirm what everyone in New Zealand seems to know but the Rebels don't; plans are well advanced for an 11-team Super Rugby competition next year that doesn't include the Rebels. "How is that fair for staff?" they ask. "All this planning and talk going on behind everyone's back?"

Stiles describes how zoom calls with Waugh - there was another one yesterday, prior to the creditors meeting - are increasingly being regarded with contempt by employees. "A few staff members have got a thing going, where every time Phil uses his key words, "anchor" or "accelerate", they stand up and sit down. Luckily it wasn't a drinking game or they'd have been hammered by the end of it."

Chapter Thirty-Nine

7th May, 2024

When it comes to the player roster, professional rugby teams are a snapshot in time. Nearly forty players, all having come from somewhere, on their way to somewhere else; a Test rugby career, a contract in the south of France, club rugby, retirement (planned or forced), a coaching career, parenthood, a regular job outside of rugby, and so on. They come from diverse ethnic, cultural and financial backgrounds. Some are ridiculously talented, others have grafted for every opportunity. Revisit in five years' time and the majority of the names and faces will be different. But the underlying fabric will be the same.

It so happens that for this particular season, the paths of this particular group of players have converged in Melbourne. For Andrew Kellaway and Josh Kemeny, this will be their final year at the club. Others, like Taniela Tupou and Matt Proctor, are in their first year. Youngsters like Ottavio Tuipulotu and Wyatt Ballenger, are developing Rebels; still an essential part of the fabric in 2024, but at the very beginning of what they hope will be many more years, where they will work their way from 'promising youngster' into the match day 23. Whatever their trajectory, professional rugby players are like ships passing in the night. The secret for any franchise is to anchor them for long enough for all of their individual inputs to gel and combine to obtain the maximum collective output.

Unsurprisingly, the player group is a treasure trove of interesting, varied life-stories. One of those stories belongs to Brisbane-born and raised David Feliuai, whose football experience began in under-8's rugby league, before continuing with 13-man game at high school in Logan, South Brisbane. Feliuai's first taste of rugby didn't come until he was 18, playing with a group of mates in a seven's tournament for Sunnybank. "It was a lot of fun, but at that time of my life, it wasn't a priority," he says.

What took precedence, necessitating a two-year hiatus from sport, Feliuai describes with great enthusiasm. "Being from a Mormon family, doing two years of missionary service was always a life priority. You don't choose where you get assigned to, but I was incredibly blessed to travel to Fiji. Fijians are such kind, outgoing, loving people. It was an awesome experience. Based in the highlands, travelling around small villages, amongst people living a traditional life, talking to them about their faith, sharing stories, spreading the word of God. I was actually one of 150 missionaries; the church is very strong there."

Naturally shy, Feliuai describes how the experience was the making of him. "At first, I wasn't the type of person to just go and talk, that takes a bit of courage. But as time passes you learn more about people and yourself, your mind opens and you become more confident. People think that the focus is on the people we talk to, and it is, but it's as much about the development of the individual. And I'm so grateful for having had that opportunity."

Upon returning from Fiji, Feliuai worked in the distribution centres for both Coles and Woolworths (he isn't getting into which one is better), before finding himself drawn back to Sunnybank. "I went down and had a run, got the groove back and really, fell in love with the game. I played for two seasons there and then I was approached by an agent, Andrew Tafa, and he got me into Global Rapid Rugby for a brief stint, with Manuma Samoa. And that was when he told me about Romania and how there was an opportunity there. I didn't know much about the place, I'd just watched a couple of Rambo movies and that was about it!" he laughs.

What transpired was a two-season stint with Baia Mare, a small city of 100,000 people in Romania's north, located near the juncture of the Hungarian and Ukrainian borders. Pre Feliuai's arrival, the city already boasted an affiliation with Australia, albeit an unhappy one; a joint venture between Australian mining company Esmerelda Exploration and the Romanian government turning for the worse when a tailing dam at a gold mine burst its banks, releasing 70 tonnes of cyanide and other toxic heavy waste into the local river systems. That waste eventually made its way into the Danube, affecting Romania, Hungary, Ukraine, Serbia and Bulgaria. More than 1,400 tonnes of fish, storks, eagles and otters died, with scientists recording the extinction of five fish species. The accident led to Hungary leading a European ban on the use of cyanide in gold processing.

For Feliuai, the immediate priority was to keep warm. "After two years in Fiji, the cold was the hardest thing for me to deal with. In winter, often there would be frozen ice on the ground, although we did have a big indoor sandpit, like 30 metres by 20-something metres, where we could train."

As for the rugby? "Now that I know what Super Rugby is like, I can say that the speed of the game was much slower. But it was definitely very physical. Although it's a simpler kind of game there, because it was my first time in a full-time rugby environment, and the coaching was good, I really got a lot out of it."

Feliuai returned to Brisbane in between seasons, got married, then returned to Baia Mare on his own. "That second time, two months on my own straight after getting married, that was tough. So that's when I decided I'd return to play for Sunnybank, although it took a while for my clearance to come through before I could play in Australia again. And that's when Stilesy came along and told me they were interested, and invited me to trial with the Rebels. That put me straight into their trip to Japan, which went really well, so they offered me a one-year contract for 2024, and since then it's been upgraded to include 2025."

That progression speaks to Feliuai still improving as a player; a remarkably mature twenty-six, but because of his limited time in the sport, and in a fully professional program, much younger in rugby years.

"It's true that last year, there were times when I really doubted myself," he explains. "After the first two weeks of pre-season I thought, 'holy smokes, what have I got myself in for, this really is another level of physical and emotional intensity'. But now, since I've had a lot of game time, I'm starting to feel more like I belong. Other players have been massive. Like Proc, especially in defence, and Carts, even though he's younger, he's been in the game and the system a lot longer, and the way he plays the game, reads the game, I learn so much from him." Feliuai takes a moment to step through Glen Vaihu's try against the Drua, where he came into first receiver with Gordon wrapping around him. "That's just a reflection of us working hard on those plays at training, but also developing that chemistry together."

What it all means for the future remains uncertain. Sitting out for a fortnight due to a heavy concussion suffered in a tackle on Caleb Clarke, Feliuai now knows he is on the radar of the Wallaby hierarchy, even if he is a little overawed and embarrassed by it. "Given the opportunity to sit in the same room as Joe Schmidt and have a discussion, it just blew me away. I had to go away and reflect on it, tell myself this is all about belief and hard work.

I realise that I'm still climbing, and I can keep getting better, keep growing, keep being there for my team, week in, week out."

Whether his team will be there for him isn't something he likes to dwell on. "Obviously I really hope we continue. I love it in Melbourne, the players are awesome, and I love the program. My partner Chelsea is settled here, we have a one-year-old daughter, named Amarje (named after a family member of Chelsea's who passed away), and while we still have most of our family in Queensland, this is our home. It really feels like we're building something special here at the Rebels. Nobody wants that to be taken away."

Nobody perhaps but Rugby Australia, whose vote against the DOCA continues to be a source of consternation amongst staff. Kevin Foote's comments in Friday's press conference have provoked a reaction at HQ, with Phil Waugh and Richard Gardham emailing all staff and players in the afternoon, calling them to a face-to-face meeting in the morning.

For Nick Stiles, it's another example of reactivism making an already tense and upsetting situation, worse. "We're playing the Reds on Friday night, it's a critical match, one we have to win to cement our finals position and to push for as high a spot as we can, to avoid an away match against the Hurricanes or the Blues. Today is our main training session for the week. The daily timetable has little flexibility, because of the way things work with the Storm. And these guys just waltz in and demand to meet with everyone, just because they're copping a bit of heat in the media about poor communication, and want to be seen to be doing something. But what they don't see, is that they're making it about them, not about the people in the club. Why wouldn't they call me first, and we could talk about what they want to do, and we could go about sorting out the best way to do that without disrupting our preparation again? Instead of spooking everyone. What do they expect people to think when they get an email like that, with no agenda, no context to it? All it does is worry the staff even more. I've had a stream of people in my office all afternoon, players messaging me, all asking what's going on; another afternoon wasted on this rubbish. And none of the staff want to hear what they have to say, anyway. Because they're actually saying nothing. It's all just waffle. What's important is what they do."

The meeting in the morning fails to move any dials. Staff are told that there are three possible outcomes; the Rebels will continue under RA management for 2025, although this is considered highly unlikely; the Rebels will fold and those players with contracts for 2025 and potentially some others will be placed at other franchises; or, the Rebels will continue in 2025 under the new consortium, but it is stressed there has been no communication with the consortium about this possibility.

Questions from staff are put respectfully, albeit some laced with barely disguised anger. Responses are dismissed as just more word salad. As for when there might be a resolution or at least some firm direction? Waugh doesn't commit to a date but hopes it will be before the end of June; notably, after the Rebels season will have finished.

Later, Kevin Foote reflects on the impact upon his staff. "What they're basically saying to people is that you should be getting another job. And some of the staff are doing that now; they don't want to, but they have no choice. And even if by some chance we do go forward with the new consortium, to the staff, it almost feels like its deliberate, that they want to break us up. So, if we do go again next year, whoever is left, we have to start anew. Cohesion and TWI, it goes deeper than the players, it's about building strength, familiarity and understanding across the coaching group and support staff as well. It's a crazy situation; these guys think you just move people around like chess pieces. Or that's how you fix the Waratahs, just cherry pick a few players and drop them in. But building a successful, lasting franchise is about so much more than that."

Chapter Forty

9th May, 2024

If the physio room really is where coaches and CEO's check the pulse of their franchise, second port of call is the team manager. Thirty-four-year-old Will Nicholson, affectionately known as 'Sausage' or 'Saus', is in his first year in the role, stepping into the formidable shoes of previous manager, Mark "Sarge" Rowe.

"It's not like I've been thrown off the deep end," he says, reeling off a work history that suggests he was born for the job. "Rowie is like a second father to me, and he saw to it that there was a smooth transition. Back in 2012 I started at Rugby Vic as a community development officer, then gradually my expertise shifted to match management, for the Rebels and then for Rugby Australia. That secured me a role at the 2019 World Cup, where I was based in Japan for seven months. That time included a lot of the pre-event preparation, working for World Rugby in conjunction with the local organising committee. For the pool matches I was based in Fukuoka, then was one of the match managers for the semi-finals and final, in Yokohama."

Despite being full-time in the Rebels job, Nicholson is still a match commissioner for Rugby Australia, and will be in charge of operations for the Wallabies versus Wales Test in Melbourne, in July. As such, he's aware he's potentially not as badly off as other staff with respect to the uncertain situation surrounding the franchise. "I'm one of the ones with a new, young family; my daughter Mila is just 4 1/2 months old, and I'm anxious and concerned like everyone else is. I hope it doesn't come to it, and there's no guarantees, but I've tried not to worry too much about things because I think I have a skill set that hopefully might provide me with other opportunities, should it come to that," he explains.

What is interesting about the two roles is that match day manager is very regimented; "there's a system, a schedule and everything has to run like clockwork." Whereas team manager, while it needs structure and regimentation, is much more fluid; "As much as I try to have everything prepared and under control, every day something different happens and you have to be able to roll with the punches and adapt on the run. There are always lots of new ideas being thrown at you from players and staff, so the job is always interesting. The spontaneity can be stressful, you can't always do something there and then just because someone thinks it's a good idea. I still have to operate around a structure where as much as possible is organised and planned."

Nevertheless, there are times when Nicholson feels more like a manservant than a manager. "I'm the first person everyone comes to when they want something. Parking vouchers, studs, kit, a new schedule because they're too lazy to check their phone… you name it, I'll get asked for it! So, I've gotten a lot better at flicking some of that stuff to Denver (assistant manager Denver Murnane) and for a lot of it, telling players to 'go and sort your own shit out'."

There are of course, some crafty players who know exactly which buttons to push. Nicholson explains; "Most of the guys are pretty compliant, especially the younger ones, because they're just establishing themselves and don't want to be seen to be causing any trouble. The coaches and S & C staff are all excellent. But there are some older ones, like Lachie (Anderson) and Lukhan (Salakaia-Loto) who mess with me. We might be away somewhere, there's a team meeting scheduled for say after breakfast, and they'll message me to say 'Saus, can you please put in an apology to Footey because I've got family to catch up with'. That kind of thing. And I half know they're joking, but I've still got to make sure they're not. If everyone isn't at a team meeting or on the bus at the right time, that's all on my head."

The nearest Nicholson has got to a major disaster of that type was in the 2023 season, when the side was in Auckland to play Moana Pasifika. "We had a pre-match team meeting in a room at our hotel, Footey had just finished his main address, then the usual process is for everyone to file straight from there onto the bus, without any diversion. That way I know whoever is in the meeting is on the bus. To make 100% certain I do a quick sweep of any toilets. This day, everything seemed normal and the bus pulled out, we got fifty or sixty metres down the road and, luckily, it's a narrow turn with an intersection so the bus didn't have time to gather full speed, and there's a tap on the window from outside and it's Andrew Kellaway! Turns out, he was in a disabled toilet, which I hadn't checked - for what I assumed were obvious reasons. And the other thing with Kells is, he's one of those guys where if you tell him the bus leaves at 5.30, he's there bang on 5.30. In this case, we'd actually pulled out a couple of minutes early. So, as a result, I've had to go back to doing it 'old school'; standing at the door of the bus, ticking off everyone's name, one by one."

Nicholson's weekly routine starts with a slot at the regular Monday morning team meeting, where he headlines anything major or out-of-the-ordinary for the week. For example, if there is a Friday night home game scheduled against a blockbuster clash at the MCG - Carlton versus Collingwood for example - then players must be reminded to allow extra travel time. Messages and timings for the week go out to the playing and non-playing groups. "Stilesy and I will sit down, after I've gone to the commercial team to see what sponsor and media commitments they have, and we'll work out which players will go to which event, and what they need to wear."

Like many of the staff however, much of Nicholson's week isn't so much around what happens in the current week, but planning ahead of time. Hotels, travel, laundry, jersey naming and so on, all have to be organised in advance. "It can be a bit tricky say for travel," he explains, "because I don't know who will be in the selected side. But I have an educated guess and the people we work through at SANZAAR are very accommodating around late changes. Jerseys are interesting because we have some players like Carter Gordon for example, who only wear one jersey all season, but there are others, like Tuaina Tai Tualima, I think I've got jerseys for him with 4, 5, 6, 8, 19 and 20. So that's extra work for Mark (Fraser), and it doesn't help that he's got a lot of letters in his name too!"

When it comes to daily training, Nicholson's role is to ensure the supply of towels, balls and other training aids. "Denver is doing more of that now, around kit for example, and he is 100% responsible for hydration."

Despite being the glue that holds the team together, one area Nicholson won't impose himself on is the player's changing room. "That's like a sanctity area for the players," he says. "Their safe spot. I don't like being in there when they're there, so basically, I only go in to take towels in and out and that's about it. I don't have to worry about cleaning it or keeping things tidy, the leadership group mostly takes care of that, and the gym as well, through Luke Vella. The kitchen though, that's a different story, it can be hard with so many people coming through there. I hate an untidy kitchen, so that's one thing I will do, get in and clean this up where it's needed."

It's clear that Nicholson, while loving the fun and camaraderie, takes his role very seriously. And there's no bigger responsibility that being in charge of the player's passports. "That is really the part of the job I hate. At the start of the year I collect all the player's passports (the coaches and travelling staff carry their own), and I keep them all in a safe at the office. Then, when we travel, I sort through which ones we need, take them home the night before, and count and recount them three times before I get to the airport. Then I'm like a mother hen at the check-in desk, handing them out individually for check-in, and then collecting them again at the other end, before we get on the bus. And obviously, for the trip home, we repeat the process over again. So, as you might imagine, that can be pretty stressful. Particularly because it's another opportunity for some of the guys to wind me up about losing them."

Thankfully for Nicholson's blood pressure levels, travel this week is only to Brisbane. "Domestic is far easier," he laughs. "No passports. Tomorrow when we assemble at the airport, I'll manage the whole thing at group check in, and then just go around handing out the boarding passes."

Which brings us to match day. Again, for Nicholson, it's mostly about routine. "Depending on where we are, some of the away games can be a challenge around setting the changing room up. Suncorp Stadium this week, that's no problem. But in general, for home games it's a lot easier, because we're on our own patch. Denver and I will take time to lay out all the kit in the morning; for each individual player there are different short sizes, cut socks or long socks, we get to learn their preference, and then we post the run sheets on the walls, and help with the sponsor signage. A few players like to come in really early; Lukhan is one of those, where he'll chill out listening to music, doing visualisation drills and so on, and then there are others, especially the kickers, they always want to be ready to go out on the field as soon as they possibly can."

"During the match itself, I don't have too much to do," he continues. "I'm on the sideline, I'll oversee the replacements and substitutions and co-ordinate those with the fourth official. And then post-match, I check things off with the officials around citings. For example, if any of our coaches want something looked at by an opposition player, we can ask for that, or if there's been a red card, like in the Drua match where there was two, I had to get video statements from Josh Canham and Alex Mafi in the rooms about what happened, and provide those to the officials."

The following day, the team gets through an uneventful 'captain's run' in the morning before travelling to the airport for a lunchtime flight to Brisbane. Nicholson is content, everything runs like clockwork. Much smoother than the chaos that is to follow on the sideline, in Friday night's match.

Chapter Forty-One

11th May, 2024

Upon the team's return from Brisbane, Kevin Foote collects his car and exits Melbourne Airport. The early Saturday afternoon traffic is light and he is in a pensive mood during his forty-five-minute drive home. Some of that is down to tiredness, having sat up most of the night in his hotel room, breaking down his side's 26-22 loss to the Reds.

"I'm genuinely proud of the effort the boys showed out there, everything we talked about during the week around intensity and attitude, they delivered on. In that respect I couldn't have asked for more," he says.

But there is more to it than that. A number of things are nagging away at him. "It was absolute chaos around the head injuries. I get what the game is trying to do and everyone wants the players protected, but the inconsistencies in how different players are dealt with, the randomness of it all, it's so difficult to understand and manage."

Indeed, Taniela Tupou was lost as early as the 7th minute, victim of direct head contact at a ruck by a player cleaning out. "I mean, Sef Fa'agase, he's had two suspensions already, he flies into a clean out and collects Taniela in the head and we're being told they're not looking at it any further. It's all okay, apparently." Foote's frustration is overt. "Hunter Paisami gets a yellow card for hitting Kells (Andrew Kellaway) in the head, Kells passes the test and comes back on, but then they test him again after the match and he fails. So now they're both in management and return-to-play protocols, two of our best players unavailable for next week, both due to foul play. And no repercussions for the offenders."

The third player forced off for a head assessment triggered a whole different kind of frustration for Foote. "We've built depth in the front row, the competition for places has been terrific, but it's also meant guys like Pone (Fa'amausili, who was sent out on loan during the week to the Waratahs) and Cabous (Eloff) haven't been getting game time. But they're professional players and when their opportunity comes they need to step up."

Foote is referring to a second-half kick-off after the Rebels had just lost Lachie Anderson to the sin-bin and conceded a try to Jock Campbell. Ahead by 15-12 but having had little territory or possession since the break, the Rebels needed to stem the Reds' resurgence, force a tough exit, and build some pressure of their own. Instead, the kick-off was received by centre Josh Flook, who was allowed to stroll through the defensive line into an open backfield. Within seconds, the Rebels were back in their own 22, with a prop, Sam Talakai forced to throw into a line-out. Eloff, in failing to get a hard shoulder into Flook and stop him escaping into the backfield, succeeded only in collecting hooker Jordie Uelese, forcing him off the field for 14 vital minutes, for running repairs to a head gash and an HIA.

Compounding the situation, replacement hooker Alex Mafi, during one of the in-match warm-up exercises the bench players conduct behind the goalposts, pinged a calf muscle and could not take the field. Regulations provide for the Rebels to nominate Talakai as a scrum replacement at hooker, so as to avoid the referee mandating uncontested scrums. But that didn't fix the line-out issue, with the Reds happily kicking to touch and getting a free shot at possession.

Foote is full of admiration for Talakai; "To go nearly the whole match like he did, some of it in an unfamiliar role, and then to still show the pace that he did, coming around the corner to set up that try for Maciu (Nabolakasi), I just can't say enough about his character."

After shipping 21 points in the sin-bin period, and being unable to construct any meaningful play from line-out while Uelese was off, the Nabolakasi try pulled the Rebels back to within a score of winning. But, despite a strong surge into the Reds' 22 in the final two minutes, they couldn't find the try-line again. It opens up another line of frustration for Foote; "Obviously, four points down, we needed a try to win. But two points down, then we're in position to force them into giving away a penalty, or perhaps setting them back on their heels just a touch, or even setting up for a drop goal. Huge difference."

Foote is referencing a missed conversion by Carter Gordon in the first half, from adjacent to the posts, a continuation of some shaky form off the kicking tee. "We all know how hard Carts works on his game," Foote says. "He's putting the practice in after team training, and going okay too. But for some reason, when it comes to the games, he's all over the place. And it's hurting us."

Foote has a short-term solution at hand. "The best kicker in the club is Joostey (Nick Jooste). It's going to be a difficult conversation but Carts is a team man, and until he can deliver the consistency we need, then we need to make that change. David Feliuai is still in concussion protocols, so Joostey will start at 12 again next week, and he'll do the kicking for goal."

There are other tough conversations to be had with bench players who didn't make it onto the field, or barely did. "I apologised in front of the team, to Jack (Maunder), Glen (Vaihu) and Strachany (Jake Strachan), because we left the starters out there. I know it's tough for them; everybody believes in themselves and they want to play. But as a coach, in the box as the match unfolds, you're constantly asking yourself, where can I get more energy from, or more impact, and you run that against what the guys on the field are doing, and what you think they have left, and sometimes, particularly if you know they're not fatigued, in certain match situations, the better outcome is to stick with what you have."

What also frustrates Foote is that, unlike all their other losses this season, this was the first lost match where they were in a position to win it at the end. "Some of that comes down to being in more of those close games and learning how to close them out," he ponders. "The Reds have been there a few times this season and came up short, so perhaps that held them in good stead for us. Okay, we know we didn't get the rub of things - we had no luck at all. But always, when it's a close loss like this, you can't help but hone in on those moments, where if guys had managed them a little bit better, that would have got us across the line. Margins are so fine at this level. And sure, we know there's going to be some mistakes; you just have to limit them and make sure they're not costly ones."

By the time Foote arrives home, his thoughts have switched to the Chiefs, and how his team will need to bring more of the same character and effort to compete at the breakdown, to disrupt their attack in the same way they did to the Reds. But to do that, he and the team will be forced to undergo another disruption, this one even more significant than Phil Waugh's flying visit, last week.

Foote explains; "We've been told by Rugby Australia that Peter Horne will be coming in to meet with players, to tell them where RA wants to allocate them next year, should they not proceed with the Rebels. I mean, what are they trying to achieve here? If there's a genuine prospect of them moving forward with us, why would they even do that? We all know that the other clubs have been circling around in the background, picking over our list, deciding on who they want. But for RA to actually action this, while there's still three rounds to go, heading into finals, it just smacks of them forcing an implosion. It's almost like, if we crash on the field it helps them justify shutting us down. So we'll have guys this week, their heads filled with worry and concern about having to relocate, maybe to somewhere they don't want to go, what that means for their families, what that means for their careers and so on. And what about the guys they don't talk to? Off contract, essentially being told there isn't a place for them in Australian rugby. What state of mind will they be in? How can we prepare efficiently with that going on? It's a crazy situation. And all I can do is say to Rugby Australia, 'if you're going to do it, at least come in on a Monday please. Not immediately before a match'."

Perhaps there's an argument to be made that the forced movement of professional athletes as if they are indentured slaves, comes with the territory. But there is no rugby precedent for this. So often a follower and a laggard, so often reactionary, sabotaging the performance of one of its own franchises is one area Rugby Australia can lay claim to being a leader in.

Chapter Forty-Two

14th May, 2024

They're the guys who TV audiences see in those cutaway shots to the coaches' box. Sitting up in the row behind the head coach and his lieutenants, eyes fixed on computer screens, tapping silently at their keyboards. Their faces become familiar to regular rugby viewers, but nobody quite knows who they are.

That anonymity sits well with Rebels analysts John Batina (JB) and Jarrod Rutley (J-Rod). To the eye, as a pair they're like Danny de Vito and Arnold Schwarzenegger in *Twins*. Complete opposites. But when it comes to their job, they are tightly bound together by their professionalism, work ethic and selfless desire to serve the team interest. Batina, as head analyst, takes overall responsibility for the function, plus specific responsibility for attack, supporting Tim Sampson. Rutley's specialised role is in defence, working alongside Brad Harris.

Batina explains how the analyst role is built around four pillars; Match Day, Review, Preview and Training. "Things can vary from place to place but that's the foundation that pretty much all coaches and analysts at sports franchises are aligned to."

Set up on match day typically starts four hours before kick-off, with cameras being set up for the provision of additional views than those provided by the broadcaster. "We're looking for attack shape (from up high behind the posts), then we also have a reverse for closer up to set pieces," he explains. "We use our cameras and tripods which are manned by our interns. These views we share with the opposition franchise afterwards as part of an agreement between us. There is an advantage however for the home team, in that instead of waiting to get all of this packaged up, the host can access those feeds live, during the match."

The analysts routinely work through connecting all the hardware and cabling before checking, multiple times, that the feeds are working. Once the match begins, the emphasis switches to the coding of events; team coding during the match, with individual actions to follow later.

Batina outlines how it works; "We sit down with the coaches in the pre-season to work out their preferences, and what parameters and KPI's they want to set for the season. There are some standard ones, things around shape play and 22 efficiency, but new coaches might bring new things they want to measure, or it might be something we identify. It's also team dependent. We work off the data from the top teams, look at what their winning behaviours are and then we'll include that in our KPI's. Obviously, we can't capture everything, and we've dropped some stuff that we were measuring but wasn't being taken to meetings or included in our match reports. Efficiency is important. We're always asking, 'why do we do this?' It's never just for the sake of it."

"Then again," Rutley adds with a wry smile, "the coach always has the final say."

So how different is the process from team to team? "Not very," says Batina. "Most teams have similar metrics, except maybe one or two things that a coach or analyst might try, just because we're all fighting for an edge."

Once the match starts, a form of controlled chaos kicks in. Rutley explains; "The first priority is coding those team actions, but I don't have my head down blindly, I'm also scanning the game, looking for things, anticipating and reacting. If the team is on attack, or there's a break, I can grab a few seconds to prepare a clip for half-time that one of the coaches might request. But you can never let your guard down. With turnovers, things can swing very quickly from defence to attack and back again. And obviously, the same applies in reverse for JB."

"On top of that," he adds, "we also have to troubleshoot on the fly. If a coach isn't getting the pictures he needs, like on the night of the Highlanders' match, then I have to find a way to solve that, while not missing any detail."

There is some help, close at hand. Batina explains; "We use up to five interns a season, so we pick one of them to code some of the generic stuff; lineouts, scrums, line breaks. He's not in the main box but in a room adjacent, but all of his data is fed into the coaches live."

While TV coverage has advanced markedly in recent years, it's an obvious observation to make that for the at-home viewer, wondering why are certain player is replaced or not replaced, the coaches are working with way more information that what they see.

At every match, the analysts are required to balance the hierarchy against the need to provide the team with the best winning chance. "We're mostly passive," says Batina, "but if I see something and I think it's been missed, then I'll speak up if I think it's going to influence the game. But we never speak just for the sake of speaking."

"We've all done it," adds Rutley. "But we're all wary of speaking at the wrong time. There's already enough good coaches in the room, and we'll always react when asked."

Post-match works like clockwork. There is the physical pack down of all equipment and cabling then, as soon as possible, they're back at their desks. "Ninety percent of the team coding will already have been done, but there'll be little fixes, things that you knew weren't quite right in the match that you didn't get time to fix. I'm six years in now," says Rutley, "and JB is ten years, so those instances get fewer and fewer. So, at that stage, the emphasis is on getting everything into a five page 'Keynote' document that the coaches and players receive on Saturday afternoon (for a Friday night match)."

Here their paths diverge slightly. Rutley prefers to stay at the office until all of the team coding is complete and a good start is made on the individual coding. That usually means a 2am finish, a few short hours of sleep, and a rush to finish the job off in the morning. For away games, Batina usually travels while Rutley and an intern work from the office. As Batina explains, "It's nice to get to travel with the team and go to different places, but for some of the away games, by the time you get back to the hotel on the bus, it's already pretty late and I'm well behind where J-rod is. Usually, our flight is pretty early in the morning, so I'll just pull an all-nighter, and try and get as much done as I can. It's not just me, the coaches will also be up, doing some of their own coding and putting little clips together; maybe something more broadly tactical, or something they want to use with individual players."

And when there is training on a Sunday morning? Where not only does all the match review material need to be completed but the training session needs to be filmed and analysed? "Those are tough weekends," nods Batina, slowly.

By Tuesday, the analysts are into preview mode; not for the coming match, but the one after that. "We work around a week and a half ahead," says Batina. "Breaking down that opposition's strengths and weaknesses. Where have they developed or gone backwards? Have there been any discernible changes over the season or since we last played them? That sort of thing."

A question arises. If the analysts are working more than a week ahead, does that mean they get to clock off a week early, at the end of the season? Batina nods his head again, like before, although this time more slowly. "The way things are… might be longer than a week off," he says ruefully.

When it comes to the fourth pillar - training - the challenge is more technical and less strategic. "It takes a long time to get a full understanding of the mechanics of it all, how to obtain the best camera views, using the drone in the most efficient way," says Batina, explaining how he has mostly stepped away from covering training, leaving that element to Rutley.

"We use the training data mostly for coaches' meetings," Rutley explains. "Extracting clips for team meetings or one-on-ones with players. We find this material more useful in the pre-season, where there are new players and new combinations. There are always obvious clips to use to help the team when they are learning new routines. In fact, for the first three weeks we don't even measure anything. Then once the cohesion improves, the coaches can then get more useful data around positioning, specific roles at the breakdown, line-out, line-out maul or in multi-phase. That then allows us to lay down markers so that we can then measure the improvement over the rest of the pre-season, so by the time we reach round one, the team is operating at around 85-90% efficiency."

With Rugby Australia seemingly in the process of shrinking the professional footprint of the game, that's not an encouraging situation for anyone in such a specialised role as rugby analyst. Particularly when Batina's rugby pathway suggests he was born for the role. "My dad is Fijian, I played rugby as a kid for Melbourne Uni, Harlequins, then Northern Panthers, the same club as Rob (Leota), Jordie (Uelese) and Fereti Sa'aga (Rebel #107). At age 16 I ruptured my ACL, then again at 20, so I started coaching kids and decided I wanted to find a professional role, at the same time as the Rebels started. I'm one of the originals; my first job with the club was ball-boy co-ordinator," he says, as proudly as if he had been the head coach.

In 2014 Batina moved into an intern analyst role under Eoin Toolan (announced in 2024 as Wallabies head analyst), and also worked as an analyst for Fiji rugby under John McKee, for the 2016-2019 World Cup cycle. Upon Toolan's departure in 2019, Batina then shifted into the Rebels' head analyst position. One of his first tasks was to hire Rutley as an intern. Increasingly, it feels like a case of Batina being all dressed up with nowhere to go. "I understand nobody has a job for life, but this is where I feel I belong and where I contribute, and I'm not really sure what will happen if things end up folding. It's a tricky time because my daughter Alisi was born the day after the Brumbies match in round one. She's as old as the season is," he concludes.

By contrast, Rutley is a self-described "late bloomer" who left school in year nine, and envisaged a life as a brickie's labourer. At age 25 something clicked in, and he decided to try his hand at university, studying sports coaching. After a spell in AFL recruiting, Rutley got a job in Sydney as a freelance analyst coding club rugby on a Sunday. "I fell in love with that, then a position came up at the Rebels. JB interviewed me and it was there we realised that we'd actually met each other before, at Victoria University. So it was kind of meant to be, we get along and we've got similar work ethics; like it doesn't matter what time of day a message comes through from the coaches, we're both on call 24-hours."

Having been interns themselves, that shared work ethic extends to the relationship with the people below them as well as the coaches above. Batina explains; "We take our experience to the interns we hire. We're absolutely genuine about teaching them, and we emphasise that, while the job can be a lot of fun, it's also deadly serious. Whatever you put in, you'll get a benefit or reward for that in the future."

Does all of that effort and commitment have a downside? Particularly if the Rebels are forced to fold? "Sure," says Rutley. "The hardest part for me is my family and partner all wanting to know what is going on. They read and hear stuff and then they worry and panic. I'd love to give them answers, but I can't. And that's been the situation for a while now. Too long."

Batina's perspective is broader. "The way I've approached it is that this is a great opportunity to show your character. To family and to work colleagues. In a high-performance sport environment, attitude is infectious, and I feel it's important for all of us to bring the right attitude. If you show up all 'woe is me' or with shit body language, that's going to affect others and spread right thought the office," he says. "I'm not going to lie and say that's not how people feel, or how I feel sometimes, because it's emotionally fatiguing. But I'm grateful for the opportunity I've been given. However it plays out, I know we can all honestly say that this is the best team, the best staff, the best alignment we've ever had."

"What we've all figured out is that there's strength in numbers. It's a cliche but we're all in it together. That means that when we're in the flow of things, like this week, we're all switched on and it feels really good. It's only when a reminder pops up on your screen, 'Zoom meeting with Phil Waugh in fifteen minutes', that you remember, oh no, we really are in a shit situation, I've only got one more pay check coming and I don't know what will happen after that."

Chapter Forty-Three

17th May, 2024

"It's been a sad morning talking about the @MelbourneRebels last home match on TV and radio. Thinking of the volunteers and fans who are going to lose their men's and women's teams."

That's Melbourne-based sports reporter Cath Murphy, in a post on 'X', echoing her comments made earlier in the morning on ABC TV's 'The Breakfast Couch', which draw a definitive line under the Rebels' 14-year existence.

It all seems so official. So final. Tonight, at AAMI Stadium, the Rebels will be playing their final home game, against the Chiefs.

That's news to Nick Stiles. "Unless Rugby Australia has told the ABC something they haven't told us, this club isn't dead yet; what is she talking about? What about thinking about the staff who have to deal with their families continually asking them what is going on, when they see unconfirmed reporting like this out there?"

Stiles is equal parts frustrated and angry. "We have an open-door policy. The ABC are welcome to come down to the club and see for themselves what is going on. See the work that the players and coaching group have been putting in. Talk to staff about their personal hardships and the stress that this ongoing situation has put on them and their families. Acknowledge, despite all of these distractions and impediments, how well the team has done to be running 6th on the ladder. But no, none of that. They haven't been near the place. Instead, they'd rather write our obituary and sprinkle a bit of pretend empathy for fans over the top."

Other media have picked up on the same theme, albeit most reporters have been careful not to be so absolute, and to frame tonight's match as 'potentially' the final home game for the Rebels. It's a natural and obvious angle; an expectation that the night will be one of high emotion.

In truth, around the club, it's been pretty much like any other normal week; normal at least by 2024 standards. The coaches have acknowledged the possibility, the players are fully aware, but nobody has made anything extra of it. As Kevin Foote acknowledges, you don't beat the Chiefs on emotion, you beat them by getting your set-piece to work efficiently, by taking your opportunities, by making your tackles, putting pressure on their breakdown and minimising the number of effective possessions Damian McKenzie gets.

One concession Foote makes is to recognise two local players who have been away with the Junior Wallabies side, Ottavio Tuipulotu and Divad Palu who, at this stage of their careers, have yet to set foot on AAMI Stadium as players. If this really is to be the end of the road, he would hate for their history with the Rebels to have such a gaping hole in it. As a result, both are invited to strip and play an active part in tonight's warm up. It's not a Super Rugby cap, at least not yet, but for these two young players, it's the closest thing going around, and a tangible experience for them to carry forward.

A few short kilometres away from AAMI Stadium, at Bells Hotel in South Melbourne, an expectant crowd gathers for a rugby lunch with a difference. The plight of Jimmy Orange, his Academy Movement business an unsecured creditor of the Rebels, has caught the attention of rugby supporters around town. An important early sponsor of Academy Movement is the Rugby Club of Victoria, whose president John Anderson, has continued to work hard to corral the support of other backers. As a result, a separate foundation has been newly established, expressly for the purpose of funding Academy Movement's operations, to allow Orange to more rapidly upscale and place more new academies into more Victorian public schools, faster, ostensibly to get in first before the Melbourne Storm does the same.

Today's lunch is a concerted effort by Orange and his backers to establish momentum for a substantial fund-raising effort. Money will be raised on the day, via donations and various activities, including a 'Calcutta' on the Rebels' first try scorer later tonight, but the bigger prize is the awareness being pushed out into the Melbourne business community, to entice other individuals and businesses to climb on board.

Orange speaks authentically about his commitment to education and outlines some of the wins - rugby, educational and social/behavioural - his program is having. One new school has been added during the week; Sunshine College, whose principal Jodie Parsons, having known nothing about rugby beforehand, acknowledges the fit for the demographic in her catchment area, and her excitement at being involved.

Also restated is the impact upon the program if the Rebels are to fold. Not only are the children involved aspirational, it is clear that identity and belonging are clear drivers and motivators for participants. Rebels branded kit is an important part of the program; not because it's a bit of free gear for the kids, but because the badge reminds them every day about how Wallabies like Rob Leota, Jordan Uelese and Pone Fa'amausili come from the same communities they come from, and that with hard work and application, on and off the field, there is a pathway for them to a life other than with a local gang or into a menial job.

It turns out that Orange has some heavy hitters in his corner. Wallaby legend and World Cup winning captain John Eales, met Orange earlier in the year, took a shine to his work, and offered to anchor the lunch around himself as a speaking drawcard. Eales doesn't disappoint, having the packed room eating out of his hand with tales and insights extolling grace, good humour and his genuine love for the game. Asking the questions, respected sports journalist Tim Lane, new to rugby but a keen and willing student, also impresses with his humility and willingness to embrace the sport and the occasion.

Local Jellis Craig auctioneer Lachie Fraser-Smith weaves his magic with the Calcutta, coaxing hefty amounts out of punters in the off-chance that the player they purchase might be the opening try-scorer. That player will later turn out to be Glen Vaihu, not even amongst the 15 listed on the team sheet, but a late replacement after Darby Lancaster is ruled out, suffering the effects of tonsillitis. One player who isn't a winning bet is lock Josh Canham, who, when told upon his arrival at the ground that his father just dropped $500 on him to be the first try scorer, laughs scornfully and shakes his head in disbelief.

With the temperature dropping and rain falling outside, the conviviality and goodwill inside the room ensures the afternoon passes quickly. When the crowd eventually thins, deep into a glass of red, a humbled and grateful Orange acknowledges; "I think my favourite part of the day was that everyone forgot all that's wrong with rugby in Australia and remembered all the good that rugby is and can be."

That theme is continued out on Gosch's Paddock where Stan commentator and ex-Wallaby Morgan Turinui, guides a bunch of young female players through a series of training drills, ahead of the Wallaroos' Pacific Four Test clash against the USA, inside AAMI Stadium. The participants are sourced from three of the state schools either currently part of Academy Movement, or originally set up by Orange and now running independent programs. Manning the bar-b-que is Rebels' director Owain Stone, while on hand are prominent Rebels Super W players, including Mel Kawa and Tiarah Minns, whose untimely shoulder injury has prevented her from making her Wallaroos debut in front of a home crowd.

Things are good early for the Wallaroos as they skip out to a 17-3 lead. But increasingly, the USA finds a fruitful pathway through their line-out maul and not only work their way into the match, but beyond, to win 32-25. While not outclassed, and improving on their loss a week before to Canada, compared to the top tier of nations the Wallaroos remain deficient in strength, conditioning and pace, as well as lacking a ruthless, clinical finishing edge.

It's the inevitable outcome of Australia experiencing a painful transition from amateur to professional. Lack of money is an issue, but it's not an excuse. USA Rugby has far less money than Rugby Australia, and a highly competitive sporting environment too, yet they have been able to develop women's participation at grassroots club and college level far in advance of Australia.

The recent announcement that Cadbury has locked in a six-year naming-rights sponsorship deal for the Wallaroos until 2029 has provided a much-needed shot of confidence. Rugby Australia's women's high performance manager Jaime Fernandez is highly regarded. But concerns remain around priorities and strategic decision-making at executive and board level, given Rugby Australia's parlous financial position. Whatever the game can or can't afford, a measly five-round high-performance franchise competition is no way to support a tier 1 Test program or to grow wider interest and participation. Particularly when the AFL and NRL are actively growing the women's versions of their sports.

As if to highlight where women's rugby sits on Rugby Australia's awareness scale, at a function up on level 2, ex-Rugby Australia CFO now COO, Richard Gardham, welcomes "past Jillaroos" players. His faux pas, confusing rugby with rugby league, is met with a hearty round of jeers and boos. With Gardham at the centre of Rugby Australia's push against the

Rebels, his words and actions only serve to reinforce to those present the real potential for short-term, austerity-driven decision-making, to override long-held relationships and sensible, balanced strategic planning and execution.

The Chiefs, currently in 4th position on the ladder, have come to Melbourne with their best available side. Within six minutes, a sweeping movement down both sides of the field sees Glen Vaihu burst through the tackle of highly-rated Shaun Stephenson to crash over in the corner. With drizzle turning to rain, and the Rebels' pack hungry to compete at the breakdown, it's clear this is not going to be the razzle-dazzle runaway victory for the visitors that many predicted.

As the game clock ticks over 14 minutes, the crowd bursts into a sustained round of applause, to mark the 14 years the Rebels have been in existence. It's a poignant moment. Emotions are mixed; there is for many a feeling of sadness and resignation that this might really be the end of the road, but there is also pride and a sense that the applause is a call to the consortium to keep fighting for the club's existence and future.

Entering the half-time break narrowly behind by 13-11, there's an opportunity to draw breath and reflect on a second consecutive match marked by chaotic, multiple, unplanned replacements. Prop Isaac Aedo Kailea didn't make it through the warm up, replaced by Cabous Eloff; Josh Kemeny has suffered a heavy concussion; Vaiolini Ekuasi has been jammed up around his hips and lower back; and Carter Gordon, victim of a high shot by All Blacks' lock Tupou Vaa'i, is undergoing a HIA. (After the match there is much laughter when Brad Wilkin, in his first match back after a long-lay off for his injured hamstring, admits, "I could see Vaiolini was struggling, but with Josh already off and me in no shape to go the distance in my first match, I walked over to him and literally begged him to keep going. I know it's selfish, but when we came in at half-time, all I could think about was how much I was shitting myself that if there was another injury I'd have to go the whole eighty.")

Geoff Parling leads a string of exhortations from the coaches that have a common theme; dominate the collision area, more urgency and awareness in contact, stay tight and look for opportunities to tip to a support player in space, greater intensity at the scrum and, from Brad Harris, to apply more double tackles, of the kind that has pressured the Chiefs into four tackle turnovers already in the match.

For the third quarter, things don't go to plan, but when some sustained phase play eventually comes together, and Lachie Anderson is twice freed up for a run to the corner, the Rebels have worked their way back to 23-23, with only four minutes of play remaining. If ever there was a time for a long, clean exit, this is it. But Ryan Louwrens hangs his head in disappointment as his clearing kick finds touch barely beyond the 22m line. It's an invitation the Chiefs gladly accept, working the ball towards the posts, trapping Maciu Nabolakasi in a ruck, preventing him from rolling clear of the ball. McKenzie chews off more than a minute of running time before he pops over what will be the winning penalty goal. There's still time to play, and the Rebels surge forward at a centre-field kick-off, forcing a ruck deep in the Chiefs' 22. In all of the desperation, referee Nic Berry fails to notice a retreating Chief's forward enter the ruck from the side, to help snuff out the attack. Instead of 26-26 and extra-time, it's a gutting 26-23 loss and another midweek apology.

Later, in the sanctity of the staff kitchen, there is widespread frustration. It's another bonus point gained, but it's still a loss, no matter how honourable, of what was a winnable match. Foote rues a couple of moments where on-field game management wasn't quite where it needed to be, and how those led to points against. On the other hand, he notes how the difficult, back-loaded draw is proving to be a blessing rather than a burden. "The way the draw is, hard matches against the Blues and Chiefs, away in Brisbane last week, it hasn't damaged us. Instead, it's given us self-belief. That we have the ability to cope with all the disruptions, and no matter who comes onto the field, stay more than competitive." He pauses for a few seconds, then adds; "We have to process the disappointment first, but already, I can't wait for next weekend in Canberra. Keep taking this group forward, keep building. And then when our luck changes, we'll be there and we'll be ready."

Even though Carter Gordon was cleared to return for the second half, news comes through that he has failed a follow up examination, post-match. Tim Sampson is frustrated by an anomaly in the process. "That's the second week in a row where we've lost a player to an HIA for foul play. Kells last week, and Carts tonight. In both cases the offender got sat down for ten minutes. That's less time than what it takes for the HIA to occur. And then our guys, because they've failed, that's now an automatic 12-day minimum stand down, so they're out of business, and the offenders receive no additional punishment other than the ten-minute sin bin. That just doesn't sit right for me. I know everyone's doing their best around head injuries. But really, if they want to be fair dinkum about it, making it fairer, making it more of a deterrent, then I think the game needs to look more closely at standing down those perpetrators for a week, to match the stand-down time for the player they hit."

There's little left to do other than for everyone present to bottle their frustration and whittle away the pile of sausages left-over from the junior women's session earlier in the afternoon. By Darwin's law of natural selection, the ones with charred (some might say burnt) outsides have worked their way down to the bottom. To an untrained eye they might look unappealing, but at 11.30pm, washed down with a beer, nobody is getting too fussy about a bit of char on a cold sausage.

Chapter Forty-Four

19th May, 2024

A string of Friday night matches has meant that, for much of the season, Sunday has become a training day. While most of Melbourne eases into late breakfast and coffee, dog walking and kid's activities, the team is already well into its work. Coaches and analysts have identified the work-ons from the Chiefs, and the players happily run out any residual soreness. Things are handled with a minimum of fuss, which clears the decks for a squad meeting, once the players are showered and fed.

Ex-Rebels director Georgia Widdup, is the public face of the new consortium and she is here to update the players on where things are post the DOCA vote. The time period for the two conditions attached to the DOCA to be accepted is nearing. Whether the players will remain Rebels in 2025 relies on Rugby Australia making the participation licence available, and she reiterates how that remains a decision out of the consortium's control. What Widdup can speak to is the detail contained in their proposal, and she sets about demonstrating to the players how a real plan, with real money behind it, with real potential to transform rugby in Victoria, will be almost impossible for Rugby Australia to ignore.

Widdup covers off the make-up of the consortium, confirming its credibility, then summarises the financials, and details the viability of the Tarneit proposal. The beauty of this aspect is that the Tarneit stadium is proceeding with or without the Rebels. While the Rebels will need to pay their way, there is little capital outlay required. Transition to the site will be gradual and orderly; indeed, many of the players present will be gone by the time the Rebels are fully established at the new base. Questions from the floor are dealt with adeptly, and it becomes clear that while the details are important and are enthusiastically received, it is Widdup's calm, authentic demeanour that wins the players over. Nothing is dodged, fobbed off, glossed over or embellished. In the court of public opinion, the directors have largely been painted as incompetent and deceitful in the way they incurred debt, and selfish and manipulative in their actions to elongate the process so as to avoid their personal responsibilities. Some critics point to a small cohort of selfish people interested only in controlling rugby in Victoria. Here, inside the fort, well away from media half-truths and social media speculation, it's a different picture. What the consortium believes is being missed by those on the outside is that they are primarily driven by the love of rugby - their love of Victorian rugby - and a burning desire not to undo all of the positive development work, and repeat the mistakes made in western Sydney, thus opening the door for rugby league to crush rugby.

Standing alongside Widdup fielding questions is Nick Stiles, whose idea it was to schedule the presentation ahead of the arrival tomorrow, of Rugby Australia's Director of High-Performance Rugby, Peter Horne. "I thought it was important that Peter didn't start talking to players about which franchises Rugby Australia thought they might place them into, without providing them with this context first," he says. "I get that Peter is in a tough position. He says that he's been kept at arms-length from the decision-making at the top, nevertheless it's clear what that direction is, given he's been asked to come and do this work."

As ever, Stiles is caught between trying to minimise distractions so as not to impact on team performance, his desire to see the Rebels continue - with as many of the current players as possible - and his duty to ensure that should things turn sour, the players and staff are best placed to find good homes. "There's obviously something not right when you're talking to players about where they might like to go next year, and having them wonder and worry about what kind of opportunity there will actually be for them at another franchise," he says. "But the reality is, those conversations are going to happen anyway with the player managers. So it's far better to pull it out into the open, be totally transparent and say, 'look, none of us want this to be what happens, the consortium is working their butt off to make sure it doesn't happen, but in the worst-case scenario that it does all turn to shit, at least this piece of work has already been started, to give everyone the best opportunity to carry on somewhere else'. That way, when RA starts talking to them tomorrow, we've given them a bit of context, plus a bit of reassurance from the consortium that, either way, people are doing their best to give them a secure future."

Kevin Foote is an interested observer, but wary about what will happen tomorrow. "I get that we need to stay in front of the players. If we don't, the whispers start up and their minds start wandering. That's only natural. And during every season, there'll always be a players having conversations in the background with their agent, looking at what other opportunities there might be elsewhere. That's how the process works. But it's never *all* of the players. And not players being forced into those discussions with a national body who plainly don't want us in the competition."

The following day, Foote makes an appearance as a guest on the *8/9 Combo Rugby Podcast*. The interview is positively received; Foote's coaching credibility, aptitude for leadership, character and humanity shining through. He speaks respectfully but with candour, admitting to being "pissed-off" at how other coaches have been circling, looking to pounce on his franchise's carcass, before adding; "We've got guys who are on contract for next year. Those players are guaranteed for next year but that's not to say they're not under stress because they don't know where that's going to be."

"Then we have this other group of players who don't have a contract next year. Some of those guys, they were right down to the wire with us negotiation wise. Some of them, their new contracts were with Rugby Australia waiting to get signed off. Those players now don't have anything. So for them, every dropped ball in training or any mistake on the field gets blown out of proportion."

Foote's point is one that has been largely overlooked. In trying to provide comfort for the players who have contracts into 2025, this exercise only exacerbates the stress and anxiety for those who don't. If there are limited spots available at other franchises, and those places will be offered first to contracted players, where does this leave them?

The sessions the following day with Peter Horne (with RUPA President Justin Harrison again in attendance) pass without fuss. One after another, players emerge with kind words to say about Horne, albeit a few are convinced he had no idea who they actually were. After he is gone, some of the coaches note that while Horne was there to enact RA's plan for redistributing players, nothing seems to have been put in place for them.

As professional and polite as Horne is to staff and players, there is an overriding sense of the club being violated; being picked over while still alive, no pretence of dignity allowed. The official line from Sydney is that no decision has been made about the Rebels' future. But on days like this, it really does feel like it's just a matter of time.

Chapter Forty-Five

22nd May, 2024

As the selected team goes through their paces on the training track, fringing around the edges are two talented Rebels players; neither of whom has played any on-field role this season, nor has any prospect of doing so. Ex-Australia sevens player and Olympian, fullback/winger Joe Pincus, and Junior Wallabies No. 8 Leafi Talataina are fully stripped and, at one end of the field, undertake their personal conditioning programs as members of the injured and rehabbing group known as 'the grafters'. Once they are finished, they linger on the sideline, watching proceedings, eager to remain connected.

It's been a long, tough haul for Pincus since his ankle injury in August last year, suffered while playing for Eastwood in a Shute Shield match against Manly. "It was one of those ugly ones," he says, with a heavy dash of laconic understatement. "It was in a corner of the field where there was a big crowd, and I could hear the groans from the people watching. When it happened it made this big noise so I knew straight away that it was bad. Someone came on and held up a blanket like a screen, so it was like I was a racehorse, waiting to be put down. It was a weird sensation because on one hand I was dealing with the pain plus a mix of 'I don't want to know how bad it is' versus 'I need to know how bad this is'. And then my brother, he was there and he took a photo of my leg and I asked to have a look, and he wouldn't show me."

Contracted until the end of the 2025 season, Pincus at least had the security of knowing he could undergo rehabilitation still part of the Rebels' forward plans. "That was critically important. Knowing that the club had shown faith in me with a long-term contract."

And why not? In 2023 Pincus appeared in ten out of fourteen matches, missing the four only through unavailability due to injury. "All the way through rehab, that's really helped," he notes. "Knowing that if I'm healthy, I'm getting picked."

Pincus progressed well up until Xmas, out of the moon boot, ticking off small performance landmarks, one by one. "But once we introduced more jumping, change of direction, more rugby movements, the ankle started blowing up and so it became a matter of getting enough work into it and balancing the reaction. Into January, I realised I was struggling, I saw a surgeon who confirmed that I needed to get scar tissue cleaned out, and that's when it hit me that it really was all over for this season."

So how has he approached both the mental and physical side of that? "When you're in rehab, what's really important is that you put your long-term career goals to the side, because that can be daunting and depressing. You have to focus on what's the next step to getting better, then the next step after that. I'm really lucky I get along so well with the medical and physio team here; I trust them completely and they trust me. They know they can set a program and I'll follow it diligently. That's such an important relationship," he says.

"It's on match days when it can get really frustrating. All you want to do is be out there playing. But it's also an opportunity to focus on other ways you can have a positive effect on the team. At the start of the year I was doing podcasts for the fans with Alex Mafi and Mel Kawa, but what I've loved is that Footey and Sambo put a lot of trust in me, keeping me busy with doing opposition reviews, and reviews of our training. It's nothing like playing, but it's an awesome feeling when something you've contributed to pays off on the field. There was a move I introduced from Shute Shield I remembered from 2017, and I suggested that would be a good one to use against the Hurricanes, and Lachie (Anderson) ended up going through a nice hole."

There's a maturity to Pincus that clearly sits well with the coaches, which extends to his outlook on the club's precarious position. "Every single player wants the club to keep going and wants the best for this group. But it's also important to acknowledge that there are guys who are in different positions. Some boys will be going overseas next year, there's a group like me who have contracts secured for next year, and there are others who are un-contracted after this year so, more than anyone, they really need the team to be around. So, we're all impacted differently. The club has done a fantastic job acknowledging all of the stuff as it's been going on; Stilesy, Baden at the start, they've always dealt with it head on. If we talk about the physios for example, they're in such a tough spot, no contract after June 30th, and I'm incredibly impressed and proud of how they've dealt with things. Footey has never taken a backward step with us. It's impossible as a player not to be motivated and inspired by that."

After being upgraded to a full Rebels contract in 2023 and logging some impressive performances for the Junior Wallabies' (Under 20's), the imposingly built Talataina might have looked forward to a prosperous 2024, if not for an untimely left ACL rupture. "In some aspects I've found dealing with a long-term injury really hard," he explains. "But I also feel like there's a big responsibility on me to do my rehab well, to set a good example to the rest of the boys. That's the thing when you're part of the grafters. Some days we're in here an hour or two before the other boys and if they can see how hard we're working before they hit the training field, I feel like it's a good example for them and gives them a bit of extra motivation."

"From the start of pre-season, in the grafters I was with Luke Callan and then Zac Hough joined with exactly the same injury as mine, then Pincus, he's been with us the whole time as well. And then there's been other boys come in and out, as you'd expect during the season. It's always difficult to see others get injured and join the group, but it makes it easier if you're not on your own. And obviously, the staff are such a big help. At the beginning I had Simon Lumb, then transitioning from medical more into S & C, it's been Luke Trewhella. And Luke Vella is always checking in on us."

Born in Wellington's Hutt Valley, Talataina's family relocated to Melbourne when he was a primary school youngster. In rugby terms, Melbourne rugby is his blood. "There's been a lot of talk about the need to develop local pathways and I've been privileged to be a part of that. I was a slow developer but was lucky enough to be involved with Jimmy Orange's Academy Movement at my school. Things really clicked in 2022 when there was a big intake of Melbourne-grown players into the Rebels, all my age. Unfortunately. I wasn't selected with that group, but because I looked at that and saw that there was a genuine pathway I spent that year working hard at my craft, performing in the Under 18's, making sure I gave myself the best chance of being selected the following year."

"That's one thing I worry about with this situation, if there is to be no Rebels moving forward. I know from my own experience how it all became real to me when I saw these boys in the pathway to the Rebels. Would I have worked the same, developed my game the same if that goal wasn't so specific? If it was, one day I might play for the Brumbies or the Waratahs? Maybe, but for me it was important that I connect with a goal I could see was attainable."

Talataina considers carefully, when asked what it feels like, knowing that having come through that Victorian pathway, he might never actually play for the Rebels. "It's disheartening. Sure, there's things happen in the game, and in life, and you realise they're bigger than rugby. It makes you think more outside the game. If it is to be the end, I'm very grateful for the time I've had here at the Rebels. It's a different system here because we don't have the large academies some of the other states do, but I actually think that's a blessing in disguise because we have our academy boys training with the full-time boys. And you can see the growth that all of us get from that, which we take back to our club sides, just from training with the top side."

There's more. "I've thought about how I'll feel if we're forced to leave, and I think for me, of course it's disappointing, but what I'll try to hold on to in the future is the feeling of Melbourne. It's where I'm grounded, it's where my family is. So, wherever I play I'll always be connected to Endeavour Hills rugby club, to Rugby Victoria, and to the Rebels."

Chapter Forty-Six

24th May, 2024

A rugby nomad in the true sense, Tim Sampson is used to balancing the demands of rugby and family, even if he doesn't like the price he pays for it. "It's quite selfish really. Everything we've done as a family has been shaped around my career. And now, if things don't work out with the Rebels, there's going to be more upheaval. After three big moves, all that disruption is on me, which certainly isn't very fair on my wife and girls. (They have been based in Perth while Sampson has been in Melbourne during the 2023 and 2024 seasons). While I don't feel like I'm ready to step away from rugby, I do feel like my head is in a different space now, and it has to be more about family."

It's match day in Canberra. Sampson has already braved the brisk morning air, met up with extended family and returned to the hotel armed with a bottle of red wine - a gift to mark his birthday.

Tonight's referee, Angus Gardner, arrives in the lobby and notices the bottle sitting on the table in front of Sampson. "Getting an early start?" he quips.

There's a light-hearted joke to be had around referees driving coaches to drink, but Sampson holds his tongue and smiles politely in return. As it happens, Gardner will be back at an adjacent table late into the evening, along with fellow match officials, Oli Kellett, Matt Kellahan and Jordan Kaminski, celebrating his record breaking 115th Super Rugby game, enjoying a couple of aged reds from his own cellar.

Hailing from Brisbane, Sampson's breakthrough into high-performance rugby came with his appointment as coach of the Canberra Vikings in the NRC, before he landed at the Force in the wake of their forced exit from Super Rugby, in 2017. "That was fun but it was like a start-up really. Three footballs, a dozen cones and 18 players. And we didn't really have a competition to play in, just a series of exhibition games."

Sampson got to know Kevin Foote through coaching against each other in the NRC, and when his contract with the Force was terminated at the end of 2022, he interviewed for a position to work alongside Foote at the Rebels, in the role of attack coach.

"Kevin and I had already developed a healthy respect for each other, and as we talked, it became clear that there were similarities in our philosophies and personalities. I also knew Baden from Canberra, and Stilesy from Brisbane. I flew across from Perth and had dinner with the three of them and we talked about how, as a head coach, I might transition into an assistant role. Even though that's fairly common in AFL, you never actually see that in rugby, so it was a fair concern. My belief was that because I knew what Kevin would be going through, day after day, week after week, I'd be an asset for him and the club, as his assistant," he says.

And the outcome? "I must say, it's been good for me. More pure coaching. Straight away I was aligned with Kevin's game model, so that made it an easy transition, me being able to add my imprint on top. On the pitch, it hasn't always been as clean as I'd like, but if you look at last week, three tries in the backline against the Chiefs… they were straight off the training track. There's no better feeling as an attack coach when in a game you find the fracture points in the defence and break the opposition down. That doesn't happen by accident, and that's what I really love the most; every week, the challenge of finding a way to crack the opposition. Obviously, the players still have to execute under pressure, but nothing happens without us doing the work up front."

Sampson describes a typical week whereby he and Geoff Parling work to get alignment on what they see as the opposition's strengths and weaknesses, then begin to form ideas on how they want to play. Working solo and with the analysts, they send preview clips out to the player's attacking strategy group for their feedback. "Carter, Joostey, Strachany, Louwrens, Pincus… these guys take the responsibility seriously and are always on point. Joe (Pincus) has been terrific behind the scenes doing preview work. Then we pull it all together, I'll finalise the playbook for the week and we'll roll it out to the team on Monday, do some walk-throughs and drills, perhaps tweak some things again, so that we're at full speed with it before the main session of the week."

As is the modern way, a lot of the backline moves involve 'back-door' plays. "I watch a lot of NRL," he explains. "Newcastle is a good example;

they score a lot of tries with a heap of movement out the back of their attacking line. Bodies in motion swinging side to side creates a blur for the defence. There are always three options minimum, preferably four."

Sampson also talks about 'space invaders'. "We want the winger and centre on the long side to be scanning all of the time, and communicating what they see to the pivots. Help them back better decisions. That first try against the Chiefs to Glen Vaihu, it was a great finish by him but the opportunity came from quick ball movement to one side, and then on the next phase, identifying the space and again, quick ball movement to where the space was. Of course, you've got to up-skill your players so they're good enough to take advantage. When the widest defenders jam in, our players have to be able to execute under that pressure. And that bullet from Vaiolini to Glen was just that; a quality player executing in the moment."

For all the talk about match strategies and processes, there is still a lot of individual coaching required. "A big part of my job is to improve individuals," he confirms. "That's where I get my biggest satisfaction. On the flip-side, if a player dips in form or doesn't have a good season, I take that to heart and I reflect; have I let this player down?"

Sampson takes a moment to consider the scorecard. "I think it's fair to say we're seeing players develop as a result of being in our program. It's always difficult singling guys out, but David Feliuai is definitely growing as a player. Vaiolini, Canham, and Jordie around the field this year… they're not just learning, but starting to put a lot of things into practice.

It's the topic of future development that leads him to the off-field situation. "The thing that really excited me was at that first dinner, when Stilesy, Bado and Kevin outlined where all this was heading. We know that whatever we do this year, we'd all be better for the experience, coaches and players, we'd be able to add a few little things here or there, another player or two, and be ready next year to give the competition a shake. (Chiefs coach) Clayton McMillan told me last week that if you guys stay together you're going to be a top four team. It's that obvious and he can't believe there's a possibility it's all going to be torn down."

In the meantime, as one of the few coaches who use social media, Sampson is aware that sections of the club have had to endure a bucketing in the court of public opinion. "There's certainly a lot of fingers being pointed at our directors for us being in the situation we're in, and also a view that because we've never won anything, we won't be any loss. Let's just say,

I'm easily able to separate those things. I access the media because I'm interested in reading articles about rugby - I like to soak up what I can. I learned in Perth never to engage in comments, and so that kind of stuff, it's water off a duck's back because I know people don't have the full story. A lot of it might be unpleasant but it's not a distraction for me. As Wayne Bennett once said, "If you listen to the people in the stands, you end up in the stands."

With a team walk about to begin, Sampson finishes by going back to what he sees as the overriding theme of the year. "We talk a lot about maintaining belief. In the future of the club, and in what we're doing as a group. We've become acutely aware around identifying and picking up on any player or staff member who might be a bit off, and getting them to have a quick chat to Andrew, or else we might have a quiet word ourselves over a coffee, or maybe post-training, out on the grass. It's a very tight-knit and aligned group. Not in the sense of 'backs against the wall' or pinning needles into voodoo dolls of Rugby Australia, because it's much more professional and positive than that. It's more that I'm thinking, every time I drive in, 'we've got to get these guys up today and how am I going to do that?' There's so much that goes into keeping things ticking over in a normal year, let alone a year like this one, and I'm not even sure a lot of the players really understand all that goes on behind the scenes."

It's a stretch to say that the sun has broken through, although it's turned out nicely enough for the team to amble for a few blocks near the team hotel, which is located on the edge of the Canberra CBD. As the players assemble in the lobby, Sampson's observation about them not fully understanding what the coaches do rings true in another, generational sense. Everyone older than thirty-five has a warm top or jacket on. The vast majority of players are dressed in a t-shirt and shorts. Did manager Will Nicholson send out the wrong schedule? Do the players think they are in Fiji already?

Chapter Forty-Seven

24th May, 2024

Like a party of Franciscans en route to a monk convention, the bus ride from the team hotel to Canberra's GIO Stadium is conducted in complete silence. It's not a result of physical barriers - only a small number of players sport personal headphones - but more a combination of Kevin Foote's final address filling their consciousness, and the overriding sense that the fifteen-minute trip, shrouded in darkness, is a perfect opportunity to contemplate what lies ahead; an opportunity to make amends against Australia's consistently best-performed franchise. On the final approach to the stadium entrance, the bus driver expertly navigates a long row of cones that to the layman's eye, seem to be set impossibly narrow. A single sneeze from somewhere near the back of the bus cuts through the silence. But that's the extent of it. Not a single word is muttered from anybody to anybody else; coach, player or staff.

As far as lion's dens go, this is an unloved stadium. That's because it's notoriously hard for visiting teams to win there (already the Crusaders and Hurricanes have failed this year), and because even the locals seem to despise it. As Canberra-based rugby columnist, 8/9 Combo podcast host and ABC sideline comments man Brett McKay, says; "It's a funny old stadium in every sense. It's exposed to the elements, and while it's only ten minutes from the CBD and is fairly central, it's not really near anything, and it's never been easier for rugby fans, especially on a cold winter's night, to find reasons not to go. We keep being told the stadium is too old and needs to be replaced, but nobody is any the wiser when this might happen, where it will be located, and what it is that will be built. So, in the meantime, apathy is the order of the day. Local people who in the same breath will cry poor that Rugby Australia don't do enough in the ACT despite the Brumbies' history of success, and then criticise the lack of crowd and atmosphere at games. All the while making the flimsiest of excuses not to go themselves."

The players dress quickly and efficiently; the icy bite to the air serves as a deterrent against lingering. Far better to be out on the field where, even with the air temperature well down into single figures and dropping, they have the ability to warm themselves up as a counter.

There is a polite knock on the door and the match officials crowd into a small, secondary room into which the forward pack is summonsed. Referee Angus Gardner begins, as is his custom, by inviting any questions or concerns from the players. As usual, nothing is raised, leaving Gardner to ponder later, over a glass of Cabernet Sauvignon in a quiet corner of the hotel, why, when offered the chance to speak before the game, players are invariably mute, but as soon as he blows his whistle to start the match, they all want to tell him what to do.

Once the main briefing is complete, Taniela Tupou takes Gardner aside and asks for clarification around a binding concern. "Stay square, keep the arm up on the bind, and that's a great picture for me," says Gardner. It works; after he is introduced to the game in the second half, Tupou follows instructions to the letter and is rewarded with a string of penalties.

Unfortunately for the Rebels, it's a small victory on a night of few wins. Already fragile at 13-3 down, with the team on a general warning, Darby Lancaster isn't able to plant his legs sufficiently strongly at an attempted breakdown steal, and is easily pushed off his feet from behind, by his own player, falling into the Brumbies' ruck. In the ten minutes he is in the sin bin leading into half-time, the side concedes 21 points; a repeat of what happened two weeks ago when Lachie Anderson was sat down for ten in Brisbane.

"We're like any side," says Foote after the match, trying to process the heavy 53-17 loss. "We train for those 14-man scenarios. But no matter, when it's Corey Toole's man that we lose, the Brumbies are going to exploit that space, and they did it well. Do we have a specific problem there? Is it easier if the player we lose is a forward instead of a winger? We'll need to have a closer look. Maybe. But then again, imagine going down to seven forwards against the Blues. They're just going to come at you even harder through the middle. I wouldn't say losing a player in any one position is better or worse than losing another."

After the match is over, the players filter into the changing room at intervals to sit and reflect. It's as quiet as it was on the bus trip, only this time the charge of anticipation is replaced by the pall of defeat. The coaches react differently, each of them true to their character and the manner in which they deal with all defeats. Foote is the most active, pacing back and forth, processing his frustration, using the benefit of hindsight to bemoan mistakes made on the field, in the box and at the selection table; filing those things away in his mind so that they are better dealt with next time. Brad Harris is phlegmatic; bitterly disappointed, but already knowing where and how things can be improved. Tim Sampson and Geoff Parling sit in the small room adjacent, out of earshot from the players, sharing snippets of conversation; unintelligible to others but, judging by the tone and the body language, just as well. Of the four, Sampson is the most overtly disappointed - it won't be until after the team has landed tomorrow in Melbourne and he is on his way home, that he will start to return to his 'normal' state. For Parling, the overarching emotion is anger. Because his forwards were prepared for the Brumbies to attack their line out, yet when the heat came, their resistance was low and brittle.

Eventually, with most of the players showered, Foote calls the team together. He acknowledges the loss and the abject disappointment, but doesn't want to dwell on it now; the review will tell everyone what they need to know and then the focus will shift to Fiji. With sore bodies all around the room, he announces that the training load will be wound back this week. No Sunday session, a tactical emphasis on Monday, Tuesday off, one solid run on Wednesday, before travel on Thursday. The immediate focus will be on recovery, then nutrition and hydration leading into the match in Lautoka. Heads nod around the room; everyone who played in Fiji last year doesn't need reminding of how cooked they were, physically and mentally, not even ten minutes into the match.

Selection is addressed, briefly. There's been talk around the office about the possibility of, once a finals spot has been confirmed, leaving some players at home, so that they can be better prepared for their quarter-final. "We're going to leave all that aside for now," says Foote. "Park it until we get through tomorrow's matches, look at the ladder and figure out where we are and what all of the options are."

Brad Wilkin, last year's captain after Rob Leota missed almost all of the season recovering from an Achilles injury, steps forward. "I can't stress enough how important it is we focus on our recovery," he implores. "We've worked so hard to get to this position, to make our first final... we can't afford to blow it by not giving 100% to our recovery tonight, to our preparation next week. No pissing up, no kava, no casino (the team hotel is attached to the Canberra Casino). It's not too much to ask." There are no team rules when it comes to alcohol consumption during the season. No curfews. The vast majority of players are mature professionals, working hard enough for starting positions they don't want to jeopardise by either impairing their recovery and performance, or potentially being involved in any incident that might bring themselves or the club into disrepute. Just turn up on time, every time, in perfect order to give your best; that's the way to show love for the club and for each other, that's the club's mantra. Wilkin's words hit the spot. Players can be easily tempted by friends and family wishing to catch up and party after long absences. Nobody needs reminding of the aftermath of the Rebels' trip to Dunedin in 2018 where, after a post-match drinking session, Lopeti Timani ended up in the boot of a car, then dumped, having been the subject of a serious physical assault by teammate (and childhood friend) Amanaki Mafi. Tonight is not the night for car boots or hi-jinks of any sort.

One more item of business remains. A guest in the changing room is Jason Callan, father of Luke, who has travelled from Perth to see his son debut in Super Rugby (older brother Ollie is player #197 for the Western Force). Parling does the honours, speaking to Callan's progress and unbending work ethic, before presenting him with his cap. Callan is Rebel #208.

Waiting back at the hotel, in the team room, there are bain-maries filled with lukewarm hamburger patties, strips of chicken breast and sweet potato fries, stationed alongside salad bowls, a selection of condiments, and a tempting display of shot-glass-sized, mini chocolate mousse. Around half of the players partake, quietly grazing, pecking as much as eating, while the travelling staff, gradually peeling off the layers of clothing that cocooned them from the Canberra chill, tentatively strike up conversation as they too refuel. It's been a crushingly disappointing day, a sharp reminder that at this level, progress is never linear.

Chapter Forty-Eight

28th May, 2024

In an article in *The Age* last week, on Tuesday 21st May, Rebels consortium figurehead Leigh Clifford, was quoted as saying; "I asked (Rugby Australia chief executive) Phil Waugh at a meeting, 'If we come up with a viable proposal for the Rebels in 2025, will you support it?' And I'd have to say that he looked around a bit, but he agreed, yes, he would. Now we want to see that case brought forward."

The article further refers to a Rugby Australia spokesperson saying that the governing body had previously outlined to the consortium that it was open to engaging on any plan it put forward. "Any hold-up is down to the lack of any details being provided around their plan, which have not been forthcoming."

On what will prove to be a landmark Monday, any hopes that the consortium might have had of those comments representing a softening in Rugby Australia's language have been rudely put to bed. Using the document sharing platform 'Data Room', the detailed consortium proposal was made available for Rugby Australia to digest over the weekend, with a view to the two parties meeting to discuss the next steps. It was the hope of the consortium that its plan, which includes the relocation of the club to Tarneit, a fast-growing development area on Melbourne's western fringe, would be compelling enough for Rugby Australia, if genuine about taking rugby forward in Victoria, to accept.

Early signs aren't promising. Able to track engagement via the software, the Rebels are aware that some people on the distribution list, including Rugby Australia board members, do not even open the proposal.

Two meetings eventuate; the first, a kind of stand-off between lawyers, circling around the merits of their respective cases, probing for holes in the other, painting a picture of the pain that lies in store should matter proceed to court. Little of substance eventuates, leading the consortium, via its advisor Korda Mentha, to fire off a letter informing Rugby Australia that they don't believe they are being taken seriously, asking Rugby Australia to indicate if they are willing to attend a formal mediation in good faith, or if that is not forthcoming, advising of their intent to proceed with legal action.

A second meeting follows. At 7pm Georgia Widdup and representatives from Korda Mentha meet via zoom with members of the Rugby Australia executive plus board member Mathew Hanning. Here it is ascertained that the Rugby Australia board had in fact met the previous day, on Monday, to discuss the Rebels' situation, seeking to make a final determination. Now, what Widdup believed was an opportunity to put a human element to the consortium case looks to her like a box-ticking exercise. The equivalent of 'junk time'; playing out the clock with the result already known.

The meeting descends into chaos; Widdup, a lawyer, mother and a person widely considered sensible and engaging, being persistently interrupted and belittled. That it is clear that Rugby Australia is not invested in the consortium proposal is one thing. But for a Rugby Australia board member to attack her in such a vitriolic manner completely catches Widdup off guard. After two hours, the meeting breaks up; the consortium knows their proposal is going nowhere, and the end of the road - the non-litigious path at least - is nigh.

By morning, a still-shaken Widdup has a second letter on its way; this one to Rugby Australia chairman Daniel Herbert, lodging a formal complaint against Hanning for his behaviour towards her, citing a breach of clause 4.1 of Rugby Australia's code of conduct.

At Rebels HQ, a quiet morning unfolds. True to his word, Foote has eased back, with players and coaches on a designated day off. Tomorrow will see a full training session, Thursday is a travel day, before a 'captains run' in Lautoka on Friday will see them ready to go for Saturday afternoon's match against the Drua.

Not everyone fully grasps the meaning of 'day off'. Tim Sampson beavers away at his work station; on such days he will typically work the morning, have a quick lunch with staff then attend to personal chores in the afternoon. Players too, drift in and out; some for a rub down or a light gym session, others simply because this is the place they are connected to, and where they know they'll find a coffee partner.

For the players in the grafter's group and/or not in the travelling squad for Fiji, it's business as usual. Lukhan Salakaia-Loto and Leafi Talataina hop off exercise bikes, dripping with sweat. Jack Maunder pushes himself through a series of strength exercises, as does Matt Proctor. Lachie Anderson puts in too, all without dislodging a strand of his immaculately tended hair. Nick Jooste works around a banged-up shoulder. Judah Suamaisue prowls menacingly, looking like he could lift a horse then eat it in a single sitting. Alex Mafi proceeds at a more leisurely pace, but the work ethic is plain to see. The medical and strength and conditioning staff are spread amongst the players. Nobody has clocked off.

Having vowed to spend more days at home on his days off, Kevin Foote is only partially compliant. This morning he meets with Luke Vella, to nail down particulars for Fiji. It's essential because playing in the islands brings such a specific set of challenges. Get something wrong and not only will this match be compromised, so will the following week; their first ever finals match.

They start by listing the players who will be released for club rugby on the weekend. The challenge for Foote and Vella is to balance the risk of impacting numbers for training next week, against the need to give these guys rugby. Their default is to the latter.

Foote has received another request from the Waratahs to 'loan' Pone Fa'amausili for their final round match against the Reds. His inclination is to help out but there's something nagging at him; "It's their last match, DC's (Darren Coleman) final game as coach… you can imagine how hard they're going to be hitting it afterwards. Pone doesn't need that, we don't need that," he says, before advising them 'no'.

Vella updates Foote on the status of the injured players. Anderson ran well yesterday and will be good to go for next week. Jooste had cortisone to his shoulder and will be okay for full training by next mid-next week. Vaiolini Ekuasi is still bothered by a hip pointer and has fluid presence around the injury. He's a hard one to monitor and is a 'maybe' for next week at this stage. It's similar for Mafi; Vella unsure whether the player has the confidence and mental belief that he is over his muscle injury.

He then runs Foote through the key messages around preparation. "We've got hydration prep in place, beginning 48 hours before, including on the plane and in transit. Carbo intake and fuelling is just as important as fluid intake. That includes electrolyte shots and gels, we've already trialled usage yesterday, halfway through the session, just to get the guys used to it, and make sure they don't react physically with upset stomachs or the like," he explains.

Although the forecast temperature isn't too bad - high twenties with 85% humidity - there were hard lessons learned last year, with every player, to a man, stating it was the hardest match they've ever played in; the penal conditions leaving them disoriented right from the start of the match. "We'll make sure the changing room is set up properly," says Vella. "We've ordered plenty of ice towels. Do your address at the hotel, the changing room is small and hot. Warm-up time is usually 38 minutes. The players will already be warm, so let's look at taking a minute off each piece."

Foote nods. "Let me check with the other coaches."

"We'll weigh everyone pre-breakfast on Saturday, post-match, then again pre-breakfast on Sunday. I expect some of the guys to lose 5% of their bodyweight, but more than that starts to become high risk. The objective is to have everyone back at their normal bodyweight by the time we leave the hotel the next day," Vella concludes.

Foote gets Vella's assent on another potential issue. "With the quarter-final to come, this has to be a 'no alcohol' situation. No kava. Just one beer in the changing room to acknowledge the debutant. That's all. I know it will be tough for Angelo, Maciu and Filipo, they'll be under family pressure. But we can't mess things up for next week."

Vella is in furious agreement. They will get the team back to the hotel and into the pool, before gathering to watch the late game.

"I'll talk to Robbie, Sam and Brad," says Foote. "That's our connection. They'll be on board. These messages need to be driven by the leadership group."

Chapter Forty-Nine

30th May, 2024

At 7.15am Nick Stiles receives an email from Kat Rottier. It's short and to the point. "What do you think? This can't be good."

Stiles has yet to open the message she's referring to; a notification from Phil Waugh requesting attendance at a meeting of staff and players at the club at 10.00am. He quickly brings himself up to speed.

She's right. Given what has played out during the week with the consortium, there is no way Waugh is dropping in for a routine update. It ties with the phone calls he received around dinner time last night from multiple journalists, indicating that there was movement within Rugby Australia's ranks, and that there would be an announcement made today.

The travelling group for Fiji are due at international check-in at 11.45am. Stiles knows there'll be messages flooding in soon from confused players. 'What is going on?' 'Are we going to Fiji or not?' It's unheard of to interrupt the player's schedule in such a way. But there's literally no time to launch into any meaningful damage control. And really, no point. (As it turns out, not all of the players are immediately aware; captain Rob Leota and Jordan Uelese don't check their phones until after it is too late for them to travel all the way in from their homes in the northern suburbs).

The office fills quickly, but this is clearly no ordinary work day. There are attempts at black humour ("wasn't expecting to see you in here this morning", and "we're going to be told how this is the beginning of an exciting new future for Australian rugby"), mixed with anger and frustration ("I wish these pricks would just leave us alone", and "every opportunity they've had to fuck with our match preparation this year, they've taken"). There's an overarching sense of sadness, although emotions are held in check. Mostly, there is understanding and resignation that this is the end of the line. For the Melbourne Rebels and for their own jobs.

At 10am staff and players shuffle into the gymnasium. Phil Waugh, Daniel Herbert and Head of People and Culture, Rachel Buckling, push their way forward, and with little fanfare, Waugh gets down to business.

Well, kind of. There is a lengthy pre-amble, akin to a parent knowing they are about to punish a child, too timid or too focused on assuaging their own guilt, to just come out and do it. Or a teacher about to deliver half-a-dozen cuts of the cane, insisting "this is going to hurt me more than it hurts you."

Eventually, after three minutes of torture, it is Herbert who finally gets to the point. "The Rebels consortium won't be offered a licence for 2025, and this means that we can't move forward with a Rebels team in 2025."

There is slightly better news for the women; "There is no decision on Super W yet". And why would there be? If the driver at the heart of all of this is money - the lack of it - the Super W team costs very little to operate.

Waugh talks about how important Victoria is and says that Rugby Australia will continue to invest in the community game. Even if that's well meaning, it feels like it's aimed at the wrong audience.

There is just one question from the floor. Rottier, whose stocks have risen as an aware, sensible, trusted voice over the season, asks for a clarification on behalf of injured and un-contracted players. There are of course other many questions - with and without added commentary - but this is neither the time or place. Waugh and Herbert have made it clear what the outcome is. Fair or unfair, justified or unjustified, they haven't come here to be persuaded or turned.

In just twelve minutes, it is all over. The players gather immediately in their dressing room, where there is brief consideration given to not boarding the plane to Fiji. It's very brief. What would that achieve? It's not going to change the outcome for next year, and they are still in this years' competition. The mood is awfully flat but there is nothing else to be done but to man up and get to the airport. Nevertheless, manager Will Nicholson takes extra care to make sure that all players are accounted for, including those who haven't made it in for the meeting.

As ever, the coaches are torn between expressing their personal emotions and the need to demonstrate leadership. Hurt and disappointment are etched on Kevin Foote's face, but behind that facade, he is already working out what he will say and do with the players so that they will have the best possible chance of success against the Drua.

Herbert and Waugh retire to the vacant office of ex-CEO Stephenson. Due at a press conference at their CBD hotel at midday, they have time to kill. Buckling waits alone outside the gym. In a repeat of the day the redundancies were announced, Buckling is gone within no time, not having done the rounds of the office workstations, not having had a single one on one meeting with a staff member to offer counselling or employment transition assistance.

"Yes, there was an offer made in the meeting," says one dismissive staff member. "But if they were serious, she'd park herself in Bado's office for the rest of today and tomorrow, and not leave until everyone's had the chance to talk things through. The only reason she's here is to tick the HR box, not because they actually care about staff, or even know who any of us are."

At the press conference that follows, Waugh and Herbert make it clear that Rugby Australia has incurred considerable financial pain in keeping the Rebels going in 2024. Waugh explains; "We stood up the Rebels for 2024. We employed 83% of the Rebels management staff. The relationship we have with the Players Association through the collective bargaining agreement ensured that the players were protected. So Rugby Australia has stood up the Melbourne Rebels in 2024."

They then go onto the offensive, targeting the Rebels' directors. "I think they've let rugby stakeholders in Victoria down and stakeholders broadly," says Herbert. "We also have claims against those directors, those former directors, if they want to continue to go down that [path]. Then there's only so many times you can continue to be threatened without pushing back." Asked what those claims were against the directors, Herbert states, "That they continued to take money whilst they were allegedly trading insolvent."

Questioning shifts to the 2027 World Cup; "Will the semi-finals and the final be in Melbourne? Is that still a deal that's on the table?" asks a reporter.

"Yeah, so as I said, we're very committed to working with Visit Victoria, the Victorian Government. International Rugby has been very, very successful in Victoria for a long, long time. And we're confident it will continue to be that way." Waugh's response is measured, but it is clear that this is a key pain point; an explanation for the heightened animosity shown by Rugby Australia towards the ex-directors. There are tens of millions of dollars at stake, with Visit Victoria, having already contributed $31m to a state rugby centre of excellence adjacent to Latrobe University's Bundoora campus, and the $16.5m package in 2017 which included Bledisloe Cup hosting rights in 2022 and 2023, tipped to bid well above New South Wales and Western Australia for hosting rights for the World Cup final. If the Victorian government withdraws from contention, or lowballs their offer, the loss of that revenue would potentially dwarf any cost saving from axing the Rebels.

Victorian state governments are notoriously parochial and suspicious when it comes to decisions made out of Sydney or Canberra. The ex-directors and the consortium considered their personal relationships with key government figures, and the government's alignment with sporting outcomes that benefit Victoria and Victorians, to be important leverage in their discussions with Rugby Australia. Rugby Australia's view appears to be that this relationship is being used as a 'blackmail' tactic against them, and there is anger that the MRRU directors have, for their own purposes, actively undermined Rugby Australia in their dealings with the government.

When it comes to the consortium and their plans, Rugby Australia's official statement reads; "The application relied upon projections for revenue growth and cost savings that RA believes are overly optimistic, raising significant doubts about the long-term sustainability of the proposed licensee."

With the consortium reluctant to be fully transparent about the make-up of the group unless Rugby Australia signs a confidentiality agreement, Waugh and Herbert are dismissive. "The information at best, what I could say, was embryonic and very underdeveloped," says Waugh.

Attention switches to the timing of the announcement, just prior to the team boarding a plane to Fiji; one reporter describing it as "brutal".

Again, Waugh is unrepentant, even going so far as to suggest that the timing is positive. "We always said that once we have the information on hand we will make a decision and an educated decision as quickly as we possibly could. We've done that. And I think it's a good time in terms of the performance of the Rebels going into a tough game in Fiji."

Herbert justifies the timing around need to get the decision to staff and players before it leaked. That reporters knew last night that the he and Waugh were flying to Melbourne to make the announcement supports this view; albeit it seems to contradict Herbert's denials from earlier in the year that information about the Rebels' situation was being leaked to media from within Rugby Australia.

"The government doesn't need us to undermine Rugby Australia," one of the Rebels' directors says, later that afternoon. "How can they possibly expect to chop us off at the knees, chop rugby off in the state, and still expect the state government to be handing millions of dollars over to them as if nothing's happened?"

Victorian State Government Minister for Tourism, Sport and Major Events, Steve Dimopolous, duly releases a statement which sides with the ex-directors.

"The Victorian Government is extremely disappointed that Rugby Australia has decided not to support the Melbourne Rebels following the team's 2024 season, after we made it clear that we expected them to commit to a team at the elite level of the sport in Victoria. We have been extremely clear that having a Victorian-based Super Rugby team would be the reason we can continue hosting large rugby events on our major events calendar - including the Bledisloe Cup and any future Rugby World Cups. That social licence has been diminished today."

Ex-chairman Paul Docherty is dismissive of the narrative pushed at the press conference. "The notion that Rugby Australia has been agonising over a decision and it's just been made is nonsense," he says. "They threw us over the side: their advisors were telling them, 'it will end in liquidation', but when it didn't and we got the DOCA up, they voted against it, again, still trying to tip us into liquidation. And then, when the consortium was pulled together, they sent a list of 40-odd criteria that had to be met, to be eligible for a licence. And we met all of them. And most of the board didn't even read it. And now they're saying it's because we didn't disclose the names of the backers in the consortium. When some of those investors wish to stay out of the limelight and RA is leaking like a sieve? They would have had every aspect of their private and business affairs raked over in the media, just like I did. For what reason? Because they're prepared to invest their money into growing and supporting rugby? And we wonder why the game is struggling?"

"There's been mistakes made at the Rebels," Docherty continues. "Different regimes, too much change, too slow to recognise that the path forward was through closely engaging the rugby community, as opposed to leading with a corporate Melbourne profile. And that's not easy to rectify because there's always conflict around specific approaches and ideas, and it's very hard to balance things around inclusion versus not getting enough action. But in 2017, when it was basically 'start again', we settled on three objectives. Grow the game; produce Wallabies and Wallaroos; and build strength in the community. And that takes time, and there was COVID in the middle of that too. But by any measure against those metrics, you would have to say we were on the right path."

"If I was afforded the luxury of a hindsight lens - given this outcome - the thing I would have done differently is to invest more time and effort into constitutional and governance change at Rugby Australia. The AFL changed their governance structure in the 1980's. The NRL changed theirs in the early 2000's. And look at how they moved forward in leaps and bounds. And so here we are again, the game being run from Sydney and Brisbane, for New South Wales and Queensland. And getting left further behind," Docherty concludes.

By the time Waugh and Herbert are finished their presser, the office has thinned out. The grafters and non-travelling players have completed their work for the day, and nobody without a compelling reason to stay feels like hanging around. A small group wanders off towards Swan Street, Richmond in search of a consoling beer, but without the conviction to hold a proper wake. Perhaps they'll feel more up to giving it a nudge tomorrow.

Chapter Fifty

3rd June, 2024

Burning through the grey Monday morning, a super-sized digital screen outside the front of AAMI Stadium defiantly projects an image of Carter Gordon. Underneath, in bold red, pink and blue, the message reads; *"ALWAYS FIGHTING, ALWAYS REBELS, WATCH US RISE."*

Does the stadium operator know something the rest of Melbourne doesn't? Has there been a change of heart from Rugby Australia?

Alas for Rebels' fans, it's nothing more than an example of a divorcing couple, upon one party throwing the other out of the house, not yet getting around to changing the locks. Another thing to add to Rugby Australia's 'to do' list.

Inside, given the rawness of Thursday's announcement, and the disappointment of the 40-19 loss to the Drua on Saturday, the mood is remarkably upbeat and business-like. Somebody rolls a clip of the Drua's first try, featuring a pass thrown by a player falling to the ground, a metre forward, and then a huge, obvious knock on. Obvious to everyone it seems except referee Paul Williams and his assistant Dan Waenga who, despite standing within touching distance, inexplicably, can be seen looking down at the ground and not at the play.

"Have you received your apology from the refs?" Foote is asked.

"No, not yet," he laughs.

It's not the time for feeling sorry about one's lot. For the first time in their history, the Rebels are playing in a Super Rugby finals match, and nobody is letting forward passes, knock-ons and a minor technicality like the forced closure of the club, get in the way of that.

To mark the occasion, Mark Fraser has provided printed t-shirts for every player and high-performance team member. 'FFF' is emblazoned across the front. *Fast, Fearless, Finals.*

The leadership group meets with Kevin Foote to complete breaking down the loss, and to align on the week ahead.

Leading 19-5 approaching half-time, and with the scrum dominating, the Rebels were well placed to surprise the rest of the competition, and seal 6th place on the ladder. Even 19-12 at the break felt reasonably comfortable. But when the second half kick-off was tapped backwards, only to be collected by a Drua player for a try to be conceded, which was then quickly followed by two more, the score had suddenly become 19-33, and with the raucous home crowd riding the Drua into the finals themselves, the game was as good as lost; 40-19 the final score.

The leaders are disappointed at the outcome, but not with the effort. And there is firepower to add back in this week; Gordon, Lachie Anderson, Vaiolini Ekuasi, Alex Mafi and Nick Jooste. Lukhan Salakai-Loto apologises for not having recovered in time; "I did my best, but it's too soon. You boys make it all the way to the final and I'll be ready for that," he says, more serious than joking.

Foote notes that he hasn't yet had an opportunity to speak personally to the boys who played on Saturday who won't be named for this week. One of those is the debutant, David Vaihu who, when he took the field in the second half, became Rebel #209. Remember that name for future rugby trivia events; David Vaihu, the last player to be capped for the Rebels.

The group checks in regarding an issue that arose coming out of the Drua match, with respect to this week's schedule. Foote's proposal to stay in Melbourne to train on Thursday, and travel Friday wasn't, at least initially, well received. A zoom meeting was hastily arranged for Sunday to lay down all of the arguments for and against, and after what Sam Talakai describes as "robust discussions", Foote's reasoning was understood and agreed to. Foote takes an extra minute to ensure that everybody is still on board, with Brad Wilkin asking for clarification that the captain's run after arrival in Wellington, will be little more than a familiarisation walk-through. Talakai puts his hand up to ensure the final decision is reinforced with the team, before everyone moves on.

Since arriving at the club in 2023, Talakai has impressed everybody. Unfailingly friendly and polite, full of common sense and rugby IQ, he carries a healthy ability to laugh at himself and with others, mixed with a strong aura of gravitas. Whenever he talks, people listen. Always one of the first to include his family in activities around the club, or spend time with his partner and daughter outside on the playing field, Talakai's move to Melbourne was seen as long-term.

"Sam's a Wallaby, he was an important part of us building front-row depth, what we identified as an essential pillar, and obviously he's just a terrific leader to have around the club," says Nick Stiles. "But it's more than that. There's no doubt that after retirement, Sam would have stayed on at the club, in a coaching and mentoring role. The growing Pacific Island player base is critical, and I couldn't think of anybody better to be at the heart of mentoring those young boys as they enter a professional environment for the first time. And with no ceiling; he's clearly a potential future head coach of the club. Now, he and his family have got decisions to make about where to go and what to do. And it's another example of how rugby here in Victoria is potentially exposed. When the league scouts come knocking, as they are already, imagine how much easier it is to counter that, and keep those kids in the rugby pathway, if you have someone of Sam's calibre alongside those young players."

Out on Gosch's paddock, it's not just the Rebels in training. AAMI Stadium is infamous for a large flock of seagulls that invariably descend on the pitch during the second half of night matches and, at first glance, it looks as if they have taken over the adjacent Melbourne Victory training pitch. On closer inspection, it's not the resident seagulls at all, but a large gathering of pigeons. On the command of their leader, or triggered by dog walkers cutting through the park come near to them, the pigeons conduct a series of fly throughs; back and forth, up and down the length of the pitch. Warming up for a day of flying and foraging, their form and co-ordination mirrors the Rebels squad, gently easing into their warm-up reps, up and back on the adjacent pitch.

As agreed, the session is of low intensity, much of it conducted barely above walk-through pace, the match-day 23 stepping through various attacking structures, and a range of match and field position scenarios. It's just what the doctor ordered; by the time the players shower, don their new FFF shirts and grab a lunch roll, energy levels are high and the mood is buoyant.

Foote too has a wry smile on his face. "I just received the apology message from the referees about the Drua game," he says. "They're sorry." He shrugs his shoulders, knowing he'd be angry if he heard nothing but at the same time, realising the pointlessness of it all. "That's it. Just, sorry."

Chapter Fifty-One

6th June, 2024

One by one, players take their turn at the mobile coffee truck stationed alongside the Gosch's Paddock training field. It's 8.30am, pleasingly mild for a June morning, and the mood amongst players and staff is happy and expectant. The Rebels have never played in a final so nobody is quite sure whether the done thing is to embrace the excitement or keep things on an even keel and treat it like a normal week. They end up doing both.

"Of course it's a special week," says Foote. "This is what we've been working for, so it's important we acknowledge that. Both as an achievement and as a challenge. But in a positive way. So we've done a few little things differently this week. Just to make it a little bit more special for the players."

One of those differences is the 9am team meeting, fronted this morning by Christian Welch and Cam Munster, two celebrated Melbourne Storm and Queensland State of Origin rugby league players. They are well aware of the Rebels' underdog status heading into the Hurricanes match and are eager to share their experience.

"In 2020 we were called the worst Queensland Origin team in 40 years, splashed all over the Daily Telegraph by Dean Ritchie, then Paul Gallen called us the worst Queensland team ever," says Welch. Running on the large screen behind him are highlights from the deciding match of that year, won by Queensland, 20-14.

Munster taps into the similarities between what their Queensland team faced and what awaits the Rebels. "New Zealand rugby sides are a lot like New South Wales rugby league. They have this born to rule mentality that automatically, by right of birth, they're better. But we know that's not true; physically we're the same. Then it all becomes about mateship and connection underpinning your motivation."

Welch implores the players; "Find your purpose. Be excited about the opportunity. These big games are decided by hunger and effort. I've been here for twelve years, I've seen a lot of Rebels sides. This is the best group I've seen in my time. Believe in yourselves."

It's a brilliant precursor to the day's business; the coaches reinforcing objectives around the game plan, and taking all of that out onto the pitch in the final full training session before Saturday's match.

It's no ordinary training run. Nick Stiles and Emily Riseley have invited sponsors, board members and a number of the club's committed fan base along to connect for what may be the final time, and the coffee truck struggles to keep up with demand. Again, the mood is celebratory rather than maudlin. Perhaps it's the presence of the board members and positive whispers around the consortium and their pending legal action, or maybe it's the lead sports story in today's *The Australian*, that is behind the positivity. Despite Rugby Australia's action, despite players very soon to be dispersed to all corners of the globe, rather than this being the final chapter, there is a perverse sense that the fight isn't actually over.

The column in *The Australian* is penned by Rod Macqueen, Australia's most celebrated coach of the professional era, and inaugural coach of the Rebels in 2011. Macqueen begins by asking; "is this decision (to terminate the Rebels) truly in the long-term business interest of Rugby Australia?"

He goes on to list multiple reasons why not, pointing to the successful expansion strategies adopted by the AFL and the NRL, whilst detailing hurdles placed in front of the Rebels, including the ludicrous situation where Rugby Australia restricted the Rebels from signing players under contract until negotiations with their existing club were completed.

Macqueen also lists some of the Victorian rugby's achievements, such as 17 Wallabies developed in Melbourne, and 25 Australia under 20 representatives, before asking; "Should the focus be on short-term fixes or long-term strategies?"

Going into bat for the consortium, Macqueen suggests that there still might be room for negotiation with Rugby Australia, that would "allow the game to build on the initiatives the Victorian rugby community has introduced such as the Weary Dunlop Club, the Rugby Academy and the Pacific Island engagement strategy." Acknowledging Rugby Australia's financial struggles, he concludes that "smarter strategies could help achieve its goals", and "Australian Rugby needs forward thinking to navigate these challenging times. It's a moment for positive, innovative solutions to secure a bright future for the sport."

One of the ex-directors present is Georgia Widdup; reeling not just from the verbal assault on her at last weeks' meeting, but from chairman Daniel Herbert's response to her going public with those claims, on Friday effectively doubling down on RA's hard-line approach.

In rejecting Widdup's account of the meeting, Herbert argued that while representatives of Rugby Australia may have posed some tough and uncomfortable questions, no-one had acted improperly. He then went on to say; "Your actions, including threats of legal action and public disparagement, are prejudicial to the interests of Rugby Australia and the game as a whole. While we understand your desire to protect your family's personal interests, it is important to recognise that such conduct undermines Rugby Australia's core value of integrity and brings the sport into disrepute. No reasonable national sporting organisation or sport governing body would award a licence to individuals who engage in such behaviour."

Fellow Rebels ex-director Gary Gray, still can't figure out how things have got to this, and why Rugby Australia has chosen to let the matter proceed to court. "We were literally one more decent meeting away from locking everything in for this year and next, with a view to re-setting after the Lions tour," he says. "Everything that we'd been working on and discussing with RA over a period of time. And now, look at where we are. One of their directors behaves abominably towards Georgia, and the chairman, instead of apologising or admonishing him, swings in behind, going just as hard. For the life of me, I really don't know where all this antagonism and bad blood came from."

Nearing the end of the run, a chant breaks out on the sideline. "Re-bels, Re-bels, Re-bels." The players stop and take it all in. They know there will be little love for them at Westpac Stadium on Saturday, but there is an abundance of it out here. Nobody is denying the underlying sadness. But in this moment, there is a collective strength enveloping the players, staff and supporters, drawn from celebrating this achievement, as well as what it means to be a Rebel.

If it wasn't already, Foote's decision to hold the team in Melbourne for an extra day is vindicated. Important players like Brad Wilkin and Andrew Kellaway didn't train on Tuesday and would have gone into Saturday underdone without this full session. Luke Vella is delighted with what has transpired. "Honestly, I was worried about how things would go this week, coming back from Fiji, then having to prepare for New Zealand. At best I might have hoped for one half-decent training run, with that compromised by having to nurse some players through. But the players have been fully professional, we got some rest into them, and now a full run today which has gone really well. Obviously, we have a huge task ahead, but in terms of prep for this time of year, I couldn't be happier."

The other vindication is the realisation of the players, as they mingle with those present, what this opportunity means to those people; not only in terms of drawing a line under their long-term relationship with the Rebels, but to be able to be there to see the team prepare, and to personally wish them well for the quarter-final.

A couple who have travelled down from Ballarat introduce themselves to Foote. He doesn't recognise them but they are part of an iconic photograph which is now a large print that fully consumes a wall inside the office. It's an image of the crowd on opening night in 2011, in full voice, cheering on their new side as they run on to AAMI Stadium for the first time. Both are in shot; she holding up a sign 'Go Rebels', but they are not together. It was as members of a Rebels supporter group that they met, bonded and later married. With them is their young son, William, who is as delighted to meet the coach as Foote is to meet him.

"We were here at the start," they tell Foote. "If this is to be the end, we're here for that as well."

It's taken a couple of days but a line from a Rugby Australia press release has found its way into the hitting zone of New Zealand radio. Gallagher, a global insurance risk management and consulting firm, has taken up a sponsorship deal as an 'official partner of the Wallabies, Wallaroos, Super Rugby W, under 16's and under 19's programs, and any future rugby competition'. "*Any future rugby competition?* What's this all about?" host of *The Platform*, Martin Devlin asks.

That last line also catches the attention of Sydney journalist Jamie Pandaram, who writes in *The Code*; "Rugby Australia chief executive Phil Waugh revealed his organisation has already had to plan for life without Super Rugby if certain financial metrics continue on a downward spiral, however is confident the challenges can be overcome."

"One of our jobs here is to ensure we've got a financially sustainable model," Waugh told Code Sport. "We're very committed to Super Rugby and we're committed to the joint venture agreement we have with NZR through until the end of 2030."

"We are also very conscious that the economics of the game need to change and we need to scenario-plan for whatever the future may hold when we go into the next broadcast cycle which starts in 2026."

Many fans have been clamouring for a replacement to the ill-fated NRC, a national domestic competition which ran from 2014 to 2019, and was a transition competition for many of today's top Australian players and coaches. The difference here, is that such a competition is no longer being touted as the elusive 'third tier' but a replacement for Super Rugby.

With so much focus on the removal of the Rebels and moving forwards with an 11-team competition for 2025, it largely slips through unnoticed, that there is ground being laid for a cessation of Super Rugby in its entirety, from 2026 onwards.

As well as reading into the line at the bottom of an otherwise standard sponsorship announcement, there are other reasons to suggest this outcome is more than possible;

- New Zealand Rugby has already strongly considered exiting Super Rugby (or creating a modified version of it with reduced Australian input), as a result of an internal review in 2020.

- Such a move would appear to be popular with the fanbases in both New Zealand and Australia.

- Both nations can't afford to maintain the status quo; Australia more acutely so. Broadcast revenue is not increasing in line with player salaries. No other revenue source has been identified that can fill the breach.

It's a running joke in rugby circles that senior Rugby Australia manager Ben Whitaker, can't see over his desk for the filing cabinets full of proposals and models for Australian rugby. Who's to say this one is any more chance of being implemented than the others?

Gray is sceptical, saying; "We're potentially about to go to court with RA over the participation licence. If Super Rugby is going to be extinct after 2025, why would they spend a fortune to fight over this? It doesn't make sense."

Then again, there are so many aspects of this sorry episode that don't make sense.

Chapter Fifty-Two

8th June, 2024

It is the way of modern rugby that genuine, David slaying Goliath upsets are few and far between. In another time, it was possible for an underdog to keep a game tight, and scrap and niggle their way to a 9-6 win. But with laws and referee applications favouring ball recycling (when is the last time you saw a breakdown/ruck end in a scrum?), and lesser sides required to score points themselves, thus exposing themselves to error and punishment, when it comes to modern rugby, fairy tales are just that.

None of which stops everyone present from believing. Last night, at a team meeting before dinner, analyst John Batina played a ten-minute video of some of the Rebels' past greats relaying their messages of support to the team. It's funny, touching and inspiring all in one.

Only days from being laid off, Emily Riseley, Neilson Campbell and Denver Murnane have paid their own airfare and hotel costs, and they are on hand to help manager Will Nicholson set up the dressing room before the team arrives. They post notes and well wishes from fans on the wall. More personal messages from family are posted in the player's lockers, without their prior knowledge. Sam Talakai takes a moment to absorb a message from each of his kids. Jordie Uelese has five or six messages from cousins and other family to read through.

Wellington has turned on a fair day for a quarter-final, its notorious wind well-behaved. Hurricanes fly-half Brett Cameron begins the action and, immediately, there are nervous moments and errors from both sides.

Gradually, the Rebels find their defensive tempo, competing with physicality at the breakdown, pressing up hard in their defensive line, and twice holding attacking players up over the goal-line. It's enough to frustrate the table topping Hurricanes into handling errors and conceding penalties. If there's a criticism of the Rebels, it's that a lot of the good work creating turnovers and fractured ball isn't quite capitalised on. A couple of times the ball spills the wrong way, or there is a wee knock on, and even a panicked kick into touch by Taniela Tupou, with men ranging free outside him.

At 39 minutes the Rebels trail by just a point and are doing enough to have home fans worried and their own fans hopeful, heading into the break. But Jordie Barrett finds a hole in midfield and frees up right wing, Josh Moorby, who wriggles over the line. Suddenly, 14-6 doesn't feel quite as tense.

Nor does 21-6 when Barrett does the same thing three minutes after the break, this time laying the try on for impressive No.8 Brayden Iose. It's been a weakness for the Rebels all season - conceding points in batches - and it's hurting them again today.

Josh Canham and Ryan Louwrens are playing what may well be their best ever matches for the club, and the combativeness is still there. But the Hurricanes lower their error rate and narrow their attack, and another two tries take the score out to 35-6, entering the last quarter. With all hopes of a win now gone, it will be easy for heads to drop, for all of the year's hardships to manifest themselves in a Hurricanes rout. The only thing left for Rebels fans to hope for is that there is no soul-destroying blow-out.

From a ruck near half-way, Carter Gordon finds Rob Leota with a loopy pass. Leota's pace and backhanded off-load catches the Hurricanes by surprise and Lachie Anderson gasses the last 30 metres to the corner for an impressive score. From the next line out following the kick-off, Alex Mafi gathers a loose ball, Leota finds a hole and an even better offload, and Vaiolini Ekuasi gallops into the backfield. Instead of running into contact Ekuasi finds Filipo Daugunu on his inside who, taken down near the try-line, lays the ball back behind him. In support, Gordon arrives at pace, expertly scoops the ball up and feeds Anderson in the one movement. There's no stopping the big winger as he crashes over, wrapped in a couple of tackles. Another superb kick by Gordon reduces the deficit to 35-20. Having climbed the gallows in the moments before their inevitable death, the Rebels have somehow found a way to tear off the black hood and crack a couple of the best gags of the year. What Anderson will go on to describe in a post-match interview as "going down swinging."

Bells Hotel in South Melbourne is a sprawling labyrinth of nooks and crannies: a conventional public bar in the front corner, a TAB and pokies down one side, a bistro along the other with a courtyard attached, then upstairs, more spaces, inside and out, before another small flight of stairs leads into a cavernous function room. At every vantage point there are TV's, and in every space, tables and chairs are filled. The whole building is teeming with people dressed in Rebels garb. Everyone is saying the same thing; who are all these people and where have they been? As a side note, publican Sam Tresise confirms that he has already taken over 350 bookings from people wanting to watch the Wallabies versus South Africa Test in August. Who says there is no support for rugby in Melbourne?

When Anderson crosses for his second, the roof of the function room is nearly blown off. The Rebels chant goes up and rings loud and strong inside the packed room. It lasts for as long as it takes for the Hurricanes to score again and fully extinguish any hope of a miracle finish.

At the final whistle the crowd stands as one; applauding the players for their pluck, but also to acknowledge that this is the very end of the closing chapter. There are hugs, handshakes and backslaps, and there are tears too; of disappointment and pride. Their club is no more.

Down on the pitch, as the match nears its conclusion, replaced players, their jobs done and with time to contemplate what is happening, begin to react. Taniela Tupou is the first to crack. Unfairly viewed by some fans as mercenary and lazy, having only had one season at the club, his reaction is telling. Unable to stop his flow of tears, he finds a spot on his own at the end of the bench and tries to shield himself from the TV cameras.

Nicholson slaps a seated Uelese on the shoulder but he doesn't move, other than to bury his head in his hands. Staff and other players who are sideline, make the mistake of looking at him and Tupou, and they too, are triggered. By the time that final whistle comes, every single one of them has been broken. Hugging and embracing becomes a way for them to hide their tears and reddened faces.

Rewatching later, it is agreed that the TV didn't do the carnage justice. That's not a criticism, staffers say, but meant as thanks to the cameramen and producers responsible for not voyeuristically over-playing what are intensely personal moments. They have the shots they need; Leota, Anderson and Brad Wilkin manfully conduct on-field interviews, the story is already there.

Winning captain Jordie Barrett hits the right note, swatting away his first interview question about the Hurricanes win, to acknowledge the Rebels.

His perspective comes from he and his own teammates knowing how hard they work to develop connection in their own team, and how much it means to them. They are not in the same position as the Rebels, but if they were they know exactly how it would feel.

Kat Rottier wanders among the players, conducting mini welfare checks, while struggling to contain her own emotions. "I've been part of a group that lost two Super Rugby finals," she says. "Plus a team that lost at the Olympic Games. In their own ways, those were crippling blows. But none of those come remotely close to this feeling. With those other sides, the players and staff all had the opportunity to come back and fight another day. But here we don't. There really is no future. And that realisation has hit everybody at the same time. Because of that, and because everyone was so invested in the club and so connected, it's really quite different. Total devastation."

Her response resonates with psychologist Andrew Waterson. "The double-edged sword of the Rebels' culture is that people have identified with it and attached themselves to it, and it's become a real place of safety for the group. And this emotional reaction is a natural response to all of that being taken away."

"I feel a lot of sadness, within the group and personally. I have no doubt that the model that Kevin has brought to the club is one that would have delivered sustainable high performance. Built around that strong connection piece and clearly defined boundaries around who is in and who is out," he concludes.

"I can't tell you how tough that last five minutes was in the box," says Kevin Foote, later. "Just the realisation that there was nothing left for us to do. We were just waiting for the game to be over. And with that, each of us was dealing with our emotions, trying to hold ourselves together. But really, it was impossible. Even though we'd known this time was going to come, we hadn't really prepared for what it would be like in the moment. All of us felt the same thing at precisely the same time. The same hopelessness. The same feeling; not that we'd lost the match, but that we'd lost everything."

Eventually, as darkness sets in around Westpac Stadium, when the players and staff have thanked the fans who gathered pitch side and there is no more reason to stay on the ground, everyone finds the sanctuary of the dressing room. Formalities are kept short; Talakai is honoured for his 100th Super Rugby match and Louwrens for his 50th. Past players who are present, receive their caps. Rob Leota is taken to a nearby medical room to have his ear stitched.

Talakai, so strong and stoic throughout the whole season, in acknowledging his award, finally succumbs to his emotions. For Moana Leilua, it comes as no surprise; "It's not just about the end of a rugby team. Sam, Nella, Khan... these guys came to Melbourne to lay down their roots. That's what people don't understand, that's why you see them hurting so much. Lukhan and his wife, they've been fighting so hard to get their daughter into a particular school. The day the school finally told us she'd been accepted was the day we found out the team was being terminated."

The leaders, Foote and Nick Stiles, offer their gratitude to everyone present but don't need to say too much. Usually, win or lose, there is space provided to absorb the physical contest and the outcome, before a quick re-set and framing of the week ahead. With no week ahead, there are instead hugs, pizza and beer, and a resolve that tonight, everyone will stay together in the team room after they return to the hotel.

Like Jim from TV's *Mission Impossible* team, mastermind Will Nicholson directs his crack crew as they pull off a stunning reverse heist on Wellington's Intercontinental Hotel. Campbell, Andrew Kellaway and Bobby Tuttle are Nicholson's partners in crime, having loaded up the team minivan at a nearby bottle shop with slabs of beer, needing a way to transfer it to the team room upstairs without alerting staff that they won't be running up a hotel bar tab. The heavy-duty black cases containing kit and equipment are emptied out in the team room and wheeled down to the car park, where they are filled with the sly grog and wheeled back up. It takes two full trips before the transfer of illicit goods is complete, and the partying can begin.

Fans who have waited patiently in the lobby for the team bus to arrive, clap the players in, and are rewarded for their persistence by being invited up to the room. Tonight there are no formalities or barriers. Tonight is about togetherness and family. And, if you are wearing blue, red and white, you are a part of that family.

Chapter Fifty-Three

12th June, 2024

There are few things sadder than a club in the last throes of its existence, as the Rebels were late on Saturday afternoon in Wellington; condemned, without any recourse or ability to change their destiny. But one thing sadder is a club in the immediate aftermath.

It's four days since the team returned from being put through the emotional wringer in Wellington. Players are dotted around the gym in what is cruelly termed 'active recovery'. By contrast, a thin sprinkling of staff sit solemnly at their workstations, the antithesis of in 'recovery'. Some are in denial; "I'm here because this is what I love doing, being with my workmates". Others are e-mailing resumes. Physio and S & C staff, ever professional to the end, are rubbing and strapping, watching over work-out routines.

In an article posted on-line in *The Guardian* on Monday, writer Angus Fontaine ran his rule over the Rebels players, urging them to move on quickly; "Like Canessa, who focused on the "generosity" of his fallen teammates, the Rebels must now set their jaw and focus on the bigger picture: strengthening the misfiring NSW Waratahs and Western Force."

It's a stunning misread on two counts; all of the blood, sweat and tears invested by players and coaches into the Rebels cannot be simply waved away and their souls transferred holus-bolus into a different entity; especially one owned and managed by the very people who sent them to this purgatory in the first place. And certainly not without a suitable time period for grieving.

Also problematic is the metaphorical reference to Roberto Canessa, a Uruguayan cardiologist and rugby player, famous for surviving a 1972 plane crash in the Chilean Andes that killed many of his teammates. Canessa's tale of survival - and the rescue of 15 other passengers - is an incredible one, involving cannibalism and a 10-day trek in the snow-covered mountains. As tough as the Rebels' players and coaches are doing it this week, to a man, none of them would equate their situation with that of the Uruguayan crash victims.

Some players are in a brighter mood than others. Isaac Aedo-Kailea walks a foot taller, named in the Wallabies' train-on squad. David Feliuai arrives and is offered handshakes for also being named. In a show of trademark humility, he is as embarrassed as he is proud. Ditto Darby Lancaster, another young man whose default setting is 'unassuming and modest'.

Carter Gordon undertakes a light weights session wearing cream-coloured 'Crocs'. "My trainers are packed away," he insists. Perhaps he is the person about to be responsible for making Crocs cool? Briefly, he considers if there is an opportunity for Carter Gordon the golfing protege, to launch a lucrative side hustle in 'Golf Crocs'. The thought passes quickly. As the rugby world is about to discover, he already has a lot on his plate.

Brad Wilkin doesn't train; "I feel like I need to rest for a bit," he says. Yet there is no place else he would rather be than amongst his teammates and friends. At home on the sofa he would inevitably be forced to go through his phone. "I can see it's full of messages. Which I really appreciate. I'm just not ready to go through them yet." He moves on, wary of triggering another emotional release.

At least any lingering effects of the team's 'Mad Monday' have been shaken off. The Rising Sun Hotel in Richmond played host to a bunch of Harry Potters, Super Mario Brothers and Matt Gibbon, who shaved his head, padded his belly and came dressed as Cabous Eloff. With no mis-steps to provide fuel for the press, in these days where any hint of misbehaviour of sportspeople can be amplified ten-fold, the day is considered a win.

But no matter the conviviality among the players, the vibrant positivity that permeated the atmosphere a week ago has been drained from the building. Conversations are fewer. Softer. Less animated. There are snatches of dark humour - Anderson is ribbed for 'tanking' in the quarter-final by failing to score a hat-trick - but the predominant feeling is one of still-raw sadness. Already, the office is looking sparse in places, untidy in others; a classic case of a tenant in the midst of sorting through their shit, packing, and moving on. The Weary Dunlop Shield sits on a bench in the kitchen, alongside a tray full of plastic tomato and bar-b-que sauce bottles. The sauce will be divided amongst staff; nobody is quite sure what to do with the shield.

Luke Vella scans the gym, still bulging with equipment, wondering where all of it might end up. Since the enforced COVID stay-home period triggered an explosion in home gyms, with the economy now sickly and many commercial gyms having closed, there is no meaningful second-hand market for this kind of gear. "I don't know if we just walk out and leave it all here, or what we're supposed to do," says Vella. "It's not like we've ever been given a plan."

Rob Taylor is the only coach present. He has a short-term job in Japan, but nothing permanent lined up after that. "Let's call it a works-in-progress", he says.

Vella has found himself a position in basketball, with the South East Melbourne Phoenix. He counts himself as one of the lucky ones. "Basketball was actually my sport when I was younger. It's a really interesting challenge, players come into the Australian season all at different stages. Some have been playing in overseas leagues, others are off a break, then in terms of match loads, some play long minutes, others in brief spells off the bench. So it's quite something to get my head around." His eyes tell the rest of the story. He knows he'll get to his new basketball club, commit to it and do a good job. But he's like everyone else around the joint. Their business here was unfinished. And now, having developed an aptitude and high degree of competency in rugby, he is lost to the sport.

Only a small handful of players put boots on and take their training outside. One of those is Gordon, who lugs a sack of balls across the carpark and invests a few minutes into his goal kicking. He's buoyed by his success in Wellington, where he kicked 4/4, including two superb sideline conversions. "I switched to using a higher tee," he says, a little frustrated by how simple the solution appears to have been. "I'm getting much better contact as a result."

Minutes later, he does the rounds of the office, shaking hands and exchanging well wishes. With a plane to catch, these hurrahs are his final act as a Rebel. By the time he lands in Brisbane, the rugby and rugby league media will be all over news of his signing by the Gold Coast Titans. Not only was this his final act as a Rebel, it's his final act as a rugby player.

Chapter Fifty-Four

13th June, 2024

Donvale, in Melbourne's suburban east is a long way from California's Silicon Valley; in every aspect. But located above a nondescript computer store is the home of Gain Line Analytics, one of the few rugby-related businesses that could, with a tiny bit of imagination, fit the description of tech start-up.

Only there is no bank of e-scooters parked outside. No common staff areas finished off with different coloured palettes carefully designed and selected to inspire or soothe team members. No Kombucha on tap. Entrance is via a narrow set of stairs, known only to staff and returning visitors. Then, via a dark, wood-panelled passageway, is revealed a couple of offices and a server room stacked with humming hardware. Is it the case that all those Twitter/X porn bots said to emanate from difficult to pronounce eastern European enclaves, might actually be being generated right here? But as soon as co-director Simon Strachan's computer monitor reveals an array of graphs containing the names of professional sports clubs, normality is restored. This is a safe space in which to chat rugby.

Strachan is an experienced rugby man who happened to coach Rob Leota and Jordie Uelese when they were kids. His business partner Ben Darwin, is a 28-Test Wallaby and was an ex-assistant coach and video analyst for the Rebels. Nowadays, the Rebels are a Gain Line client, one of a number of Super Rugby franchises utilising their services. Darwin is at home today nursing a fever, but Strachan is eager to talk through how Gain Line's metrics for cohesion can be applied to the Rebels' historical performance, and also, to where they might have been headed.

"When the Rebels started in 2011 things were set up in a way where the impact wouldn't be too severe on the existing franchises," he says. "The Rebels were allowed ten non-Australian players, and while that sounds nice, it actually impeded things from a cohesion perspective because of the disparity of the relationships and the age profile of the squad. So, from the get-go, the Rebels had this automatic, high turnover, low cohesion structure, which you could describe as built-in obsolescence. A ceiling baked into their performance."

Strachan's comments align with those of ex-Wallaby coach John Connolly, in an article that appeared in *The Roar* last week, where Connolly stated, "When rival codes – and the AFL is the gold standard here – set up expansion teams away from their home state, they give them huge financial support, the pick of the new crop of young star players and every other incentive you can think of.

When the Rebels were setting up in Melbourne, they were locked out of access to top players in NSW and Queensland and were forced to spend too much of their start-up money to attract talent."

Echoing Rod Macqueen's comments, Connolly becomes yet another respected figure in Australian rugby to express horror and concern about how events have unfolded: past and present. "The Rebels always felt like they were outside the NSW-Queensland tent," he writes. "And they were. We needed people right at the top of the game who could see through the NSW and Queensland bias and deliver what was needed to successfully grow the sport nationally."

"What's RA doing? Killing teams. They can't even call themselves a national competition anymore. The money from the private consortium would have been a Godsend and anyone at RA who thought it was a good idea to walk away from Victoria needs their head read."

From those initial years, the Rebels paraded a stream of high-profile players through the club; names like Mortlock, Cipriani, Beale, Horie, O'Connor, Somerville, Mafi, Genia, Cooper and many others, but as Strachan is at pains to put out; "Tony McGahan's last season as coach (2017) really exposed the absence of a strong system and a lack of continuity. It was patently obvious that the Rebels continuing as they were, just adding the odd star player here and there, meant that they would never going to be able to catch up to the better teams. Things took another turn when a group of Western Force players and coaches arrived, but the benefits of that were overstated. What was gained on one hand - a group all from the same club - was offset by the low cohesion markers that existed between them and the existing players."

As a result, Strachan is sceptical about the notion that by expelling the Rebels from Super Rugby, the performance of the remaining four franchises will improve. "For a start, that just stimulates players into seeking opportunities overseas - either the Rebels players or players at other franchises who fear being replaced or getting less game time. And for those who do get redistributed, again, they'll typically be new and having to start all over again in that new environment. So, any perceived benefit about improved player strength, in terms of cohesion markers... that benefit, if there is one, quickly dissipates."

Strachan talks more generally about how Australian franchises have typically struggled for Super Rugby success. "It's very difficult in Australian rugby to develop the same cohesion levels as say, the Crusaders or Leinster. Despite those sides being in very different competitions on opposite sides of the world, when we apply our measurements, because of their pathway systems and the way they bring their players through, they look almost identical," he states.

"By comparison, in Australia, the Brumbies don't have strong internal pathways but they've been great at identifying the type of player they want in their system, bringing them in and retaining them. The Reds, they're now beginning to reap the benefits of what Nick Stiles did; basically starting again with a group of inexperienced players, bringing them through together. He copped a bit of stick for it too. That was carried on by Brad Thorn, through the NRC and Super Rugby, and now they've got a team where a lot of the players have been together a long time, and they're still relatively young."

"In 2014, when the Tahs won, their data reflected the lowest number of changes made by any team during the season. As well, pretty much everything that needed to go right, did go right. But look at this year, with all of their injuries and changes, and it's no surprise to see them at the bottom of the ladder. We can even apply the same principle to the Wallabies at last year's World Cup, where there was a strong correlation between the data around change and the team missing the quarter-finals."

Strachan then points to a key advantage held by the New Zealand franchises; "New Zealand teams can get away with making more changes than the Australian teams, and still be successful. That's because they have more cohesion depth - their players play more rugby, and play more rugby together."

Other factors contribute too. Strachan relates a story about All Black prop Greg Sommerville arriving to play for the Rebels, taking part in an indoor line-out 'walk through' drill. "Almost all of the players were slouched on furniture or leaning on a wall. Somerville automatically assumed his set position, crouched over, in set position to perform his role as a lifter. In an instant, it was possible to spot who the player was that had come from a high-performance environment, compared to everyone else. In low cohesion settings, where players are thrown together, young players aren't sure who to listen to. But when players come through together, where high standards are set by the senior players and the coaching group, what the normative behaviours are, are set and universally understood. In this case, what was normative behaviour for this group, was a notch or two below the normative behaviours Sommerville was used to."

So, what about the Rebels in 2024? Strachan points to improved cohesion markers aligning with the Rebels making the quarter-finals for the first time. "The reason why we're seeing forward progress is because Stiles has actively recruited in batches, and by relationship as well as talent," he says. "They're working hard to develop combinations and to stick with them; Canham and Salakaia-Loto; Louwrens, Gordon and Feliuai; so that this breeds more familiarity and more clarity in their roles. It's also resulted in the Rebels having a much stronger bench."

"It's still a works-in-progress," Strachan continues. "Lack of cohesion manifests itself more in defence than attack, and we saw a number of times during the season, the Rebels concede points in quick succession. High cohesion teams don't rush or overreact compared to low cohesion teams. They deal with pressure as a collective. So that's the next phase if you like. If this Rebels team was to have continued into next year I'd expect to have seen defensive tightening and their points conceded drop. And when that happens, teams start to win more games."

But now there are no more games to win? "I can understand how incredibly frustrating that must be for everyone at the club," Strachan says. "To reiterate, because of the different pathways and competitions that exist in New Zealand, the system isn't built to allow the Rebels or any Australian franchise to be truly competitive against the best of their franchises. No third tier, no 'B' matches, no out of season matches. What Stiles has done well is to 'MacGyver' the Rebels into a position where they are now able to make the 'best from the worst'. Making themselves truly competitive, and from there, being able to compete in the top section of the competition. This current group, with their age profile, the promise of continuity… I'm sure there would have been a few more seasons of positive improvement."

Chapter Fifty-Five

14th June, 2024

It's a cool, wintery Friday night, but the main function room upstairs at Bells Hotel is well heated and welcoming. The space fills quickly; players with their partners, and all of the staff. It is too late for a few players who are already on their way to new assignments, but everybody who can and should be there, is present. It's a mostly casual, standing affair; drinks and finger food to share, along with recognition and celebration of the year's best performers. It's also an opportunity to say final goodbyes.

To one side a gathering of players includes the three Rebels halfbacks; Ryan Louwrens, Bobby Tuttle and Jack Maunder. Each of them has reason to reflect on how events took an unexpected turn for the club, and how this has impacted on their personal situations.

"Obviously, it's been very frustrating," said Maunder, a few days earlier. "It became clear quite early on that the way the coaches wanted the team to play, that there wasn't quite the fit I'd hoped for. The game here is more highlights based. In the UK, it's a bit more results based, more of a territory game, and the competition is a bit tighter. So, because I wasn't getting the minutes, I then had to focus on figuring out my role, how I could push my personal disappointment to the side and help the team in different ways. Because I felt like there's still a lot of growth there, untapped, amongst the younger boys."

"It helps when you really get along with the lads," he explains. "Don't get me wrong - if you ask my girlfriend, you've got to have a safe spot to sulk and get your frustrations out, but I'd like to think I've been a good teammate, and that they would all say I've been helpful and supportive."

S & C coach Luke Trewhella might disagree, having suffered the humiliation of being snubbed by Maunder after the halfback's arrival at the club. A fellow Englishman, Trewhella was briefly a teammate of Maunder in an Exeter junior side, showing off the team photo to prove it. As Trewhella tells it; "When I heard he was coming to the Rebels, I thought, 'that's great', being able to have someone from home around the club. And I thought that might be good for him too. And so I told a few people about it before Jack was introduced around the office. I shook his hand and welcomed him by name, and he looked straight through me - it was obvious he had no clue who I was!"

Their mutual embarrassment a source of great mirth for everyone else, Maunder is still mortified, months later. "Obviously, it wasn't deliberate," he maintains. "And fair play, we were just thirteen!"

Maunder finishes off by looking towards the future; "I'll still be able to look back when I'm eighty, with a whiskey and a cigar, and say that I got to play against pretty much all of the main Super Rugby teams, and I got to travel to New Zealand for rugby. So it hasn't been all bad."

Indeed. Despite finding himself third-ranked by the Rebels coaches, Maunder, having secured a 2025 contract with French Pro D2 side Agen, is the only one of the halfbacks with a job. For a committed red-wine drinker, relocating to a pretty provincial town in the south-west of France, midway between Toulouse and Bordeaux, hardly feels like a fate worse than death.

For Tuttle, it's also been a frustrating season. Already the sufferer of serious injuries throughout his career, his wrist continues to prove troublesome. He is playing well enough that, should he actively pursue it, some kind of contract might eventuate, perhaps in the USA. But he is also cognisant of the sacrifices made by his wife, in support of his career. Now in their later twenties, it feels like time for them to become a more traditional husband and wife. To spend time together; at home, in the same city. For him to begin to pay back some of the sacrifices made on his behalf. For some players, when the first thoughts of hanging up the boots surface, retirement doesn't so much loom, as swoop.

It comes as no surprise when the third of the trio, Louwrens, is awarded the 'Ubuntu' prize. Always strong and competitive, Louwrens this year took his contribution to a higher level; strong and combative in defence, accurate on the pass, and an inspirational leader in the gym. His reliability and consistency allowed his coaches and teammates to focus on their own responsibilities, knowing that 'Hundy' always had things covered at halfback.

Surprisingly, Louwrens is without a contract for 2025. Like others, he returned to Melbourne with a young family, looking to put down roots; a Rebel for life. Says Nick Stiles; "Undoubtedly, we were looking to sign Ryan on for another two years. His on-field performances warranted that, and he's such a great influence around the club. Like Sammy (Talakai), I've got no doubt he would have gone on to be a great contributor for the Rebels in a coaching role."

For now, Louwrens isn't panicking. He is, after all a veteran when it comes to clubs being cut from underneath him (incredibly, this is his third time, after the Western Force and the Austin Gilgronis). He feels like he has more to give the game and is confident something will present itself. "We're going to head to Perth for a bit, take some time to think through everything, and then see what happens. There's a sniff of something in France, so we'll see."

The awards list is kept short. Louwrens, the player who most demonstrated the spirit of Ubuntu; Filipo Daugunu, voted as the 'player's player' for the men, Jayme Nuku, the women; Sam Talakai and Mel Kawa are popular winners of the 'Spirit of Weary Dunlop' award for men and women; and Keven Foote takes home the 'Mark Rowe Employee of the Year' award' as voted for by all staff and players.

It was never intended to be this way, but Foote's speech is a bookend for his stirring address on the day of the pre-season launch. He talks not of the season results, nor the events that have seen their club swept away. Instead, he restates what Ubuntu means, specifically referencing the people who make up the club - made up the club - urging everyone to carry their relationships and their experiences with them. He singles out the people who have made this possible, the partners of the players and the staff. Selfless people who have made enormous personal sacrifices to allow others to pursue their personal dreams. Some people have a knack of, when they speak, making each person in the room feel as if the address is intended solely for them. Foote is one of those people. In three short minutes he does everything to justify why he won the award. As if there was ever any doubt in the first place.

Despite everyone wanting to celebrate the past, conversations inevitably turn to the future. 'Have you got anything?' 'Where are you heading?' 'What day are you leaving?' Good news is celebrated. Next week, Kat Rottier and Jarrod Rutley will join Geoff Parling in the Wallabies set-up. John Batina has a short-term assignment with Fiji. Alex Parr will join Luke Vella at the South East Melbourne Phoenix. Bryn Savill serves as doctor for multiple sports teams and will be able to extend his hours.

Others have irons in the fire but nothing confirmed. Brad Harris is one of those. "I turned down a multi-year extension in Fiji to come here," he says, raising his eyebrows. "It was the right choice at the time; with what we had I was delighted to join the program. And it feels like I still have a lot to offer Australian rugby. There's no regrets, but… I had no idea things were this tenuous and events would play out like they have. You could say I'm up shit creek without a paddle." Harris pauses, before his phlegmatic nature kicks in. "There's a little bit around. Something will come up."

Geoff Parling, despite being one of the few with a job to go to on Monday, is feeling frustrated and angry. "It's like double whammy; I'm both a Rebels coach and an ex-player. This club has become a huge part of my life. A big one for me, is that I always felt we were shackled by being based at AAMI. I get that it's central, and that it's part of the sporting precinct. But our facility, even after the improvements, it's not exactly world class, is it? And it locked us in to high operational costs. Perhaps we could have done more with one of the clubs and built ourselves a genuine world class home base, without all of the high overheads? But even so… I still can't really believe this is happening."

Parling is also exhibiting signs of survivor guilt. "That's what really gutting. You look around at all the good people in this room. What a waste."

Tim Sampson is humbled by an offer of support and a job in Perth, outside of the game. "It's terrific knowing I have something to fall back on," he says. "But…" His eyes tell the rest of the story. He's not yet ready to step out of rugby.

Nick Stiles is faced with a similar choice; stay in Melbourne and leave rugby, or put himself forward for the vacant position of General Manager, Rugby at the Waratahs. Still grieving, it feels like Hobson's choice. "I just need a few days… some distance to clear my head, then I'll be better placed to make a decision," he says. (That decision would be taken out of his hands when, two weeks later, the Waratahs appoint ex-Fiji World Cup coach Simon Raiwalui, to the role).

Foote has a decision to make too, although he knows what he won't be doing. "I'm not putting myself forward for the Waratahs. I can't do this again, not like this, not so soon. Especially when I don't know the people behind the club, what kind of a fit there would be, and so on." First things first, he'll enjoy being a dad for a few weeks. "If I stay in rugby, there's a short-term opportunity for me in Japan, and then longer-term, an exciting opportunity coming up in Cape Town. It was never in the plan to go back there, but it's not out of the question either. As a family, we're very settled here in Melbourne. It's a great place to bring up the kids. And I've potentially got a career opportunity around leadership coaching and culture development. I'll have a good look at things over the next few weeks with my wife, then we'll decide what to do."

For every person staying in Australian rugby, there's another who is in the process of being lost. Is that the fair and reasonable collateral damage that comes with a necessary financial decision, or is it another self-inflicted blow that Australian rugby can ill afford? Rugby Australia has been highly visible in communicating the cost of keeping the Rebels. But were the costs of axing them ever properly thought through?

On the matter of financial cost, Stiles notes the irony around an anxious Phil Waugh seeking to lock down details with him prior to this event, trying to ensure expenses are kept to a minimum. "I mean, it's a pretty modest night. At a pub, not a function centre or five-star hotel... basic finger food... but there were hoops I had to jump through around keeping the guest list to a minimum, only inviting certain Super W players and so on." (By contrast, the Waratahs end of season event is held, the following week, in the Grand Ballroom at the Hyatt Regency, Sydney).

"They were also worried about us potentially having media here too; as if RA thinks this night is all about them and protecting their image. Well, it's not, it's simply about our team and our staff spending our last bit of time together."

As if to frank Stiles' take on things, staff and players clamour for their photographs to be taken, candidly or posed in a group, against a Rebels sponsor backdrop. Something by which to record the moment for posterity.

With pics snapped and food platters long since cleared away, the first signs of alcohol taking over begin to emerge. Truth serum. For Foote, that's a signal for he and his wife to head home. "It's nothing much but I can sense a couple of people starting to get a bit negative. That's understandable but it's not how I want to remember my last night. I've got so many good memories I'd much rather focus on."

Chapter Fifty-Six

18th June, 2024

It's now ten days since time was called on the Rebels in Wellington. As desolate and depressing as the office felt last week, the vibe has sunk another few notches lower. Most people have gone; there are some who remain on the payroll for a few days, but with nothing to do there's simply no reason for them to be there anymore. There's also been a change in colour palette, from navy blue with red and white trim, to green and gold. Not the traditional, bold, triumphant Aussie green and gold, but this years' tasteful, pastel version. For a few days this week, the office has become a temporary training base for those local players and staff involved with the Wallabies, until they shift camp and unite with the whole national squad for the upcoming matches against Wales and Georgia.

Geoff Parling and Jarrod Rutley tap away at their workstations, looking resplendent in their new 'Team Wallabies' garb. Along with her colleagues, Kat Rottier is working on players in the physio room, albeit yet to make the switch from blue to green. Wallabies scrum coach Mike Cron is also present, delighted at how the cold, bracing morning reminds him of Christchurch, while a chirpy Peter Horne busily prepares for the on-field training session, eager to run the players through their paces.

That playing group is a severely diminished one; now down to those players named in the Wallabies train-on squad only. For some of them, like Lachie Anderson, Matt Gibbon, Jordie Uelese and Josh Canham, it will only be another ten days until they too are cut, as Joe Schmidt's squad is reduced to 38 players.

Those who have arrived early take the opportunity for a rub down or some light gym work, before the session proper begins. For captain Rob Leota, it is both a relief to be named in the train-on squad, and an opportunity, with a home Test match against Wales on the near horizon. His last home Test will forever be remembered as the occasion where French referee Mathieu Raynal extravagantly called a time-wasting violation on

Wallabies' fly-half Bernard Foley, and a Wallabies win became another heartbreaking Bledisloe Cup loss. After some effective first-half involvements, Leota ruptured his Achilles tendon and saw out the rest of the match on the bench, with a pair of crutches sitting alongside.

Reflecting on this season, Leota (Pati to his teammates; a shortened version of his Samoan name) is happy and proud that the side played in a quarter-final. But, he's also pensive about what he feels is a missed opportunity. "Obviously, we would have liked to have gone further, and I feel like the potential was there for that," he says. "But being a realist, with what we had to go through, with all the outside noise, everyone trying to figure out what their next step might be, in the event we didn't go on… as well as try and play our best footy… it feels like an achievement that we all stuck tight together as a group, and that's a memory I'll hold close."

Picked out by Kevin Foote as captain for the 2023 season, Leota never played a game, recovering from the Achilles rupture. He's cognisant of the contrast between being captain in both years, in two totally different sets of circumstances. "It was really tough trying to be a leader while not playing. It's just not the same, because you can't show your leadership through your actions out on the field, in battle. The best thing I could do was help with the vibe every day - keep good energy amongst the boys. Moving into this year, I felt a bit inexperienced at the start, but the thing I learned as the season progressed was not to let captaincy take away from my game. The leadership group stepped up and took a lot of weight of my shoulders this year; Sammy, Khan, Josh, Brad and Carts. I learned how to lean on those guys, because why not, they're great players and great leaders themselves. So I figured that the biggest way I could impact a game was through my play, to lead in that area. And towards the end of the season, once I figured all that out, and my body was right, I felt like I played some of my best footy. And on top of that, the group kind of came together and helped with everything else."

Already, Leota is missing the teammates who have left. "It hasn't really sunk in yet," he says. "Just that connection with the boys, it's been broken. Not just like at the end of a season, but obviously moving forward. And for me personally, I've come through the Rebels and been here for nine years now, in Melbourne all my career, so that's tough to process. I really feel for the Melbourne rugby community and our loyal fans, what's happened is terrible for them. And I'm worried about the rugby pathway; how that will affect kids."

As disappointed as he is, Leota knows he has to, when he's ready, make an adjustment and focus on his future career. But he's also very aware of the future rugby aspirations of other Melbourne kids like him. "I really enjoyed my time here, this has been my rugby life. And I'm very grateful I've had that opportunity and experience. I just hope it inspires other local kids who are chasing the dream, that they use those of us who have come through to professional rugby and become Wallabies, as positive role models. What I would say to those kids is that, you never know what life is going to throw at you, like what's happened this year, but opportunity can come from anywhere. What's important for those kids is that, Rebels or no Rebels, they overcome any adversity or hurdles and grasp every opportunity that comes their way."

Without a full squad present, the training session has a skills and conditioning emphasis as opposed to teamwork and unit components. It's a useful blowout, with the tackle bags getting a good workout, until Leota pulls up, grabbing at a hamstring. An hour or so later, after a shower and a coffee, he limps to the medical imaging centre located adjacent, tucked under a large bank of stairs that carries fans into AAMI Park. The scan tells him what he already knows; it's a bad one, a six-week injury. There'll be no opportunity to make up for his home Bledisloe experience. Another adversity to add to the list. The sight of the captain hobbling forlornly back to the carpark is not only a devastating personal blow; it serves as a fitting metaphor for the plight of the Rebels.

Chapter Fifty-Seven

30th June, 2024

"One thing I've learned through all of this is that it's almost impossible to get anyone at Rugby Australia to engage for long enough and remain focused on solving this part of the game. Part of it is that once Super Rugby finishes everything revolves around the Wallabies, but more than that, I'm convinced that once people go inside that building (Rugby Australia HQ in Sydney's Moore Park), there's something in the air-conditioning units, a different kind of air they breathe, that drives a whole different way of thinking. One that seems to omit a national approach to the game and ignores the Federated model."

Inside a busy suburban cafe, Paul Docherty sips at a green tea, still trying to rationalise how the Rebels came to be cast adrift, apprehensive for the future of Australian rugby, but very committed to ensuring that Victoria has an influential role to play in determining that future. Imminently, a statement of claim is to be lodged with Rugby Australia's lawyers, via the administrator, on behalf of the Melbourne Rebels Rugby Club (MRRC), that has the potential to shake the foundations of the game, with ramifications extending far beyond the matter of the Rebels' participation in Super Rugby or not.

"Whatever the game looks like, however little or much money is in the game, all we have ever wanted is to be part of that conversation. Which we were before: we're a positive contributor to Australian rugby and our contribution is only going to increase. I mean, where are the other genuine expansion areas and opportunities to grow rugby in the future? We should be and must be part of that shaping of rugby, instead of being pilloried as some kind of blight on the game."

As Docherty describes it, that statement of claim will detail in depth, a history and world view that reads very differently to that which has so far informed the public debate. "Rugby Australia have had their few months in the sun, telling their story. Now it's our turn to tell it like it actually is," he says.

As Docherty explains it, this legal claim isn't the desperate, swift-response action of people intent on saving their houses and having Rugby Australia pay for their financial misdeeds, that many people might expect. Instead, the emphasis is on the nature of the relationship between the governing body and the franchises, the rights of member franchises, and how professional rugby is administered.

"This all goes back to the conversations and work that happened in 2017," Docherty explains. "It was then that it was decided that, for various reasons, including pressure from New Zealand and South Africa, and financial concerns around Australia's sustainability, we would reduce our footprint to four teams."

He pauses to note how the Rebels are on record supporting the retention of five teams, before continuing. "As everyone knows, it was the Force who were dropped, but in 2021, because of COVID, it suited Rugby Australia to bring them back, because they needed a fifth team to keep the broadcast deal alive. That readmission occurred without the formal agreement of the member franchises or the proper admission process provided for in the constitution. And then because the deal made with Andrew Forrest was that the Force would fund themselves for the first two years only, in 2023 we were back to a situation where we had five teams, diluting the distribution made to us and the other franchises. At the very same time where the financial outlook for the game was worse than what it was in 2017 when the decision was made to go to four teams."

"What's important is that during this period, after 2017 when we went back to four teams and before COVID, the franchise chairs, Jeff Miller, Roger Davis, Matt Nobbs and myself, were all aligned. We were talking together regularly, working on how we could all get better together. It was almost like we were humming along, trying to drag Rugby Australia with us. (Then CEO) Raelene Castle's response was built around getting competitive tension and putting a new broadcast deal to tender, but that all fell in a hole. Partly because of COVID, but also because the inherent flaw in our model is that these deals cover both the Wallabies and Super Rugby, and the Super Rugby season is so short, when we get to the end of it and the franchises want to knuckle down and put the work in in the off-season, everyone at RA is off running with the Wallabies. So, even though Super Rugby is supposed to be the premier professional club or franchise competition, which it undoubtedly was in a global sense, it's been compromised at every turn;

unable to maximise its own revenue potential, poorly promoted, and used by the national unions as warm-ups and trials for Test rugby. Hence there developed this sense in the rugby community that the magic of the old Super Rugby brand had diminished. The excitement, the quality… where it all stood with Japan, Argentina and South Africa… it was like nobody quite knew what Super Rugby's identity was any more, and that tied as well to a lack of promotion. And simultaneously, Rugby Australia is having these huge internal battles; you've got the Israel Folau stuff going on, there's Wallaby ex-captains trying to bring down the CEO, there's a concerted media campaign against rugby, the relationship between RA and New Zealand Rugby is volatile, SANZAAR as an organisation is no help to anybody, and then we run into COVID… and what happens is that all of the franchises revert back to protecting their own patch."

Leadership and relationships are a recurring theme. "So, we've got Cameron Clyne as chair," Docherty continues, "the aircon has got to him, he and Raelene (CEO Raelene Castle) are under siege… and we all come to realisation that he's tired of all those battles and he's not the kind of leader the franchises need. And to Cameron's credit, he realised that too and cleared the ground to enable the game to find someone else. But by then, the rot had set in, they just weren't able to attract the right calibre of new people to the board. There were people who had the right profile, but once they looked closer, they wouldn't touch it, or it wasn't worth it for them to come back from overseas. So they kept narrowing the requirements until such time they basically ended up with a homogenous kind of board with a more narrow and shallow view of the game. And with that, there's not the same kind of relationships and inherent understanding of the age and everyone's role in the eco-system that there was before."

"As a result, we've gone from in 2019, everyone agreeing, 'this has got to be a game of partnerships' to a time of severe upheaval and change in Rugby Australia, coupled with a changing of the guard at the franchises, with Jeff and Roger stepping away. And it's not a united front any more, it's 'here we go again', because we've got the Force back in, who are not only parochial, but after what happened to them in 2017, they're understandably very bitter."

Docherty orders another tea then goes on to outline the failed attempt to instal Peter Wiggs as chair before Hamish McLennan eventually took on the role. "It's fair to say that everyone had reservations about his style. I remember a senior media executive telling me that 'he will fix things, but there'll be a lot of heartache and blood along the way'. But there was a void and the game was so bereft of leadership it was seen as a risk worth taking."

McLennan proved to be a double-edged sword for the Rebels. "Hamish definitely had a vision for what the game needed, and he had the courage to fight for that. Even as late as at the World Cup in France, he was still saying, 'don't worry, we can solve all of this'. And that was a continuation of that relationship and shared responsibility piece, and the multiple assurances that were made to us and all the franchises, and our reliance on them, which will come out strongly in the detail of our legal claim. Contrary to how it's been painted, we were never acting alone, in financial isolation. But for Hamish, having aligned himself so closely with what was a failed World Cup campaign, ultimately the board determined that his position was untenable."

There's another revelation around finances. "What's also not well known is that during this period we went down a PE path ourselves, which we had all set up to go. And Rugby Australia asked us to pull back because they were pursuing a PE deal for the whole game and didn't want to dilute that. So in good faith we said, 'fair enough'. At that point we've got a massive potential state government investment in the game which we'd brought to the table being knocked back, plus our own PE solution being sidelined, and what happens? We discover the reason is because they're doing a deal with World Rugby to take an advance on the World Cup revenue - for which they trade away all the upside - because the certainty of that money provides them with the security they need to take up a debt facility with PEP (Pacific Equity Partners). And then Hamish gets rolled and into the void steps the consultants and the toe cutters, and without the depth of historical relationships to draw upon, the other franchises all start scrambling for solutions for their own financial issues, and we become sitting ducks."

In this context, Docherty is keen to point out the prevalence of short memories. "It's not very long ago I sat there and voted for Queensland to receive millions of dollars in emergency funding to that they could keep the game alive up there. We understood how important that was for the national game. Did we whinge about it or litigate it through the press? No, because we wanted to do the right thing for the game. And let's not forget too, how Rugby Australia was spending money at the World Cup like a drunken sailor. They've communicated Eddie's unauthorised overspending; and what does that say about their governance? But what about the authorised overspend?

All of that plus nearly a million bucks on psychologists. Millions on a rugby league player. And then they've got an arrangement with celebrity chef Guillaume Brahimi, where he's being paid to put swanky events on for board members and selected guests in France; and there's no transparency around how much they're spending on that but it's said to be in the millions of dollars as well."

"And yet, when we asked for one million bucks, everyone goes, 'no way, who the heck do you think you are?' Suddenly, it's not the game that has a money problem any more, it's the Rebels who have got a money problem. Well, we know what the other franchises are losing every year, and how many millions in debt the Waratahs were and are – and how much the game is losing - and yet the message Rugby Australia pushes out is that 'you guys can't run a franchise properly'. I mean, that's so nonsensical I don't even know where to begin arguing that."

Perhaps not, but he makes a start; "We're a strong, contributing franchise. I've got no doubt that the previous Rugby Australia CEO's, Raelene (Castle), Andy (Marinos) and Rob (Clarke) would endorse that we were the most constructive contributor and easiest to deal with of all of the franchises. We've had Baden as an effective, constructive voice at that table; we put women's rugby properly on the table, we did the leg work and were well advanced with putting together a replacement competition for Super Rugby which included four Japanese teams, including facilitating the commercial backing for that, which got brushed aside; we had Tim North put in the hard yards for Rugby Australia to re-write the constitution so as to make a transition away from the federated structure which everyone agrees is holding the game back, which got ignored; everyone could see how well our rugby program was coming together; we're starting to make much stronger connections into the community; and we had the state government, off the back of our relationship with them and their vision for rugby, basically prepared to underwrite not just Victorian rugby but the whole game, so as to help Rugby Australia avoid taking on the $80m debt funding. That one is something you won't see Rugby Australia leaking to the media. Other franchises bring their things to the table; Queensland and New South Wales have history and size, the Brumbies have a killer program, and the Force have Twiggy's backing and support a national game. Our 'super power' if you like is to deliver the Vic state government, and new growth corridors for the game, but I really worry that Rugby Australia doesn't understand that by casting the Rebels adrift, they're turning their back on tens of millions of dollars of government assistance to help grow the game at both the community and professional level."

Docherty is leaning into to the increasing animosity that has developed between Rugby Australia and the Rebels' directors. "In October last year, things were cordial and constructive and we were in the process of accepting centralisation. It started to become adversarial from mid-November, when we were told by RA to get legal representation because administration was becoming an option. And that stand-off continued all the way through the appointment of the administrator to the DOCA, which they voted against. My view is that their anger, which we really saw manifested in how they treated Georgia, comes from them adopting the recommendations of their consultants and lawyers, and proceeding with a plan that included a media campaign which linked in my personal business challenges, that framed a narrative around the debt and incompetent management, through to getting PwC in to liquidate, and that plan not playing out like they thought it would. And so, not only are they angry that we didn't crawl away and die, they're upset that we're actually fighting back. They think we've turned the state government against them; which is just nonsense, they've done that themselves through their actions. Add in the fact that we got Leigh Clifford to lead the consortium and come up with funding for that, and that's why we're seeing this full-on assault against us. A fight which I must say, we've avoided playing out in the media."

Docherty pauses for a moment before continuing; "Unfortunately now, it's gone too far for them to walk back. And without that gravitas and depth of experience, without that understanding and vision for what the game really needs and the courage to fight for that, then we're just subject to the same old power bloc. And because they're so backed into a corner, because they'd long made up their mind and pursued this extermination path, when the consortium proposal went up - and I promise you it was totally comprehensive, fully funded, a no-brainer if they were genuine about wanting to maintain a credible rugby footprint in Victoria - they were forced to say 'Leigh's not good enough'. I don't care who you are but if you're in corporate Australia and you're watching someone sledge Leigh Clifford, you're thinking, 'what on earth are these people thinking'?"

Despite the consortium proposal being knocked back by Rugby Australia - or as Docherty insists, never being seriously considered - Docherty explains how everything is still in place. "The investors are still keen to be involved, whatever the pathway looks like at the end of all of this. The short-term challenge is for us to maintain the DNA that resided around Stilesy and Kevin, somehow keep that intact, help keep Jimmy Orange going, back Rugby Victoria and help keep the government keen and invested, while all the legal stuff gets sorted out. Because whatever the outcome, the game will still need to move forward in Victoria. And with all that they have to say about us, we're not hearing any detail or strategy from Rugby Australia about how they might do that."

Chapter Fifty-Eight

5th July, 2024

If there is one person in Australian rugby qualified to speak on matters pertaining to both the Melbourne Rebels and Rugby Australia, that man is Rob Clarke. A former Australian Schoolboys rugby representative, upon entering administration Clarke served as CEO for the Brumbies (2003-2005) and the Rebels (2013-2014) before taking up a position as chief operating officer on two separate occasions at the Australian Rugby Union (ARU) in 2006-2007, and Rugby Australia (2015-2017) until his departure in 2017. In 2020, he was coaxed back to Rugby Australia serving as interim CEO for ten months, following the exit of Raelene Castle.

Observing the events of the last few months with close interest and some sadness, it isn't a surprise to discover Clarke pointing to relationships and mutual respect - or the absence thereof - as an explanation for why things have played out the way they have. "Our federated model brings with it certain strengths," he says, "but it also brings unique challenges, one of which is that Rugby Australia and the people who sit around that table, can lose sight of the fact that it's a member-based organisation. Those members are the individual states and Territories. Those at RA are only in that role because the members have voted or supported them into those positions, and therein lies the tension that at times can develop: because head office controls so many of the purse strings, yet ultimately it's the members who see themselves as having significant influence on the game to the point of some even wishing to actually be in charge."

"In my experience at Rugby Australia, ensuring a high level of communication and connectivity from the top down to the members is probably the most important role to be fulfilled. Without that being in place, what happens is that when you're facing important decisions, like this one recently with the Rebels, then you bring into play all of the emotion, parochialism and politics from all state and territory members. As a result, if you don't have strong, respectful relationships, with consultation and open communication, the combination of uncertainty and speculation - which is fuelled by the media - unfortunately breeds suspicion and distrust. If you don't have those relationships and good communication channels in place, then you're on a hiding to nothing."

"I believe that's a primary factor contributing to what we've seen play out in this situation with the Rebels. On one hand, a misunderstanding or underestimation on the part of RA of that need for genuine and respectful connectivity, plus when you look at the history of the Rebels and all of the different iterations and ownership over time, I think there was very little trust between the parties. That means there wasn't a pathway, with the requisite goodwill required, to solve any deep-seated problems. And that compounded the lack of trust on both sides. And rugby history shows, when that happens, that's when you get people behind their fortress walls, lobbing grenades."

If Clarke is critical of the way matters were handled, he fully understands how Australian rugby's bleak financial position precipitated action from Rugby Australia. "We've ended up in this weak financial position through multiple circumstances over time. One is the fact that with Australia's population of around 25 million, and being in the most competitive winter sporting market in the world, and there's only so much money that can go around to sustain all professional sports. We know that the AFL and NRL have done a very good job at capturing a sizeable portion of the money that is available, and that other sports - men's soccer, netball, Olympic sports and rugby - suffer by comparison. On top of that, our federated model has limited our ability to develop a comprehensive and aligned strategic plan which allows us all to put our hands in the middle and say 'we're signing up to these commitments for the game to flourish and grow.' That historic inability to align all our entities towards a common goal has certainly hindered our capability when it comes to generating revenue for the game."

Clarke expands on the financial imperatives; "Generating sufficient revenue has become the number one area of concern when it comes to the survival of the game. In rugby, we all talk about the strength that comes from it being a true global sport, but salary inflation driven by Europe and Japan has created a nasty spiral which impacts us even further. So, if we tie this back to decisions being made about the Rebels, in my view, the decision to cut the club was less about strategy and more of a tactical reaction to financial pressures."

He runs through the numbers quickly; "There's an $80m line of credit Rugby Australia secured through PEP (Pacific Equity Partners), which they're probably $60m or more into already. They're desperate for the Lions tour next year to kick in another $100m or so, and they've negotiated with World Rugby a guaranteed payment of $100m for hosting the World Cup in 2027. My understanding is that amount is capped, which on one hand is somewhat unfortunate, but Hamish (McLennan) made a decision at the time, looking over the horizon, and accepted it was a necessary trade-off to secure the line of credit and keep the lights on in the short term. Obviously, it's essential for RA to make certain they cover the PEP debt, otherwise PEP will be owning the professional game. RA will also need to fund whatever debt is still existing on the balance sheet between the Lions tour and the World Cup, and then hopefully there'll be enough left over to fund the game for a period after 2027."

Clarke insists that there are no magic rainbows with pots of gold with Australian rugby's name on them. The NRL and the AFL have lucrative associations with gambling, but even if Rugby Australia was to go down that path, there are increasing ethical headwinds that suggest any material opportunity may well have passed. But what about the prospect of rugby tapping into Saudi and other middle eastern investments, like what are being made into sports like Formula One, soccer and golf? "As uncomfortable as something like this might be, I suspect rugby is going to be forced down this path," he says. "If you haven't got the money from billionaire owners; if you haven't got enough money from broadcasters; and you certainly haven't got the money coming out of the corporate market like it used to; if your crowds don't deliver that kind of revenue; and you set all that against the mounting costs of running the game, then what other options are there? Professional rugby franchises are hungry beasts to keep feeding."

So why wasn't the Rebels' consortium taken seriously by Rugby Australia, given the quantum of new money it was potentially bringing into the game? "Whilst clearly I wasn't at the negotiating table, if Leigh Clifford and the Victorian consortium genuinely had the money to put in and were committed to investing that money into rugby to sustain the Rebels, then from my perspective, Rugby Australia should have done everything possible to secure a future for Victorian rugby via that initiative. So we've read about various reasons put forward why the consortium wasn't acceptable to RA, but I suspect this decision had very little to do with the consortium itself, and instead, was more about having another model for rugby in mind and pursuing that at all costs. What some people describe as 'shrinking to greatness'. Who knows what discussions have gone on with New Zealand about the future of Super Rugby? Certainly in my time, the Kiwi's always said to us: 'you've got too many teams in Australia to be competitive, you need to cut back to three', so I strongly suspect the politics 'across the ditch' have fed into this decision to kill off the Rebels, and also accounts for RA's unwillingness to work with the consortium."

What Clarke is describing is a situation that feels equal parts opportunistic and inevitable. "Yes, definitely," he says. "Those conversations have gone on for over a decade around having too many Super Rugby teams and not being financially viable. So, from Rugby Australia's point of view, what's happened wasn't sudden, but it was addressed quite conveniently by the Rebels going into administration, thus opening up an opportunity to reduce the number of teams."

Given all of the conflict and impact upon the Rebels and the Victorian rugby community, does Clarke think Rugby Australia could have handled things in another way? "I'm sure it could have been dealt with somewhat differently had there been deep relationships and trust between key decision-makers. That would have allowed for meaningful discussions that could possibly have led to a different outcome. I don't know how many more new consultants we need to come in and write reports for RA because there's already filing cabinets full of them from previous consultants. At the end of the day, yes, Rugby Australia is a corporate entity, but there's no substitute or compensation for people with a deep understanding of the game in the Australian context, with the necessary gravitas, strong personal relationships and relevant rugby administration experience, who have been around the blocks many times, to be able to manage the competing considerations through those trying circumstances. And it's fair to say that there's a lot of new blood at the executive level and around the board table who don't necessarily have the history, the depth of understanding, and probably the respected ability - so far as the members are concerned - to navigate around the federated structure, and work all of that for the common good."

Clarke touches on the differences between administering sport and operating a 'normal' business. "You can't come in from corporate land as a CEO or director of a corporate entity and lob onto a board like Rugby Australia, or a board running a Super Rugby franchise and expect it to be a mirror of the world you operate in day to day. It's a totally different environment with a different level of expectation and understanding required." He references the Sydney Swans, and more recently, the Gold Coast Suns and Greater Western Sydney, as new AFL franchises given resources, encouragement and time in which to become established and successful. "AFL clubs, and the sport as a whole, understand the benefit that accrues from growing cohesively with a very long-term view. We don't seem to have grasped in rugby that the optimal sum is greater than the sum of the individual parts. Some of that is down to lack of resources, but whichever way you look at it, it's fair to say rugby hasn't been good at supporting and sustaining new ventures like the Rebels."

With a number of factors in play, Clarke pulls them all together. "Unfortunately, because those important, respected relationships didn't exist, because of the grim financial outlook for the game, when the opportunistic moment presented itself, that timing was such that it allowed Rugby Australia to act as they did. I know many of the Rebels' directors very well and I count a number of them as close friends. I've never met a group of more committed people who have put in herculean efforts (and significant financial contributions) over the years into the Rebels and into the growth of rugby more broadly in Victoria. These people have rugby in their veins, and the goodwill and intent to put rugby on the map in a tough sporting environment like Melbourne; and to have this outcome happen in the way that it has, it's just so gutting and bitterly disappointing for them. So, it doesn't surprise me at all that they are pursuing legal avenues and I don't underestimate for one minute the ability of Tim North - one of the sharpest legal minds I've ever come across - to prosecute the case on behalf of the Rebels through the courts. They don't call him 'The Alsatian' for nothing! I haven't read the statement of claim but I understand it's been considered very seriously, and the action isn't being taken frivolously."

Stepping outside the specifics of the claim as they relate to the Rebels' exclusion from Super Rugby, Clarke foresees an end-game where the action could have a positive impact on the future of Australian rugby. "I believe that the game is going to have to go through a fundamental restructure which recalibrates both the approach to high-performance and the current commercial model, which in turn may recalibrate the whole governance model. In other words, 'how do we recut our cloth and reshape the game so it is sustainable and successful?' This legal action may well be an opportunity to bring all of this to a head: to highlight to all members the deficiencies of the federated model; to determine if any processes weren't properly followed in reaching these dramatic decisions, and to point out any actions contrary to the constitution as it currently stands. This process will almost certainly force people to the table to address these issues and will hopefully lead to a revised and future-oriented constitution. If this happens, it could well lead to a wonderful outcome for the game, where we might settle on a structure that allows the community game to thrive, and at the higher level still underpins and supports the development of top-class players for Super Rugby and the Wallabies and, importantly, is financially sustainable on an ongoing basis."

"Because at the moment it doesn't. And it can't. And therefore, it won't."

Chapter Fifty-Nine

10th July, 2024

Despite it being such a tough year for rugby in Melbourne, a healthy crowd of over 240 people has gathered for dinner in the Olympic room at the MCG, ahead of Saturday night's second Test between the Wallabies and Wales. The entertainment is provided by the Melbourne Men's Welsh Choir; nearly 30 in number, upholding the traditional reputation of Wales as a producer of high-quality vocalists.

Also on the roster are the two coaches, Warren Gatland and Joe Schmidt; both Kiwi's, both ex-Ireland coaches, both formidable figures in the game. What they also have in common is that their adopted countries have slipped well down the international rankings (going into this series Australia is ranked #9, Wales #10). Unquestionably, it is Australia and Wales of the 'Tier One' rugby nations, who have coped worst with the commercial reality professionalism brought to the sport in the 1990's. As a result, Rugby Australia has determined that it will again revert to four professional franchises, whilst the Welsh Rugby Union is in the midst of yet another review of its regional structure and how it best might remain competitive and financially sound.

The mood in the room is positive and, despite their different styles, both men connect warmly with the audience. Gatland might be less of a natural performer, whereas a relaxed Schmidt often hits the funny bone, but both men give generously of their opinions and themselves. Another guest, Wales president Terry Cobner, regales the crowd with tales from his past - a Lion on the 1977 tour to New Zealand, where for three and a half months it was "just thirty players on a bus with one coach, John Dawes and a manager loaned to us by the New Zealand union", which necessitated Cobner stepping up to the dual role of player/forwards coach part-way through the tour. Given the cast of thousands and high stakes that accompany Lions tours today, perhaps things have changed for the better. Or have they just changed?

No-one is quite sure what triggers it, but at some point during the evening a familiar chant starts up in the room: 'Re-bels, Re-bels, Re-bels…" No slight is directed towards Australia or Wales; it's merely a sign that, when it comes to rugby in Melbourne, despite all that has happened, there's a wee bit of fight still left in the dog.

Amongst the audience is Nick Stiles, here in an unofficial capacity. It's Test week and tonight is all about the Wallabies and Wales, but it doesn't stop people coming up to him to question him about the Rebels' season. "What's been really difficult these past few weeks is watching our guys sign for other clubs," he says. "Of course, I'm happy for those players continuing their careers, but I'm not going to lie and say that it doesn't hurt when you see all the excitement around those clubs and their fans have, from picking the eyes out of our team."

The termination of the Rebels has hit Stiles as hard as anybody. He knows he has to move on, and he will, but that doesn't mitigate what he and others at the club have gone through. "Anyone in a position like mine, you know there are no guarantees around security," he explains. "We all know how unstable professional rugby is in Australia. And it's a high-performance environment; you're judged on your results. When I was sacked as Reds coach, that was tough, because I felt we were on the way to delivering longer-term, sustainable success - which we're seeing some of now. But at the end of the day, we didn't win enough games and so the decision was made. And if results are the ultimate measurement, then you cop that and come to terms with it."

"But this is different. We haven't been punted for non-performance. Anyone who looks inside the club can see what's been put in place; the recruitment of the right people, the development of a great culture… everything to set the club up for ongoing success. Not just for a few more wins here and there, but through establishing a pathway for the talented local juniors, building cohesion levels so that when they're ready for Super Rugby it's not just individual players coming in at random, but groups of players already tightly connected to the club and with each other. So, that's a lot harder to take; being sacked for reasons out of your control. Knowing that no matter what you did, no matter what you built and all the heart and soul that so many good people put into this, that it was all kind of doomed. Because some people who don't really understand those things had a different agenda. And the power to make it happen. And some people who did understand it, chose to look the other way."

Stiles is touching on the same relationship elements identified by Rob Clarke. "That's been incredibly frustrating. And at times, demeaning. People who I thought I had strong personal relationships with, who, for whatever reason, felt that they weren't able to communicate with me like rugby colleagues should always be able to do. Because they were too embarrassed about what was happening. Because our fate was pre-determined but they had to keep up this pretence that we were a chance of surviving. Or because they felt - or had been advised - that they had to treat me as an adversary. And the sad thing is I don't see how that helped anything. In fact, it only made things harder than they needed to be."

There are other negative outcomes too. "Say for the Junior Wallabies, I would normally get phone calls; 'how's so and so going?', 'who should we be looking more closely at?', 'who needs more rugby?' and so on. But because we've been cast aside, the U20's team that went to South Africa had just one Rebel in it. And it's not just that someone like Judah (Saumaisue) isn't in the team when he plainly should be, but that nobody is even talking to me about him and other boys. I'm not saying there's a conspiracy against Melbourne, but it does feel like we're back to the bad old days where it's too easy for people just to focus on what they know, drawing from what happens in schools and club rugby in Sydney and Brisbane."

These are familiar themes for Stiles and others from throughout the year - the lack of planning, and failures in communication and professionalism. "I mean, they have these summits - which we're no longer part of - but they're mostly re-sets or looking at the lay of the land; updates on the situation for rugby in Australia. But it almost feels like the only plan is to centralise everything. And that's fine as far as removing duplication in some admin areas is concerned and if there's a genuine cost-saving to be had. But to what extent are they proposing to take control of the professional franchises? How will the connection with the local communities be fostered and maintained? The important piece around identity? Who drives the decision-making and is ultimately accountable? Does anyone genuinely believe that RA can be sufficiently invested and operate the franchises better than the franchises do themselves? Who are the people who are going to deliver all of this? What happens when they all get busy with the Wallabies? We've got Rebels players now who are contracted by RA to play, who should be playing club rugby, but they're not; they've just decided by themselves to take a break. And who is looking after them, monitoring and managing all of this? Nobody, that's who. After we went into voluntary administration and Baden left we still had around $350k in pledged sponsorship that I know the sponsors were happy to pay, to keep supporting the team. But when things started going south, because nobody at RA followed them up, because nobody was on the ground understanding what was going on, those amounts never got paid."

Anyone who has rugby in their blood as thick as Stiles does knows that no matter how many times the game knocks you down, there is something in that connection that drags you back up again. But in this case there is a sense that, if he was to be lost to rugby as a result of the Rebels demise, Stiles is at peace. "I understand that rugby is political and how it can be rough and tough, and you have your wins and losses. But one thing I've increasingly embraced in my time here in Melbourne is the importance of culture and integrity in relationships. Perhaps there'll be an opportunity for me to remain part of something in Victorian rugby which fosters that, via the consortium and the state government and their plans. But if not; if rugby here does all turn out to be something that RA ends up paying lip service to, and things end up like they have in Western Sydney… then I'll be frustrated and extremely disappointed, but at least I'll be able to move into another field knowing that I've given it my best shot."

Chapter Sixty

21st July, 2024

Separating the Gosch's Paddock training ground from an adjacent car park there is high netting that runs along the western side of the pitch, designed to prevent stray touch-finders from denting car bonnets and roofs. This morning, a chill, July wind comes in heavy gusts, testing its integrity. The netting ripples insistently but holds firm. The fabric and the large poles it is attached to are black, but there is colour in the form of plastic cones - red, blue, white and yellow - that have been tied at intervals, at a height where a line-out forward with outstretched arms, might be at the top of his jump.

Now six weeks after the Rebels' season ended, there are no hookers around to hone their throwing skills; to lob balls at these improvised targets. In future years those cones will instead serve as a subtle reminder to anyone who knows the game, that there once was a rugby team based here. And to strolling families and passers-by unfamiliar with the dark arts of line-out play, they will be the source of questions from curious children to parents who have no idea of their purpose, but who will make something up anyway, just to keep them quiet.

Kevin Foote is well rugged up as he cuts from the Olympic Boulevard footpath towards the training field. With only the Storm using the pitch it's in remarkably good condition given the cold and wet of the last week. Immediately, it's apparent that this isn't an easy place for Foote to be. Six weeks isn't a long time to come to terms with the emotion of the season being finished, of there being no next season to plan and prepare for, to deal with the uncertainty of what career chapter comes next, and to consider what all of that means for his family, who are settled and happy in Melbourne.

But it's also an opportunity for closure. And reflection. "During the season I think I accepted that things could go against us," he says, "but because we were so focused on the rugby at that stage, the emotions around what was happening to the club probably weren't so real. Then after it all finished, it was incredibly draining, and I've dealt with a lot of anger and different emotions. Now, I still feel a bit angry, and definitely disappointed. Could the situation have been avoided of things done in a different way? Perhaps, but the reality is that it's happened now and we've got to move on."

"Being here today though, the biggest thing I'm feeling is gratitude. For the opportunity I was given. Towards the people who provided that. Everyone who showed they had confidence in me to do a job; the board, Baden, Dave (Wessels)."

Foote knows he is in the process of moving forward, but for today at least, it's okay to look back. "There's so many memories walking on here. The section near the road where it's all gridded… where we used to do drills, where we cranked the music up loud and put in all the hard work… and here on the main field, this is where it all came together. It's a special place."

Stepping lengthwise down the field, it is obvious that Foote - despite attractive options outside of rugby - isn't finished as a rugby coach. "I think for the first few weeks, maybe because of the anger, but also because I was looking at some really good opportunities in corporate leadership… I was thinking, 'that might be the end of it'. But walking on here now, and looking at the opportunity that has come up in South Africa, it feels more and more that I still belong on a rugby pitch. The juices are starting to flow again."

He hasn't had long to contemplate a return to his homeland, and it's clear that it's not something he would have considered had things not turned sour for the Rebels. "I've tried to give everything back to Australian rugby. Because that's who gave me the opportunity as a coach. And I've been loyal, I called Australia my home, and we decided as a family to be here for the long haul. But that door has now been closed, that's the reality and so, if we have to go back to South Africa, that's how it is. And the great thing about this opportunity is that I get to develop young men - as rugby players and in terms of their maturity - and that's something I really love." (Within two weeks Foote will be formally appointed head of South Africa's junior national program, under 20's head coach, with oversight of the under 18's, based at Stellenbosch).

"There's an incredible amount of talent there," he says, enthusiastically. "The school program is incredibly strong and competitive, so the young players are used to performing under high pressure. But there's an opportunity for me to look more closely at skills development and also, the player's connection to country. To look at creating the environment I think will be most conducive, and building relationships with coaches and staff.

The starting point though, is that everything over there is just so aligned and supportive. From Rassie (Erasmus) and the Springboks down, now with Dave (Wessels) in the role of GM of Rugby, it makes a huge difference if you feel like everyone in the game is pulling in the same direction."

That's not intended as a slight on Australian rugby, nevertheless for Foote, the differences are obvious. "Look at the players here who, despite a Lions tour next year, despite many of them being in the prime of their career, despite having their family support networks at home, are signing up and playing overseas. And in some cases that's about money, and that's fair enough. But it's not only about money. It's about the state of the game here. More than anyone, I don't want Australian rugby to be so poor. The negative criticism, I feel like I'm part of that - I've been part of it for twelve years now - so that makes me think, 'what have I done to help change that?' To be part of turning that into a positive story? And so we all do our best as individuals. But you never feel as though you're part of anything cohesive. Rugby in Australia is very political. And so, when you add that to the financial challenges, it becomes very reactive. And unstable."

Foote is struggling to understand how cutting the Rebels is any kind of solution for Australian rugby. "You hear speculation that Super Rugby in 2025 might be the last season as we know it, with Rugby Australia potentially moving to a domestic competition, maybe with crossover matches against New Zealand and possibly Japanese sides. And then you hear from someone else that they're going to continue on as it is. It all comes down to planning, doesn't it? I was actually reading this morning about the difference between action and planning. Simplistically how, if you're building a skyscraper you don't just put columns into the ground and then decide what kind of building you're making along the way. Every little detail is planned beforehand. In Australian rugby, everything is reactive. And that's when you get decisions made for the short term. And things become emotional. And really, that's a failure of leadership," he says.

"So, if they do end up changing Super Rugby after next year, you'd have to ask, what was the point of all of this? And if they don't, and Super Rugby continues, why wouldn't they embrace the consortium? Either way, if they'd let us be, kept things as they were for next year, then if there is a change and Australia and New Zealand announce there's going to be a restructure, then we're all still part of the family and there'd be a better chance of the keeping more players and coaches in Australia. Plus, they wouldn't have to go through this legal battle. I mean, it's all hypothetical at this stage, and that's really the point - nobody knows what's going to happen. Because nobody really does know what's going to happen. There's no plan, there'll just be some decisions made, they'll get leaked, everyone argues, then there's changes made and more people are lost to the game. And then two or three years later, that whole cycle starts again."

Foote extends the theme to address the history of the Rebels. "When you think about it, how were the Rebels every going to survive anyway? The depth of planning required, the financial investment required, the ability to build a competitive team - all while the environment for rugby was getting rockier and rockier - with what was actually provided, it was an almost impossible task. Instead, it was more like, 'Here's your licence, good luck'!"

"Look at the Pasifika population here in Melbourne," he continues. "If this had been set up properly from the start - proper planning, proper investment, more foresight, genuine commitment - imagine after 12-13 years, the players that would be coming through now. Everyone that's been involved with the Rebels has all done their best with what they had to work with, but really, forget about AFL and how tough the Melbourne market is for sports teams - with the demographics here now, this place should be pumping as a rugby city. And now, just when some of that is starting to happen, it's all being shut down again. I can't say how sad and disappointing that is for the game. So then you ask, right from the start until now, 'was there ever any serious intent on the part of RA to make this work?' You'd have to say there wasn't."

Discussion returns to the 2024 season and how, despite the Rebels making the quarter-finals for the first time, and despite all of the mitigating factors, on-field results were still disappointing. "Of course, there are things I messed up – like misreading the opening match against the Brumbies and getting my selection at halfback wrong. Things like that haunt you. And while we're all certain we would have climbed the ladder next year, the fact is, that's unproven. Our record as it stands is not that good, and so that hurts. What helps is to look at guys who have come through and knowing that you've had an important role to play in their development as players and young men. Not just (Josh) Canham and Isaac (Kailea), but all of them, whatever level they've come up to. Many of those players are just going to get better and better. And we would have got better and better. The other thing that happens is that when your program develops and starts to click, you get players and agents coming to you, wanting to be part of it. So, in terms of recruitment, where we'd got this squad to, we would only have added more quality on top."

"But it's not just about what would have happened in the future," he adds. "Look at this year. We all know this competition is hard enough as it is. Imagine being able to take all the distractions we had away? Even towards the end, when we had three games to go, I felt some players… they were still invested, they still wanted to win, but they were already focused on next year. Dealing with their managers, sorting out their future, not 100% focussed in the now. We spoke about it as coaches: when we weren't able to convert one of those later games into a win, we could feel the group slipping out of our hands. Out of our control. And that was very hard for us to deal with."

Foote looks across again at the stadium and the curved, studded 'soccer ball' design that encases the structure. "I'm going to miss AAMI. As the side has come together over the last couple of years and when we played some good rugby and got the crowd doing the Rebels chant again, there was a sense that this was becoming a real home for us. Somewhere where opposition sides were starting to think; 'this really is becoming a difficult place to play.' There's something else I regret too, something that hasn't really been mentioned. One of the hardest things is losing the opportunity to play against the Lions next year. We've been thinking about it and quietly planning it for months. Those midweek games in between Tests are always important. It's our job to soften them up and disrupt their week, and that's a responsibility we really had our hearts set on."

It's time to get out of the cold wind and retreat to the nearby London Tavern, where a welcoming open fire and a hot lunch awaits. As he steps off Gosch's Paddock for the last time, Foote's final summing up is brief. "While being here today is emotional, I still feel like there are many positives to take away. As time goes on it all starts to feel more like a chapter as opposed to it consuming my whole life. And so then I start to think about all of the good things that make up that chapter."

"One of the big ones for me is seeing so many staff move on and do great things. In real life, we were never going to stay together forever anyway, and while none of us have left on our own terms, many of the staff are going on to take the positive and happy experiences from here into something new. There's a real sadness around the Rebels, but when I think of the people involved, that makes me happy."

Acknowledgements and Author's Comment

There were times when this story felt like it was an account of a condemned murderer from America's south. Where, despite the prisoner fighting to escape death row, and believing he had proved his innocence, an intractable Texas governor pulled the pin regardless.

It's what Joni Mitchell referred to in her 1976 song *Hejira*: the simultaneous hope and hopelessness that comes with all of us being mere particles of change orbiting around the sun. In terms of what the Melbourne Rebels were able to control, on the field this was the best of their 14 seasons. But despite their self-belief and optimism, because they were hindered from having a better year, and prevented from parlaying that into an even greater 15th season and beyond - because the governor pulled the pin, because events were bigger than what the team or staff could control or endure - they suffered the ultimate fate. Termination of the club. The hope and the hopelessness.

In such a setting, where external events create an uncertainty which feeds into stress and fear, there were opportunities for individuals to step up into leadership roles. To provide belief, to chart direction, to help colleagues navigate through the tough periods, and to hold things together, just in case circumstances changed and there might have been a pathway forward. Some of those people at the Rebels were designated leaders, others were not. But if this whole chapter of events was to be framed as a chance for people to demonstrate their best qualities, then person after person within the organisation grasped that opportunity.

Note that I write now in the past tense, because the past, most certainly, is where the Rebels reside. If this book happens to be criticised because it paints only one side of their picture, then so be it. I searched far and wide in my observational memory, notes and taped conversations, to find and draw upon negatives or events that might help contrast the narrative. To show people getting things wrong or doing things to the detriment of the club or the game. To uncover and report flashpoints, tensions and incompetency. And it is true not every happening, every person or every decision made was perfect. On some days the room temperature was cooler than others. The team lost more matches than they won. But if failings or arguments occurred, they were mostly inconsequential or happened behind doors I never found, or formed part of conversations that somehow must have been abruptly cut-off whenever I arrived and re-started after I left.

More likely, what I observed was the authentic product of the love culture instilled at the Rebels. The living embodiment of Ubuntu. The belief of a whole bunch of individuals, in that what they were contributing to was the sum of something highly valuable. Something that, even if it wasn't yet the finished product, was on its way to being something quite special.

In that context, whatever this book is, it is the story of the people within the Rebels organisation, told through their eyes, through their words or my direct observations. If there are quotes or phrases or happenings here or there that have been slightly modified, this has been done only for the purpose of readability, not to materially change the truth of anything. Importantly - and undeniably - this is their story, not my interpretation of their story.

For the avoidance of any doubt, I had communication early in the year with people at the most senior level at Rugby Australia about my coverage of the Rebels issue - deemed to be too one-sided, in favour of the Rebels' directors - and later on, about this book project. I was told that I was being given part information only from the Rebels' side, and an offer was made to sit down and discuss. Unfortunately, when that time came, because things had deteriorated between Rugby Australia and the MRRU directors, and because I was said to be "closely associated" with those directors, I was informed that advice had been given to Rugby Australia officials not to participate in discussion related to this book.

For the record, I have no association with any of the MRRU directors, other than a shared interest in the health and advancement of rugby in general, Australian rugby and rugby in Victoria. Some of the directors I have never met. It is of course a shame that I have not been able to provide a deeper account of Rugby Australia's position other than what is on the public record, but that is Rugby Australia's choice, not mine. In that regard, it is only natural that because this book is the telling of the Rebels' season from inside the Rebels, by the Rebels, it is naturally going to reflect the views and beliefs of people from a perspective, in some instances, consisting of opinion and comment unflattering to Rugby Australia. While, for the reasons stated above, it is not possible to directly counter that, it should be noted that between Daniel Herbert and Phil Waugh's public-record commentary, and official Rugby Australia press releases and statements, there is ample material available from which to report Rugby Australia's position. Much of that material is fairly represented in this book.

That you, the readers, have the opportunity to share in the Rebels' season as I did, is due to the generosity and foresight of the people who green-lit the project, and the willingness of everyone in the organisation to give of their spirit and their professional wisdom, whilst going about their business as if nothing was distracting them.

I first pitched the idea to Kevin Foote and Baden Stephenson after the completion of the 2023 season. I went to Foote first, thinking that if I didn't have the coach on board the CEO could never agree. In practice, I needn't have stressed. Both men were immediately enthused; not just warm to the idea, but effusive and determined to assist in whatever way they could.

My one non-negotiable was that such a book would only be worthwhile if the writer was provided unfettered access. Again, I needn't have worried. Both men were clear from the start; nothing would be placed off-limits. There was to be no right of veto. Whatever would play out, warts and all, would be what made the page. And so, with their assent, and that of Nick Stiles as GM of Rugby, we set about opening a window into a professional rugby franchise to a degree that has never been done before.

For that I am expressly grateful. Not only for that window being opened, but for the bravery shown in never closing it, despite the occasions where matters got uncomfortably dark, and when emotions came to the forefront. That this episode has resulted in these three men - Foote, Stiles and Stephenson - and also others, being lost or potentially lost to Australian rugby speaks to the heart of what ails the game. Partly this is because the game can't afford to accommodate every talented and committed individual that it should. But irrespective of financial constraints, surely Australian rugby must search within itself and find a way to stop shooting itself in the foot, and unearth a solution that values inclusivity; not just the modern, box-ticking meaning of the word, but genuine engagement with all of the game's stakeholders. A strategy that emphasises growth over constriction. That retains talent and IP within the sport. A path forward that embodies the values and spirit of 'old rugby' within the umbrella of its professional necessities. Everybody understands the importance of sound balance sheets, but when it comes to a sport like rugby, the people responsible for compiling these financial documents should always be a contributory voice at the table; one of many voices shaping the future of the game but, if you like, always a backing singer, never the lead vocalist. Relationships and a common understanding of the values of rugby, matter.

Hearty thanks are due everyone in the club - staff and players - who made me welcome and contributed so warmly and wholeheartedly to this project. Rather than repeat their names here, you will have seen them listed at the front of the book. There are many champions on that list; people who can and should hold their heads high, and who will certainly go on to success in other fields. For some, our contact was only fleeting or not at all. To others, inside and outside the Rebels, who gave generously of their time to be interviewed in depth, please accept my sincere thanks.

To my partner Nicole, and our little band of helpers - Elsie, Lulu, Tiggy and Kwazii - thanks again for going the distance and putting up with my heavy-handed typing and self-absorption in getting this book done.

To my publisher, Ian Hooper of Leschenault Press, and his small team, many thanks for being a breeze to work with - straight and true, welcoming and supportive. Leschenault Press has previously published non-fiction books on all manner of topics - self-awareness and self-love, 'slaughtered' nursery rhymes, Irish dancing - but never before on rugby. Maybe I'll convince Ian to one day do another one; but next time with a happier ending.

To the editors I have served under at *The Roar* - Tony Harper, Daniel Jeffrey, Patrick Effeney, Tristan Rayner and the Zavos clan; Spiro, Zac and Zoltan - who provided me with opportunity and the luxury of a weekly soapbox on whatever rugby topic caught my fancy - and were crazy enough to pay me for it. I am profoundly grateful.

To the staunch rugby men of *The Syndicate* - Trev, Digger, Chook, Rob C, Hazza and Brett - as always, great chat!

To the many talented musicians - Ruth Moody, Emma Donovan, Lass, Adeem the Artist, Arooj Aftab, Bokante, Angel Snow, Little Axe, Aoife O'Donovan, Sarah Jarosz, Neil Finn, Fergus McCreadie, MC Taylor and others - who provided the soundtrack to the hours spent compiling this book; my admiration and thanks.

To Rebels fans, thank you for reading and… let's do better next time! Harness the atmosphere that was present on the day of the Rebels' final match, capture the support there is for rugby in Victoria, and turn this into something tangible, in behind whatever rises from these ashes.

My 2017 book, '*A World in Conflict: The Global Battle for Rugby Supremacy*' was grounded in empathy for administrators in Australia and New Zealand. Sinking the boot in is something that is done hard and often; usually by people who pay no heed to the daily 'Hobson's choice' scenarios that our rugby administrators face. It seems every man and his dog knows what isn't working and is happy to vocalise that, but constructive, realistic alternatives, that take into account forces local rugby bosses have little or no control over, are almost always never proffered.

That book was thus an attempt to explain the global commercial and political rugby world, and provide an understanding of why things are like they are. In short, there are no easy solutions for Australian rugby. The commercial market for rugby in Australia is small; paltry compared to other global rugby markets, and a small piece of a crowded domestic sports market. Even so, in the years since writing that book, my sympathy for those in leadership positions in Australian rugby has softened. Unquestionably, all who take office have done so with admirable intent. But the game here will not be saved by ten ex-Wallaby captains hounding out an 'outsider' CEO. Nor will it be saved by a 'my way or the highway' chairman hell-bent on conducting a phoney code war against a counterpart with profoundly deeper pockets. And the game most definitely will not be saved by rugby's over-reliance on consultants and corporate lawyers; smart people perhaps, but too often lacking the deep understanding and connection with rugby required to carry the whole game forward. Perhaps the hardest pill to swallow in all of this is that many of the key people involved in the decision to terminate the Rebels - consultants, accountants, lawyers, board members - actually had very little genuine understanding of what it was they were tearing down.

Over this time period, the situation and outlook for Australian rugby has only got worse, not better. In that respect, the Rebels are merely a 'canary in the coal mine'; a symptom if you like of rugby's deeper woes. But it is one thing to make austerity-driven financial decisions. It is another thing altogether to make a decision about cutting the Rebels under the guise of saving money, without there being transparency around the cost of the alternative, or explaining the reasons why some cuts are more palatable than others. And it quite something to do that in a manner which goes against what most rugby people consider are core values - a shared love of the game, fellowship, respect, the development of deep-seated relationships and the ability to do battle on the field and laugh it off over a beer afterwards.

Almost certainly, the costs of this course of action taken by Rugby Australia will be felt long after the effects of any benefits have subsided. Rugby Australia has chosen to allocate its scarce resources to its traditional power bases of Sydney and Brisbane; a reconnection of sorts, with past glories. To a degree this is understandable; a desire to re-hitch to the tribal, domestic and distinctly Australian rugby landscape that existed before the game went professional. But, unlike the NRL and AFL, Australian rugby doesn't get to choose to exist in a vacuum of domestic bliss; the sport is undeniably global and, at the highest levels, the competitive arena unrelentingly professional and commercial. Any such 'return to the past' also flies in the face of Australia's growing and future rugby demographic; instead, seemingly impeding development of a longer-term strategy to secure the future of the sport. Similar to other states, Victoria and Western Australia are awash with Pacific Island, New Zealand and South African families, whose boys and girls, if rugby wants to and works at embracing them properly, could potentially underpin participation for years to come. But to use just one example, by fracturing its relationship with the Victorian state government through this episode, and blowing up its local pathways, Rugby Australia has not only put the government's ongoing injection of tens of millions of dollars into the sport at risk, it has thumbed its nose at this large constituent catchment, and in the process, likely consigned the new Victorian Rugby Centre of Excellence at Latrobe University (courtesy of a $31m investment by the state government), into becoming a white elephant.

And so now it will be for a court to determine where fault and responsibility lies. Irrespective of that outcome, the fact the game has got to this position is, of itself, a considerable failure of leadership. No matter, rugby has survived all manner of crises over its history. As distasteful and unpleasant as much of this episode has been - and the unfortunate outcome for the Rebels, and for rugby in Victoria - rugby will, in one shape or another, survive this too.

One other aspect surrounding this saga bears further examination. The Gell Mann Amnesia Effect is a phenomenon attributed to people who distrust a news source because they know that news source to be unreliable and inaccurate on matters they have detailed knowledge of, yet those same people are prepared to treat information on matters they have no knowledge about, from the same supposedly unreliable source, as gospel.

Throughout this year I was frequently astonished to observe how easily people without a detailed understanding of the matter made definitive statements about the Rebels' situation - about the propriety and motivations of the management and the MRRU directors in particular - often a result of them parroting something they'd pulled from a source they'd otherwise be disparaging of. The dark side of social media is also a contributory factor, but it is far more than that. We've all been there, whether it be in an on-line rugby forum, a What's App group or shooting the breeze with mates over coffee or a beer. Think of two young political staffers entering Parliament House in the early hours... without any of us knowing the facts of what occurred, it is nevertheless determined, with no little authority, that one of them must be a rapist or the other must be a conniving, lying cow. And so it was for the Rebels. Incompetent. Crooked. Or both. Case closed. Perhaps that is one potential good that might arise from court action in this matter - that some of us might in the future, stop to consider the pointlessness and in some cases hurt, that comes with drawing conclusions and contributing to debates we really should have no business involving ourselves in.

This book was always intended to be a window into how a Super Rugby franchise operates - any professional rugby franchise, not just the Rebels. Events took over, and the book - unavoidably - took on a whole new life. Or should I say more accurately... death. Even so, it is my hope that underneath all of the off-field drama and the bigger concerns around the direction of Australian rugby, those insights are visible, and there remains at the core, a story of decent people doing a decent job, working individually and collectively to turn their side into a decent team. The book's unavoidable conclusion may emphasise the 'death', but the true beating heart of this story are the people involved, and how they bought life to the Melbourne Rebels.

About the Author

Raised in a rugby family in New Zealand's King Country, Geoff Parkes has become a prominent and respected writer on rugby. Now based in Melbourne, Australia, his weekly column 'The Wrap', written for www.theroar.com has become a regular Monday morning staple for rugby followers all around the globe.

Published in 2017 his book, *A World in Conflict: The Global Battle for Rugby Supremacy,* provided insights into the commercial and political factors at play in determining rugby's future, arising from the sport becoming professional in 1995. His writing seamlessly blends a deep understanding of how rugby is played on the field with an ability to explain how boardroom battles and off-field machinations impact upon and influence, on-field outcomes.

In November 2023, Geoff embedded himself into the Melbourne Rebels franchise. This book is a first-hand account of everything that occurred over the course of the 2024 season; the high of the Rebels' first-ever Super Rugby finals appearance to the lowest low imaginable; termination of the club.

Geoff is also a novelist; his crime fiction book *When the Deep Dark Bush Swallows You Whole,* will be published by Penguin Random House in February 2025.

Printed in Australia
Ingram Content Group Australia Pty Ltd
AUHW020407041124
402215AU00002B/5